Theatre and Adaptation

Theatre and Adaptation: Return, Rewrite, Repeat

Edited by Margherita Laera

BLOOMSBURY
LONDON • NEW DELHI • NEW YORK • SYDNEY

Bloomsbury Methuen Drama
An imprint of Bloomsbury Publishing Plc

50 Bedford Square
London
WC1B 3DP
UK

1385 Broadway
New York
NY 10018
USA

www.bloomsbury.com

Bloomsbury is a registered trade mark of Bloomsbury Publishing Plc

First published 2014

British Library Cataloguing-in-Publication Data
A catalogue record for this book is available from the British Library.

ISBN: HB: 978-1-4725-3316-6
PB: 978-1-4081-8472-1
ePDF: 978-1-4725-2241-2
ePub: 978-1-4725-2221-4

Library of Congress Cataloging-in-Publication Data
A catalog record for this book is available from the Library of Congress

Typeset by Fakenham Prepress Solutions, Fakenham, Norfolk NR21 8NN
Printed and bound in India

For David Kohn
With all my love, always

Contents

Acknowledgements

This book brings together an extraordinary group of theatre-makers and academics whose work I deeply admire, and with whom it has been a pleasure to collaborate. I am very grateful for the time each has contributed, and for the resulting rigour this has brought to the project.

The idea for this collection emerged from a series of 12 public interviews I organized in 2012, entitled the Leverhulme Olympic Talks on Theatre and Adaptation. They took place at Queen Mary, University of London, at the ICA and at the Barbican Centre. The project, generously sponsored by the Leverhulme Trust, also received support from Queen Mary's Drama Department and Olympics Committee. I want to thank the Head of Drama, Michael McKinnie, and the Olympics Committee Chair, Evelyn Welch, for their endorsement. I am also indebted to Jules Deering and the technical team for providing exceptional assistance to the series of talks, and to Harriet Curtis and Nicola Lee for helping it run smoothly. The European Theatre Research Network at the University of Kent kindly teamed up with Queen Mary and the Barbican to support the last talk of the series, with the director Grzegorz Jarzyna.

I am also very grateful to Matthew Cohen for his advice on the subject of Indonesian puppetry performance, and to my patient colleagues who transcribed the interviews: Harriet Curtis, Diane Gittings and Susan Higgins.

Many thanks to the editorial team at Methuen Drama, especially Mark Dudgeon and Emily Hockley, for making this book happen.

Lastly, I want to express my gratitude to my family for their love and encouragement while I worked on this project.

Introduction: Return, Rewrite, Repeat: The Theatricality of Adaptation

Margherita Laera

Theatre returns, it always does. It returns to places where it has already been before and to times in which it has already appeared. And while it does so, it sends us too, the spectators, to those places and times, performance after performance. Theatre also rewrites. It constantly does. It rewrites history, relationships, stories and rules. It refashions beliefs, recycles old and used objects and reassembles them into new embodied experiences. Above all, theatre repeats, and incessantly so. It repeats itself and the act of returning and rewriting, as though it were struck by an obsessive compulsion to reiterate and re-enact, again and again, the vestiges of its past. In so doing, it adapts itself to present contingencies and situations, like an animal species struggling to survive through evolution. Theatre, however, does not reshape its coordinates simply to remain alive or to remain itself through time, but also to change the world around it. Theatre, one could say, never stops adapting its features to the world and the world to its features. In this book, theatre makers and academics discuss the many modalities in which theatre returns to, rewrites and repeats its objects and desires. Through 17 commissioned interviews, the contributors to this volume explore the notion of 'adaptation' and its multiple relevance to theatre and performance in the twenty-first century.

While the mechanisms of the cultural practice we now call 'adaptation' have been associated with theatricality for longer than written historical evidence can account for, they are certainly not limited to the theatre. In *After Babel*, George Steiner proposed that 'invariance within transformation' is at the basis of what we call 'culture'.[1] For Steiner, 'a culture is a sequence of translations and transformations of constants' relying upon mechanisms such as 'paraphrase, pastiche, imitation, thematic variation, parody, citation in a supporting or undermining context, false attribution (accidental or deliberate), plagiarism, collage and many more'.[2] The production of community, therefore, is rooted in the repetition of cultural units of meaning through the rituals of sociality and belonging, otherwise known as 'tradition'. But what role does theatre play in the perpetuation of traditional practices? How does theatre contribute to the formation, deformation, and hybridization of 'cultures'? What relationship is there between adaptation, performance, and change?

In the interviews that follow, the term 'adaptation' is applied to a wide variety of theatrical operations, uses, and contexts, in which a transformation of sorts takes place. It not only refers to the dramaturgical practice of turning, for instance, a novel into a play script, a domain traditionally covered by playwrights. It also covers the work of directors and their *mise en scène*, that of actors in performance and rehearsals, that of translators in transferring a text from one language to another, and that of audiences in co-authoring and responding to a piece. A focus on the *processes* of adaptation, that is, on the modalities in which theatre makers adapt existing cultural material of varying form into performance, can be traced throughout the volume. Here, artists reflect on *how* they practise adaptation as well as *why* they serially do. While theatre venues continue to bank on the attractive familiarity of adaptations, and more and more university drama departments offer practical and theoretical modules on how to devise and analyse them, scholarship has so far concentrated on literary and cinematic practice or on specific subfields of Shakespeare Studies and Classical Receptions.[3] Through conversations between theatre and performance academics and internationally renowned 'serial adapters' working in Europe, the Americas, Asia, and Africa, this book wishes to explore a variety of approaches and contexts in which stage practitioners make theatre by constantly returning to, rewriting and repeating their methodologies, histories and inherited narratives.

This volume explores the idea that the mechanisms of adaptation and those of theatricality have something fundamental in common, not least in their relationship with temporality. As approximate repetitions of cultural fragments, adaptations obsessively return to the past and continuously repeat it, even if their intention is to reject it. In adaptation's logic, time is no linear progression, but a spiral that keeps turning on itself, causing cyclical reoccurrences while ensuring evolution. This logic is seamlessly matched by the ghostliness of performance, its apparatus of reproduction and representation, its 'restored behaviours' and recursive apparitions.[4] One might say that both adaptation and performance are nostalgic in their 'ache for return', their desire to come 'home' again and again, wherever 'home' might be. In *The Haunted Stage*, Marvin Carlson writes that '[t]he retelling of stories already told, the reenactment of events already enacted, the experience of emotions already experienced, these are and have always been central concerns in all times and places'.[5]

As a memory machine, theatre is the site for the recollection, re-elaboration, and contestation of readily available cultural material, and for the production of new, and newly adaptable, ideas out of established ones: this makes the position of the theatre spectator uncanny, since, as Herbert Blau states, '*we are seeing what we saw before*'.[6] According to Blau, it is our mortality which dooms 'us' to repetition.[7] He states:

> What is being repeated in the tautological cycle of performance – replay, reenactment, restoration, the play within the play within – is the memory of the origin of the memory which is being solicited and resisted. It is in this recursive way that performance is a testament to a life that seems to look like death because it is always being left behind.[8]

One could speak, therefore, of the theatricality of adaptation. One could say that adaptation is a 'theatrical' device precisely because it contains, extends and multiplies those principles that are already at the core of performance: restored behaviour, representation of the world and a relentless repetition lacking the exactness of machines. This book examines both works that avowedly adapt from a source and other, less evident instances, in which adaptive mechanisms pertain to the everyday practice of theatre makers. The series of 17 interviews uncover methodologies proposed by stage artists who have repeatedly practised a kind of theatre-making that we might call recursive, stubbornly repetitive, or even productively obsessive.

Definitions and modalities of adaptation

Contributors explore the rich signifying potential of the term adaptation and many of its possible metaphorical uses, without following a unifying definition. Our keyword is a multi-faceted term that allows many uses and interpretations, from the constant adaptation of an actor's performance to that of other members of the cast in each rehearsal or run (see Woods, p. 157), to the quick changes made to the performance script in response to sudden requests from sponsors in Java (see Escobar, pp. 137–8), to the variations introduced by each collaborator throughout the creative process (see Radosavljević, p. 266), or those brought on to adapt a production to a new venue (see Davids, p. 31), or again those ushered in by a new audience, whose interpretative work understands the production from a different perspective or language (see Read, p. 186).

However, in Adaptation Studies, a growing field of scholarly research, the term adaptation primarily refers to a kind of interpretative intervention – much like Steiner's intertextual practices – which involves transposing a source or stimulus into a different language, medium, or culture, seeking 'matches' for certain features of the source and proposing 'mismatches' for others. Meanings, therefore, may wilfully and/or unwittingly be distorted, parodied and subverted as part of a process of translative refashioning, which can include juxtaposing different sources, compressing, or expanding sections of larger works, and adding new material to the old. Evidently, there are several types of adaptation, depending on the nature of the adapted work, the kind of engagement with it and the product resulting from this process. In this intertextual sense, the process of adaptation implies negotiations of numerous kinds, such as interlingual, intercultural, intersemiotic, intermedial, but also ideological, ethical, aesthetic and political. Comparative Literature scholar Linda Hutcheon defines adaptation as 'an acknowledged transposition of a recognizable other work or works; a creative and an interpretive act of appropriation/salvaging; an extended intertextual engagement with the adapted work'.[9] However, the terminology concerning intertextual practices of rewriting is contested. Some theatre artists and scholars prefer the term 'appropriation' to define their work (see Johnson, p. 112) because adaptation is perceived to be too linked to literary practices and text-based theatre, or because it suggests the idea of a derivative endeavour of lesser value than an 'original' work. Others, like English Literature and Drama scholar Julie Sanders, have sought to distinguish between the terms 'adaptation' and 'appropriation', the latter being more removed from its source.[10] However, I find it more useful to think of adaptation as a synonym of appropriation, because it is too problematic to draw the line between a 'faithful adaptation' and an 'unfaithful appropriation' (faithful or unfaithful to what, anyway?). If any difference can be elaborated between the two terms, appropriation emphasizes the idea of 'taking for one's own use' and therefore of conscious manipulation, and is thus often preferable in contexts in which there is little or no concern, and productively so, with 'staying true' to the source. It is clear, though, that the multiple modalities of adaptation, stretching from accurate interlingual versions to radical reuses of a stimulus and intra- or intermedial renditions, make categorizations complex but necessary.

Let us then sketch a taxonomy of adaptation as intertextual practice – where 'text' may refer to performance, film, and other non-literary sources. I shall start by considering negotiations between languages based on Roman Jakobson's classification of translational practices into the intralingual (or rewording, between the same language), the interlingual (or translation proper, between two different languages), and the intersemiotic (or transmutation, between two different semiotic systems, such as a verbal sign system and a non-verbal one).[11] Following Jakobson's distinctions, one could say, for instance, that the English script for Split Britches' and Bloolips' *Belle Reprieve* (1991), a feminist rewriting of Tennessee Williams' *A Streetcar Named Desire*, is an intralingual adaptation (see Harvie, p. 146); that Daniel Veronese's *Los hijos se han dormido* (2011), an Argentinian rewriting of Chekhov's *The Seagull*, is an interlingual version (see Graham-Jones, p. 71); and that Romeo Castellucci's productions *Inferno*, *Purgatorio* and *Paradiso* (2008), which feature almost no speech at all, are intersemiotic appropriations of Dante's epic poem (see Ridout, pp. 100–3).

However, things get more complicated when we consider the different mediums, genres, cultures, and historical periods that are involved in the act of stage transposition. Intramedial adaptations work within the same medium, such as a written play script adapted into another play script, which is the case of Rio Kishida's adaptation of *King Lear* (1997) for Ong Keng Sen's performance (see Peterson, p. 171). Intermedial adaptations, on the other hand, transpose a source into another medium, for instance Elevator Repair Service's *Gatz* (2005; see Monks, pp. 203–7), a stage version of Fitzgerald's novel *The Great Gatsby*. Moreover, every *mise en scène* of a play can be considered an intermedial adaptation of a script into a live performance. By the same token, intrageneric adaptations retain the same genre as their source, such as Two Gents Productions' two-hander *Two Gentlemen of Verona* based on Shakespeare's comedy (2008; see Woods, pp. 156–61), while in intergeneric ones we witness a genre shift, for instance with Emma Rice's and Spymonkey's comedy version of Sophocles' tragedy *Oedipus*, renamed *Oedipussy* (2012; see Welton, p. 228). An intracultural adaptation involves a transposition within the same culture, such as Simon Stephens' stage version of Haddon's *The Curious Incident of the Dog in the Night-Time* (2012; see Radosavljević, pp. 255–66); while intercultural adaptation (also known as transculturation) transfers one source from one culture into another, such as Ong's two versions of *King Lear* (1997 and 2012; see Peterson, pp. 169–73).

The distinction between intratemporal and intertemporal adaptations is perhaps more complex than one might imagine. It depends on whether the setting of the target text is located in the same period as in the source or in a different one, though there is a distinction to be made between the time of writing/publication, the fictional time in which the source and the target texts are set, and the time alluded to in the performance. Most projects featured in this book are intertemporal, but Nick Stafford's and Handspring Puppet Company's 2007 stage adaptation of Michael Morpurgo's 1982 novel *War Horse* can be considered intratemporal, as the fictional action is set during World War I in both source and adaptation (see Davids, pp. 23–4 and 29–31). An intertemporal adaptation that relocates an old source (either written or set in the distant past) into more recent times is also known as actualization: Katie Mitchell's *Women of Troy* (2007) transposed the story of Queen Hecuba and the Trojan War prisoners into a World War II context, with the female characters wearing 1940s dresses. We could debate whether Mitchell's adaptation constitutes an actualization proper, seeing as it still placed the fictional time comfortably far away from the contemporary world; nonetheless, it did bring the adapted work closer to its intended audience in terms of temporal context by way of costume and cultural references. On the contrary, a *mise en scène* can become a reconstruction if it attempts to stage a play in the manner in which it is supposed to have been staged at the time of writing or publication. Renditions of Shakespeare's tragedies in period costume, especially if in reconstructed venues like Shakespeare's Globe, may qualify as more or less accurate reconstructions.

Ideological shifts are perhaps the most important to note: intraideological transpositions retain the ideological landscape of their source, while interideological ones do not. A clear case of interideological appropriation is Catur Kuncoro's *Wayang Mitologi* (2010), in which the Javanese puppeteer reuses myths from Yogyakarta to lampoon contemporary Indonesian politicians (see Escobar, pp. 122 and 130). It is difficult, however, to find an example of intraideological adaptation, as the shift in language, culture, or medium always entails a refocusing and repositioning of the adapted work, and consequently of its emphasis on specific issues.

Another distinction to be made is between the two largely opposite – but not diametrically opposed – approaches of 'domestication' and 'foreignization'.[12] These terms, coined by Lawrence Venuti, are now commonly used in Translation Studies to differentiate between interlingual translation strategies that aim to make the source text more (domestication) or less (foreignization) familiar to the target reader, preferring or avoiding idiomatic expressions and standard dialect tropes of the target context. These two terms can be usefully employed in the context of our discussion on intertextual stage adaptation given the interpretative nature of theatrical transposition. Venuti argues that domesticating approaches, which are predominant in the Anglo-American literary translation industry into English to boost sales, can be considered an instance of cultural colonization because they obliterate the source culture and its difference.[13] Although adaptations often do not even try to be accurate and complete renditions of the source text, their intertextual engagement with their so-called 'original' often betrays attempts to make the audience relate more strongly to the adapted work. This often comes hand in hand with actualization (relocating an old source to more recent times), recontextualization (relocating a distant source to a different context, often more similar to the receiving one), transculturation (relocating a culturally specific source to another cultural context, often the target one) and various other mismatches, such as changes in the plotline, that are introduced to turn the 'foreign' elements of the source into more familiar characteristics to facilitate reception in the receiving culture. While domesticating and actualizing approaches can be seen to be vital to the survival and continuing relevance of theatre to its audiences, domestication and actualization can easily become entangled in conservative discourses, reinforcing dominant views and the status quo. On the other hand, foreignizing techniques are often accused of alienating audiences and creating elitist works that can be understood and enjoyed by few.

In this book, several approaches along the continuum that connects the domesticating and the foreignizing poles are represented. For instance, Javanese *dalang* Catur Kuncoro champions the need to actualize *Wayang Kulit* in order to make young Indonesian people engage more easily with this traditional art (see Escobar, p. 131), while Noh actor Udaka Michishige only makes very minor concessions to the idea of updating the centuries-old Noh tradition to please audiences (see Pellecchia, pp. 77–88). Active foreignization is practised by Julia Bardsley, Simon Vincenzi (see Johnson, pp. 110–17) and Romeo Castellucci (see Ridout, pp. 96–105), whose appropriations of Western 'classics', mostly familiar to their target audiences, provoke an unsettling sense of alterity through the use of anti-realist images, non-standard bodies, and radical rewriting techniques. More often, though, practitioners combine several approaches at once and it becomes difficult to assign a particular production to either of the two 'camps': in Katie Mitchell's *Waves*, for instance, Woolf's novel is both made more approachable through a reduction in size and simplification of the plot, and more unfamiliar through the self-reflexive blending of several live mediums on stage – performance, cinematic projections, and foley art – and a refusal to conceal their machinery and processes. Here, the British audience's expectation of a familiar, illusionistic type of realism was disturbed by actor-cameramen shooting close-ups, live footage, and foley artists performing their sound effects on stage.

As already suggested, the act of 'updating', 'recontextualizing', and 'dusting off' old or foreign narratives to make them 'relevant' and easy to digest in the present day can end up consolidating dominant forms, canonical sources, and current power relations. As Venuti has demonstrated and as I have investigated elsewhere in my work, transferring pre-existing material into another language, culture, or medium involves an exercise in self-definition through an act of appropriation of the foreign, which raises issues around a given society's self-representation and the reiteration of ideological exclusions.[14] But how might adaptation be an agent for political resistance, rather than a tool for reinstating the norm? Foreignizing techniques, in which the otherness of the source material is exposed and not altered, appears as one possible way forward, because they engage spectators in an act of self-redefinition through unfamiliar encounters at the theatre. Foreignization does not, however, equal exoticization: in the former approach, as Venuti suggests, the inevitable act of domestication inherent in any translation is reduced to a minimum, and the cultural differences are allowed to shine through; in the latter, difference is highlighted and spectacularized to capture and indulge the spectators' voyeurism. The difference ultimately lies in the instrumentalization of the foreign, which characterizes exoticization. Another politically productive approach is parody, which often contains elements of domestication but avoids the latter's ethical deadlock by critiquing the source. Feminist and queer parodies of canonical 'originals' and popular culture, for instance, have proved subversive of dominant heteronormativities (see Harvie, pp. 135–47). Ultimately, however, in every attempt to challenge the politics of a source through adaptation there lies a contradictory stance which accepts to reiterate the 'norm', however briefly and fleetingly, in order to denounce it.

Book structure

The volume is divided into four parts which examine similar issues, approaches, and debates. Part 1, Return, Rewrite, Repeat, focuses on artists whose work reinterprets existing sources, often canonical in their respective cultures, in order to find new meanings or rediscover old ones; their relationship to the chosen stimulus is predominantly one of exploration through performance. Here, TR Warszawa director Grzegorz Jarzyna talks to Paul Allain about adapting the 'classics' in a changing Poland to promote debate on important issues for society: Greek tragedy, Shakespeare, and Pasolini, as well as films such as Vitgenberg's *Festen* and Murnau's *Nosferatu*, become malleable material to tell stories that activate an 'emotional code [engrained] in our bodies' (see p. 41). Nadia Davids speaks to Handspring Puppet Company and their dramaturg Jane Taylor about, amongst other projects, the development of animal movements and personality in the blockbuster adaptation *War Horse* (2007) and the company's response to the horrifying testimonies of apartheid abuse presented at the Truth and Reconciliation Commission, entitled *Ubu and the Truth Commission* (1997) and based on Jarry's sinister character. Peter Boenisch considers *mise en scène* as a form of adaptation in his conversation with the director Ivo van Hove of Toneelgroep Amsterdam, whose projects include innovative, multimedia stagings of canonical plays by Shakespeare, O'Neill, and Euripides, and stage adaptations of film scripts by Bergman, Pasolini, Antonioni, and Cassavetes. In a conversation with Jean Graham-Jones, Argentinian playwright/director Daniel Veronese reflects on his meta-theatrical adaptations of Ibsen and Chekhov, in which the stories are radically rewritten to reflect on issues of performance and theatricality. Lastly, Noh actor and master Udaka Michishige is interviewed by his pupil Diego Pellecchia about the fine balance between innovating the repertoire and respecting Noh tradition in his interpretations of canonical Noh plays and his compositions of new Noh, which adapt historical narratives and figures into the language of the oldest surviving Japanese performing art.

Part 2, Defusing Tradition, takes its title from a phrase employed by Italian theatre artist Romeo Castellucci (see p. 97). It features conversations with practitioners whose relationship with sources, or with the traditions and cultures in which they work, is one of more or less overt antagonism; using appropriation as a tool for resistance, they challenge the politics of the 'original' on issues like gender, race and power relations, or demonstrate 'iconoclastic' dispositions towards the canon. Nicholas Ridout discusses Socìetas Raffaello Sanzio's work with Castellucci, touching upon the often disquieting 'literality' of his adaptation approach, such as the moment from *Inferno* (2008) featured on the cover of this book, in which a climber ascended the steep façade of the Cour d'Honneur of the Pope's Palace in Avignon to offer spectators the sense of vertigo that Dante describes while descending into hell (see p. 101). Jen Harvie talks to the feminist performance artist Lois Weaver, whose work with Split Britches investigates queer sexualities by appropriating and subverting popular culture from within, through techniques such as lip-synching. Dominic Johnson converses with live artist Julia Bardsley and choreographer/director Simon Vincenzi about projects which radically appropriate dramatic and cinematic characters, such as King Lear and Fritz Lang's Dr Mabuse (Vincenzi's *The Infinite Pleasures of the Great Unknown*, 2008), and Medea (Bardsley's *Medea: Dark Matter Events*, 2011). *Wayang Kulit* master Catur Kuncoro, the enfant terrible of contemporary Indonesian shadow puppetry, is interviewed by Miguel Escobar about innovating and disrupting a centuries-old tradition, whose canonical repertoire is based on retellings of the Indian epics *Ramayana* and *Mahabharata*, in order to engage young audiences.

In Part 3, Intercultural Encounters, we investigate the politics of a theatre that travels across cultures, contexts, languages, and traditions. Here, artists and their interviewers consider not only transculturation and hybridization of culturally specific material, but also the politics of adapting to transnational collaborators' conventions and foreign spectators' expectations. William Peterson talks to director Ong Keng Sen of TheatreWorks Singapore about his transnational Shakespeare plays featuring several languages and performers from different Asian backgrounds. Arne Pohlmeier, Denton Chikura, and Tonderai Munyebvu of Two Gents Productions, a multicultural theatre company based in London and Harare, share their thoughts with Penelope Woods about their 'post-cultural' three-hander company and their experience of adapting Shakespeare's *Two Gentlemen of Verona* (2012) into Shona, one of Zimbabwe's official languages, for a London audience during the Cultural Olympiad.[15] Finally, Alan Read's meandering conversation with the Latvian director, Alvis Hermanis, touches tangentially upon his adaptations of several Russian works, such as *Sonya* (2006), a short story by Tatiana Tolstaya and Pushkin's verse novel *Eugene Onegin* (2013), preferring to dwell on his piece without words, *The Sound of Silence*, which transports Simon and Garfunkel songs into a 1970s Latvian context. Read and Hermanis also discuss how different attitudes within European theatre cultures shape reception of touring shows and how theatre 'adapts' itself (or otherwise) to audiences on tour.

Part 4, Crafting Adaptations, examines adaptation as a creative process and includes conversations in which practical techniques for turning novels, essays, plays, and fairy tales into performances are investigated more prominently. Here, artists share aspects of their methodologies such as verbatim dramaturgy, group devising, and improvisation. John Collins of the US collective Elevator Repair Service is questioned by Aoife Monks about the ways in which the group developed a trilogy based on three American modernist novels: Fitzgerald's *The Great Gatsby*, Faulkner's *The Sound and the Fury*, and Hemingway's *The Sun Also Rises*. British director Katie Mitchell tells Dan Rebellato about how she tackled the notoriously intricate writings of Virginia Woolf, Dostoevsky, Sebald and Strindberg to stage subjective experiences, but also how she collaborated with children in creating a musical version of *Hansel and Gretel* (2012). Martin Welton speaks to Emma Rice of Kneehigh, the Cornwall-based company whose internationally successful work includes popular adaptations of fairy tales for children and adults. German directors-collective Rimini Protokoll's process for devising adaptations with non-professional performers, such as *Karl Marx: Capital, Volume I* (2006), is examined in my interview with Helgard Haug, co-founder of the group. Finally, Duška Radosavljević talks to playwright Simon Stephens, whose adaptations include the multi-award-winning *The Curious Incident of the Dog in the Night-Time* (2012), and English-language versions of Jon Fosse's *I am the Wind* (2011) and Ibsen's *A Doll's House* (2012), carried out from literal translations.

Many if not most practitioners working in theatre and performance today have practised forms of adaptation for the stage. But some artists, including all of those who have been invited to contribute to this book, have returned to it again and again throughout their career, suggesting that they find the acts of returning, rewriting, and repeating particularly fruitful and congenial to their creative processes. The selected practitioners reflect a desire to cover as many approaches to adaptation as possible through different forms of theatre (playwriting, live art, puppetry, among others) from a wide range of contemporary cultural contexts. It has been crucial to cover work devised in European languages other than English, from Latvian to Italian, German, Polish and Dutch, as well as work by artists from Zimbabwean, South African, Singaporean, Indonesian, Argentinian, Japanese and US backgrounds, even though their identities may not be defined by nationality, language, or culture alone. I have mainly included early or mid-career practitioners, and those whose work is still relatively under-explored in dominant academic discourse, while excluding late-career artists such as Robert Wilson, Ariane Mnouchkine, and Suzuki Tadashi, whose adaptations have already generated lively debates. It is my contention that each practitioner featured in this collection of interviews has played a pivotal role in developing current understandings of adaptation and its relationship to performance, experimenting with its possibilities and expanding its definition. From Catur Kuncoro's ground-breaking *Wayang kontemporer* style to Romeo Castellucci's scandalously 'literal' responses to Western 'classics', from Split Britches' feminist appropriations of popular culture to Rimini Protokoll's work with non-professionals and their biographies, the practitioners featured here have pushed the boundaries of adaptation for the stage.[16]

As partial and approximate repetitions of cultural material, intertextual webs connect past and future in a metalanguage that participates in the transmission of ideology through the dissemination of mythologies.[17] As such, then, adaptations have a role to play in prompting social, cultural, and ideological change. It is my hope that this book will enable those practising and studying adaptations to begin to think of ways in which change might be initiated by transforming, reformulating, challenging, and subverting inherited narratives.

Selected bibliography

Baines, Roger W., Christina Marinetti and Manuela Perteghella (eds). (2011). *Staging and Performing Translation: Text and Theatre Practice*. Basingstoke: Palgrave Macmillan.

Carlson, Marvin. (2001). *The Haunted Stage: The Theatre as Memory Machine*. Ann Arbor, MI: University of Michigan Press.

Carroll, Rachel. (2009). *Adaptation in Contemporary Culture: Textual Infidelities*. London: Continuum.

Cartmell, Deborah, and Imelda Whelehan (eds). (2007). *The Cambridge Companion to Literature on Screen*. Cambridge: Cambridge University Press.

—(eds). (2010). *Screen Adaptation: Impure Cinema*. Basingstoke: Palgrave Macmillan.

Chapple, Freda, and Chiel Kattenbelt. (2006). *Intermediality in Theatre and Performance*. Amsterdam and New York: Rodopi.

Forsyth, Alison, and Christopher Megson (eds). (2009). *Get Real: Documentary Theatre Past and Present*. Basingstoke: Palgrave Macmillan.

Friedman, Sharon. (2009). *Feminist Theatrical Revisions of Classic Works: Critical Essays*. Jefferson, NC and London: McFarland.

Hall, Edith, Fiona Macintosh and Amanda Wrigley (eds). (2004). *Dionysus since 69*. Oxford: Oxford University Press.

Hammond, Will and Dan Steward. (2008). *Verbatim, Verbatim: Contemporary Documentary Theatre*. London: Oberon.

Holledge, Julie, and Joanne Tompkins. (2000). *Women's Intercultural Performance*. London: Routledge.

Hutcheon, Linda. (2006). *A Theory of Adaptation*. London and New York: Routledge.

Kennedy, Dennis (ed.). (2004). *Foreign Shakespeare*. Cambridge: Cambridge University Press.

Krebs, Katja (ed.). (2013). *Translation and Adaptation in Theatre and Film*. London and New York: Routledge.

Laera, Margherita. (2013). *Reaching Athens: Community, Democracy and Other Mythologies in Adaptations of Greek Tragedy*. Oxford: Peter Lang.

Leach, Thomas. (2007). *Film Adaptation and Its Discontents*. Baltimore, MD: Johns Hopkins University Press.

MacArthur, Michelle, Lydia Wilkinson, and Keren Zaiontz (eds). (2009). *Performing Adaptations: Essays and Conversations on the Theory and Practice of Adaptation*. Newcastle upon Tyne: Cambridge Scholars.

Massai, Sonia. (2005). *World-Wide Shakespeares: Local Appropriations in Film and Performance*. London and New York: Routledge.

McCabe, Colin, Kathleen Murray and Rick Warner (eds). (2011). *True to the Spirit: Film Adaptation and the Question of Fidelity*. Oxford: Oxford University Press.

Radosavljević, Duška. (2013). 'Devising and Adaptation: Redefining "Faithfulness"', in *Theatre-Making: Interplay Between Text and Performance in the 21st Century*. Basingstoke: Palgrave Macmillan, pp. 56–84.

Sanders, Julie. (2006). *Adaptation and Appropriation*. London and New York, Routledge.

Schneider, Rebecca. (2011). *Performing Remains: Art and War in Times of Theatrical Reenactment*. London and New York: Routledge.

Steiner, George. (1998) *After Babel: Aspects of Language and Translation*, 3rd edn. Oxford: Oxford University Press, 1998.

Venuti, Lawrence. (1995).*The Translator's Invisibility: A History of Translation*. London and New York: Routledge.

—(1998). *The Scandals of Translation: Towards an Ethics of Difference*. London and New York: Routledge.

Notes

1 Steiner (1998), p. 448.

2 Ibid., p. 449 and p. 437.

3 For a general introduction, see Hutcheon (2006); for cinematic adaptations, see Cartmell and Whelehan (2007, 2010); Leach (2007); McCabe et al. (2011). For popular culture, see Carroll (2009). For literary adaptations, see Sanders (2006). For Shakespeare adaptations, see for instance Kennedy (2004) and Massai (2005). For Greek tragedy, see Hall et al. (2004) and Laera (2013). Useful chapters on stage adaptations can be found in Carlson (2008); Chapple et al. (2006); Hollege and Tompkins (2000), and Radosavljević (2013). Krebs (2013) analyses both film and theatre adaptations. MacArthur et al. (2009) focus exclusively on

performance. The *Journal of Adaptation in Film and Performance* is also a useful resource.

4 For the notion of 'restored behaviour', see Richard Schechner, *Performance Studies: An Introduction*, 2nd edn. London and New York: Routledge, 2006, pp. 28–9 and pp. 34–6. See also Herbert Blau, 'Universals of Performance, or Amortizing Play', *SubStance*, 11.4/12.1 (1982–3), pp. 140–61, (p. 149).

5 Carlson, p. 3.

6 Blau, p. 149, emphasis in the original.

7 Ibid., p. 150.

8 Ibid., p. 150.

9 Hutcheon, p. 8.

10 See Sanders (2006), p. 26.

11 Roman Jakobson, 'On Linguistic Aspects of Translation', in Lawrence Venuti (ed.), *The Translation Studies Reader*, 2nd edn. New York; London: Routledge, 2004, pp. 138–43.

12 See Venuti (1995), pp. 1–34.

13 See Venuti (1998), pp. 8–30.

14 See Venuti (1995 and 1998) and Laera (2013).

15 See p. 155.

16 What is not included in the book is an exploration of dance, operatic, verbatim and documentary theatre, historical re-enactments and live art remakes of famous pieces by other performance artists, since these genres have received dedicated attention in recent years. For documentary theatre, see Forsyth and Megson (2009) and Hammond and Steward (2008). For re-enactments, see Schneider (2011).

17 I am referring here to the notion of mythology as articulated by Roland Barthes in *Mythologies*, trans. Annette Lavers. New York: Hill and Wang, 1995.

Part One

Return, Rewrite, Repeat

1

'It's Very Tied to the Content of the Play': Basil Jones, Adrian Kohler, Jane Taylor and Mervyn Millar of Handspring Puppet Company in Conversation with Nadia Davids[1]

Introduction

The Handspring Puppet Company was founded in 1981 in Cape Town and is still run by co-founders Basil Jones and Adrian Kohler. Since its inception, the company has worked intimately with and through processes of adaptation, drawing on stories, texts, performance methodologies, and puppetry techniques that traverse both globe and form. Jones and Kohler understand their work as existing at a productive intersection between theatre and fine art. They believe that in drawing on the skills of different art practitioners, such as 'musicians, sound designers, lighting designers, choreographers and […] actors', the work 'creates a web of communication' between disciplines: their collaborations with the artist William Kentridge and the Malian Sogolon Puppet Troupe are good illustrations of this.[2] Their productions, striking, unsettling, insistent, technically innovative and moving, have reinvigorated and reimagined the parameters and performance terminologies of puppetry, shifting register seamlessly between rural/urban South Africa and London's West End. Complex and collaborative in idiom, they have blended African, Asian, and European puppetry traditions, allowing the form to alternately stage and narrate intersections and angles between memory and forgetting, the private and the public, complicity, victim and perpetrator, breath and death.

Their plays draw into close proximity rotating themes of war, frailty and power, and raise questions around liveness, the animated object, cultural ventriloquism, the often-vexed relationship between 'scriptocentric' and physical 'texts' in post-colonial and post-apartheid performance, utilizing theatre to make visible the invisible, to make possible the impossible.[3] Below, Kohler and Jones refract some of those themes and questions through a discussion of the processes of adapting four of Handspring's major works: *Ubu and the Truth Commission* (1997), *Woyzeck on the Highveldt* (1992), *War Horse* (2005) and, most recently *Crow* (2012), an adaptation of the Ted Hughes poem by the same name.

While Handspring's work is often described as ground-breaking and experimental, their audience, diverse, large and global, is testament, too, to the accessibility of their productions – for instance, the multiple award-winning *War Horse* based on Michael Morpurgo's 1982 novel, is now running in London, New York and Berlin, has been seen by over four million people and has inspired a blockbuster film by Steven Spielberg. Concurrently, the site of some of their most fertile and important creative experimentation occurs within the zone of The Handspring Trust for Puppetry Arts, a non-profit organization that works predominantly in rural areas and townships in South Africa to promote engagement with puppetry arts.

The adaptation and the re-imagination of source material is central to Handspring's work, as is the understanding that puppetry is capable not only of shifting the idiom of performance, but also of prompting a new kind of 'authorship' of the text *through* performance by staging what Jones describes as '*ideas that are incommensurate with script and script-writing*'.[4] *Ubu and the Truth Commission*, an adaptation of Jarry's *Ubu Roi*, embodies Jones' ideological approach. It is a work that seeks to unpack, explore, and mediate a critical moment in South African history: in 1997, the Truth and Reconciliation Commission was underway and the nation listened for the first time to the testimonies of the victims of apartheid government. These narratives, often harrowing and unimaginable, were, through the act of testimony, being moved from the secret to the public, from the unspoken to the spoken. In allowing puppets to narrate and theatricalize these stories, Handspring circumnavigated the dangers of merely replicating testimony through verbatim theatre, allowing for gaps in testimony, for fragmentation, for silence. In this, they invited audiences to participate in co-authoring the un-scriptable. Similarly, in *War Horse*, the horse puppet's muteness combines with an intense and articulate physical presence to encourage an audience to co-author, to imagine, the horse's internal world. Handspring productions create worlds in which puppets articulate the silent, invisible components of the source material, and yet remain, in Kohler's words, 'very tied to the content of the play'.

Mervyn Millar and Jane Taylor join Handspring founders Kohler and Jones in the conversation that follows. Millar is the foremost exponent of Handspring's style and philosophy in the United Kingdom. In 2012, he was charged with the creation and direction of *Crow*. Prior to this, he worked in development and production on numerous shows including *War Horse*, for which he directed puppetry in the London, Toronto, and New York runs. His book *The Horse's Mouth* (2009) charts the development of *War Horse* from novel to stage.[5]

Taylor is a scholar, writer, and director who has worked extensively with Handspring and her work weaves together theatrical, creative, archival, and philosophical aspects of the company's work. Currently Dramaturge with Handspring, she is the author of the play-text *Ubu and the Truth Commission* and has written extensively about Handspring's work. She has held Visiting Fellowships at Oxford and Cambridge, and a Visiting Professorship at the University of Chicago. Taylor has recently been appointed Wole Soyinka Chair of Theatre at the University of Leeds.

Interview

Nadia Davids: 'Adaptation' is a term inextricably linked to processes of literary production, literary practice, and text-based theatre, whereas 'appropriation' is often understood as operating at a more pronounced remove from the original. It strikes me that the work of Handspring does both: for instance, they offer a measure of faithfulness to the original texts of *Ubu Roi, War Horse*, and *Woyzeck*, but they re-imagine each production entirely through the use of puppets and animation. In what way do you think these works negotiate both approaches?

Jane Taylor: Part of what puppetry does is to denaturalize the relation between physical and metaphysical presences on stage. The body/consciousness matrix is disrupted. Within traditional 'live' embodiments by the human performer, the audience tends to stitch that system – body/consciousness – together, in terms that are reassuring and stabilizing. My sense is that puppetry necessarily always makes the text at least in part *about* the conventional character of the 'thinking thing'. In such terms it shifts the focus of attention, the centre of gravity, of the play-text. At the same time, a Handspring production generally seeks to engage in a dialogue with a tradition of theatre making that includes the literary text. It is a very inter-textual undertaking, if one understands performances as texts.

ND: *Ubu and the Truth Commission* is a work concerned – amongst other things – with the resonances of a particular and very charged political moment in post-apartheid South Africa, and it speaks to that moment through performative mechanisms that are often disorientating, disturbing, and revealing. It is, in tone and subject, a very South African work, yet it is adapted from the 1896 play, *Ubu Roi* by the French writer, Alfred Jarry. Mobilizing a European work to tell a specifically African story is in and of itself a political act – one of subversion, resistance, and post-colonial entanglements. Was this, in part, what drew you to using the text?

JT: There is certainly a sense in which the post-colonial disruption is in mind as a political intention, but as with all such endeavours, the relations of power escape and evade control. The Ubu figure, once on stage, assumes too vulgar, too funny, too charming a seductive power. Here that 'too' is not negative: rather, I mean to sound that feeling of disquiet at discovering a generative life force inside the work of art that exceeds intentionality. I am reminded theoretically of Michael Taussig's rather astonishing *Mimesis and Alterity*, a study that explores the volatility inside the mysterious processes of mimicry.[6] There can be a particular intention in that relation, but one can never fix that intention into any art event. Critique and mimesis are a Janus-faced pair. Nonetheless I think we were interested in the anarchic impact of Jarry's purposes, and wanted to mark that the twentieth century had been underscored, through Ubu, by a monument of such irrationality.

Adrian Kohler: When the Truth and Reconciliation Commission (TRC) was happening we were looking for a piece to do. We wanted to do a piece about waiting, and we tried to do *Waiting for Godot* with puppets and adapt the show to a South African context. When the TRC began we realized we had the most amazing story to tell, that our own history was being revealed to us every day, every week, on television.

Basil Jones: To connect to Adrian's comment about waiting: we had thousands of people around South Africa who were waiting to tell their story, and when the TRC started these people all began to actually tell the story having waited sometimes a lifetime to be able to speak in public about what had happened. Some of them were perpetrators and some of them were victims, but there was a tremendous outpouring of stories. In terms of adaptation and translation, it was agreed that all these stories could be told in your own language and that they would be translated for the audience so there were always translators who were listening to what the people were saying and translating immediately, which was quite a difficult thing for them because they, the translators, were saying things like, 'And I walked forward and I saw my son's skull open on the floor … and I reached down and I picked up pieces of my son's brain.' Because of those 'I' words that they were having to use every day about atrocities that were being narrated, the interpreters somehow started to inhabit those lives and those moments of terror themselves: it was a very trying thing, they then themselves needed therapy and were given therapy at the time. So those kinds of translations of speech, those forms of ventriloquism – maybe Jane might talk about them – were in the forefronts of our minds when we were making the work.

JT: There is apparently a bio-medical effect that is a consequence of the utterance in the first person, that there's something in the information circuitry that distils information that we say about ourselves in the first person, in particular biochemical ways, the neural information is held in particular kinds of ways. And so part of what's interesting in the piece is that you've got these intensely subjective first-hand accounts of somebody else, and it was pretty astonishing to watch because the people who were doing the interpretation had no idea what was going to happen in the account because they were speaking in the moment in which they were discovering what it was that they were hearing. With somebody who's actually giving their own testimony, they know what's possible, they know what the degradations of the human being are, they've been inside the environment in which the atrocity has happened, whereas the person who is doing the translation on their behalf is in that environment for the first time and they are speaking the trauma in the moment in which they are being traumatized. At certain points in the translation process, Archbishop Tutu would actually acknowledge how much distress the interpreters were experiencing and give the interpreters moments in which to recover themselves and say, 'We as a nation understand what you're going through, let us just take a minute or two for you to recover your composure because the burden of speaking in that present moment, a trauma that you are seeing for the first time, is a very unnatural task.' Usually, when one is speaking, one has at least made mental representations to oneself, of what it is that you're going to give an account of.

AK: Artists were responding to the TRC in many ways and the difficult conundrum of it was how do you actually repeat, as part of a dramatic context, words that are a personal testimony? Is it anybody's right to perform those words in public? And we felt that maybe a puppet could attempt this. Maybe it could say those words.

ND: If we could turn for a moment to the question of the actual writing of the text and that process of adaptation: within the TRC, one of the crucial parts was about speaking, but the other was listening – the way in which people listen, the quality of listening that was needed in those moments. Jane, you wrote that one of the things that moved you to work on this text was you were dismayed by 'those perpetrators who seem to have some capacity for remorse, appear to be shocked at observing, as if from the outside, the effect of their behaviour. Others simply show no response at all, so profound is the denial, or the failure of moral imagination.'[7]

JT: If one's thinking about the idea of adaptation, in Jarry's *Ubu Roi* the Ubu figure parades around the world plundering, eating, destroying everything. He goes without any understanding of the consequences of his actions, and it seemed to me listening to the testimony from the TRC, that a lot of what one was becoming aware of was the ways in which people were acting in the world without any sense of consequence, in an infantile way. Part of what one realized was that people who had the capacity for these behaviours had no sense of themselves as ethical agents and as being tied in a reciprocal relation to the rest of the world. And it seemed to be extraordinarily interesting to take the capacity for destructive mayhem inside Jarry's play and to situate that in relation to a universe where text and information was being generated about the consequences in people's lives. So I was in the first instance thinking about the form of the Jarry piece and what happens to that if you embed the testimony from the TRC inside the given shape of the play. So it was the disruption and the agitation of the Jarry piece in relation to the historical archive that was so interesting to work with.

AK: In designing the environment for Pa and Ma Ubu, in which the witnesses also had to exist, we chose a quasi-military style tent:

an overstuffed armchair was the one comfortable place to sit in the room with very over-sized brutal furniture. The Ubus lived in this rather temporary accommodation as the country was going to shift and the witnesses simply appeared in and around their furniture. But the Ubus never saw them: the witnesses were not recognized as part of their own world even though they were in the same room. And that seemed to translate the situation in South Africa, visually, through the text.

ND: What was the process of animating the text through puppetry?

JT: There was a very particular process in the making because we actually had enclaved a space and time for a workshop. The TRC was unfolding at the time – it was 1996 – and I had put together a series of cultural explorations on what the TRC was meaning and we were beginning to hear testimony coming forward from it. So Handspring set aside a week of creative time to work together and just see what happened inside that space. I would spend a morning setting in place one or two kinds of possibilities and I got a friend who was doing data gathering for the TRC, and each day she would send through bits and pieces of recording and information. I would listen to testimony and try and find powerful metaphors for what they had experienced. In one scene, the woman whose son is burnt describes watching his mouth open and close, and open and close, like a bird's – a moment in which the intensity of the event for the person who was testifying attaches itself to a very rich metaphoric image. And then in the afternoons and in the evenings Basil and Adrian would go into a kind of creative mayhem in which we were asking, 'What does this actually mean in the world? Where would we situate this piece of testimony? What does one want to do in order to implicate the audience?' Part of what we were exploring was the texture of laughter, of culpability.

BJ: I think one of the things that we were learning, and all these things we only learn in retrospect rather than being conscious of doing them in the moment, was the fact that the puppet is an object that struggles to live. That struggle to *live* in the context of this piece was a metaphor for the struggle to *tell*. Everyone found it difficult to tell their story, because they had often been very traumatic events. Puppets have to struggle all the time to be alive on stage; every second that a puppet moves on stage corresponds to the struggle of the puppeteer: if at any moment I stop that struggle the puppet stops living for you. Somehow there was a very moving equation between that struggle that is normal and natural for a puppet and the struggle in the TRC for people to speak their witness.

ND: In a sense, all forms of puppetry are intrinsically linked to adaptation because there's this transformative effect that starts when you're working with puppets. Mervyn, do you have any thoughts on this in terms of your production of *Crow* as well as your experiences with *War Horse*?

Mervyn Millar: I think puppetry demands a new dramaturgy. You've got performers visible onstage picking up objects and making them behave as if they are alive. Any time anyone picks up an object, this object potentially has the ability to become alive. This opens an enormous can of worms, which the writer and director have to navigate progressively through the process of adaptation, which is why that process for us is long and difficult and costly. It's very difficult to make a puppet show.

BJ: One of the things that you're doing immediately is you move away from the word and into a parallel visual language, a visual semiotics. We're talking about the hapticity of performance: namely, the language engendered when people touch one another and move between one another on stage. We're very interested in that as puppeteers; we're interested in exactly the way we may reach out and touch a face. Puppets don't touch very easily, certainly puppets don't touch fleshy things very easily. So we've got to be careful that when a puppet reaches out to touch someone, there's a special language for that, that we begin to develop. And we have this word, 'micro-movement', where every movement is very important. Why? Because when you move away from the words, particularly if I happen to be manipulating an animal and I'm not capable of using words, and I have to communicate to you, an audience member, you are hungrily interpreting and trying to make meaning of every tiny movement the puppet makes. *War Horse* was a text which was presented to us at the beginning of rehearsal, there was no real text as such for the horses because the horses don't say anything, and yet the horse had to be on stage and say things to an audience for two hours. That horse had to speak to the audience. So we had to move into another form of text, namely the text of movement and of relationships, of hapticity. It's an area of semiotics that is not much written about, but it is really essential for us. It was one of the very important parts of the adaptation of *War Horse,* not only from a novel into a piece of theatre text, but from a theatre form that has been developed over millennia for human expression, into one that can incorporate the life and expression of horses, and the understanding of animal beings.

JT: The original novel by Morpurgo is written in the voice of the horse, so there's a kind of an anthropomorphic claiming of the sensibility of the horse in the way that the narrative is told. And so initially we asked ourselves, 'Is that what we're going to do? Are we going to make this in the voice of the horse?' And I think pretty early on we decided that was so implausible and counterproductive for us as serious theatre makers, that what we had to do was to find a performable sensibility that had all of the linguistic and expressive capacity of a first-person narrative, which is the most complex instrument that Western culture has produced: it's the heart of the production of the bourgeois self.

BJ: So what we were doing, looking at it in retrospect – we didn't realize it then – was that we were staging, for the first time in theatre history, a first-person narrative of an animal.

MM: I think the first-person third-person thing is really interesting anyway when you're going from a novel to a stage of any sort, and the first-person narrative is completely controlling: it tells you where you're looking and at what, and everything else is excluded, like a camera shot. The stage can't do that, it doesn't do that, you can always see the characters the playwright has allowed to be on stage, you can always see and you can choose to watch from different narrators' perspective, and that's a choice that *you* can make as a spectator. Because we're working with puppets and puppeteers, there's this other layer of experience which we can tune in and out of. So there's this kind of tiering of perspectives around the focus that you want the audience to find because the story is there: even in rehearsals that's what we're talking about, 'We need to make sure the audience sees this moment, we need to make sure they see this man look at this horse at this moment.' It's an on-going question as we move into an animal mind and try to make that animal real on stage. Animals are unpredictable and so not only is there this enormous quantity of un-notated knowledge around 'the script of the horse', but also the horse changes from night to night, performance to performance, so that we can keep it as unpredictable as an animal would be. The adaptation of *War Horse* continues also as we go from theatre to theatre. We will move at one point towards a final adaptation and we'll write down everything, but you can make a new *War Horse* every time. Every single time you go into a new rehearsal room with a different group of people and with a different architecture of the theatre, it changes the entrance times and the exit times and the rhythm of the scene, then lines need to change, so the text responds differently.

JT: In *Woyzeck* there is a primary manipulator, who is generally the one who is speaking on behalf of the character and then there'll be a secondary manipulator. The Woyzeck character is a soldier who's been brutalized by war, so he's a very complex man because at some level he's a philosopher, so he's got quite a high order of existential sensibility, but he's also been a blunt instrument, he's just been turned into a kind of technology for destruction as one is in a militarized context. Part of what was interesting in the interpretation was that the Woyzeck figure is being performed by Adrian, who is the world's angel in terms of puppetry manipulation and embodied sensibility; and Louis Seboko, who brings such an intensity to the character, was the secondary manipulator, but also spoke on Woyzeck's behalf. Our Woyzeck is those two practices: in the hands of Adrian and in the sensibility of Louis's voice. So the kind of rupture in the heart of Woyzeck, the schizoid construction of the character of Woyzeck, is available in performance precisely because the body is an abstraction: the carved abstraction that is the residue of Adrian and Louis's performance practices and their embodied idioms. So a third being comes into existence in a kind of Trinitarian wonder that is neither Louis nor Adrian.

ND: In Handspring's productions, design often precedes writing and text is decentralized. Why then start with, say, a Ted Hughes poem and use that as a point of departure?

MM: I don't think we always do decentralize text and start from design. But it cannot be *not* textual, you know, it has to come from somewhere, and there are bits in *Crow* that have come from paintings that the designer thought of when she read the poem. Responding to any bit of text or situation is no more or less legitimate than us constructing a show from scratch.

ND: I think what's really extraordinary about the process of decentralization is that the audience have a certain agency in reading actively what they're seeing; there's room for visual interpretation. *Crow* was specifically geared towards interpretation.

MM: There's a first script for that show which differs significantly from what happens on stage, but it attempts to describe what might be communicated by theatre or dance. That first text is then taken into the rehearsal room and adapted into something. It demands an audience to invest; the ambiguity of the puppet's carved face demands that the audience follow the puppet-character's thoughts and processes carefully. We talk a lot about the gaps between the movements when you're allowing the audience to construct the meaning of the action.

BJ: So the authorial audience is really what we talk about and in a way the moment when you take away the most usual semiotic, namely the semiotic of words, the spoken word or the written word, you force the audience into a much more interpretive space: the moment you have no words, you have to, as an audience member, work harder than if there are words.

AK: The process that goes into achieving a puppet that fits the show is always a very interesting one because if you simply repeat what you did last time it won't fit the new story: it always comes out of the text that is developing and the conversation that you have with the dramaturge or the director. It's very tied to the content of the play.

Links

Handspring Puppet Company: http://www.handspringpuppet.co.za/ (accessed 18 January 2014).

War Horse: http://www.warhorseonstage.com/ (accessed 18 January 2014).

Selected bibliography

Millar, Mervyn. (2007). *The Horse's Mouth: Staging Morpurgo's 'War Horse'*. London: Oberon.

Taylor, Jane (ed.). (2009). *Handspring Puppet Company*. Johannesburg: David Krut Publishing.

—(1998). *Ubu and the Truth Commission*. Cape Town: University of Cape Town Press.

Notes

1 This interview was part of the Leverhulme Olympic Talks on Theatre and Adaptation. It took place at Queen Mary, University of London, on 5 July 2012.

2 See Handspring's website, http://www.handspringpuppet.co.za/artistic-profile/ (accessed 3 September 2013).

3 Conquergood, Dwight, 'Performance Studies: Interventions and Radical Research', *The Drama Review*, 46.2 (2001), pp. 145–56.

4 Jones in Taylor (2009), p. 266, emphasis in original.

5 See Millar (2007).

6 Taussig, *Mimesis and Alterity: A Particular History of the Senses*. London and New York: Routledge (1993).

7 Taylor (1998), p. iv.

2

Social and Theatrical Adaptation: Grzegorz Jarzyna in Conversation with Paul Allain[1]

Introduction

Polish director Grzegorz Jarzyna emerged at a difficult time for Polish theatre as it attempted to re-establish its purpose and renew its contract with audiences in a non-Communist culture post-1989. He graduated from the Kraków State Drama School directing programme in 1996, alongside the equally celebrated Krzysztof Warlikowski with whom he is often compared, and soon gained a reputation as a provocative young Turk, exploiting European classical sources from a range of genres in challenging ways.[2] Already in 1998 he was appointed Artistic Director of Warsaw's Teatr Rozmaitości, now called TR Warszawa, of which he became General Manager in 2006. A widely fêted early achievement there was that he brought new audiences, especially young people, into the building. Only in such ways could Polish theatre revitalize itself.

During his formative years as a student, Jarzyna's world had been transformed and opened up to numerous new influences and possibilities. With the fall of the Berlin Wall in November 1989, Poles could travel abroad, censorship was greatly reduced, and while theatre subsidies dwindled, the frames of reference of Polish culture altered and expanded, cemented by Poland's entry into the European Union in April 2004. Initially theatres struggled to compete as audiences stayed at home to watch widely available rentable videos. Polish Romantic writers had previously provided classic texts that directors had used allusively to comment on their continuing oppression.[3] Following the example of his teacher Krystian Lupa, Jarzyna turned instead to other sources and novels for his inspiration, several of which he adapted himself – most recently Bram Stoker's 1897 *Dracula* (for *Nosferatu*, 2011).[4] The Romantic dramas had ceased to serve as a nation's mouthpiece and fresh materials and approaches were needed.

In the widespread quest to find new means of expression, alongside novels, Jarzyna also turned to films, including Thomas Vinterberg's *Festen* for a 2001 production of the same title, and *Theorem* by Pier Paolo Pasolini (*T.E.O.R.E.M.A.T.*, 2009). Jarzyna is looking for what he calls a 'strong partner' with which to dialogue. But in the way that cultural consumption today happens across multiple platforms, many now digital, so does Jarzyna cast his net widely. He also looks to work across and between genres, using music and film and other media within many of his pieces – in his 2006 opera *Giovanni* his actors sang (quietly, not mouthing) to loud pre-recorded professional singing. Such stagings are dramaturgically and technologically complex and rich, but a core collaborative team holds Jarzyna's ambitiously expansive net together, many of whom have worked consistently with him across several productions.[5] They have become familiar with his approach, enabling and supporting such experimentation. It is only recently though, in his collaboration with novelist Dorota Masłowska on *No Matter How Hard We Tried* (2009), that he has started to work with living writers, preferring usually to do any script work himself before the adaptation evolves collaboratively in rehearsal.

Jarzyna's spirit of enquiry and playfulness does not just extend to using non-dramatic sources but also reaches into play texts. His *2007: Macbeth*, produced in fact in 2005, was a radical intermedial response to the Polish army being deployed in Iraq and emphasized how mediated our experience of war usually is. His 2006 *Medea* all but abandoned the source text, and in *4.48 Psychosis* (2002) he added characters and shuffled scenes around. It is difficult to ascribe any specific methodology to his process of adaptation which begins with a desire to use the theatre to contest taboos, be it child abuse (*Festen*) or more recently the other/outsider (*Nosferatu*). The controversies many of his works have aroused demonstrate not only how conservative Polish society still is but also why there is a need for works of this nature. Adaptations need teeth to go beyond aesthetic and merely formal exploration.

Post-1989, Polish theatre might have lost its very explicit political efficacy but in Jarzyna's eclectic works it has rediscovered its role as political and social irritant and as a meeting place for the exploration and contestation of contemporary European values, seeking out new audiences as it does so. As Poland has adapted to huge changes, so too has the theatre, led boldly by the likes of iconoclasts such as Jarzyna.

Interview

Paul Allain: On your company website you state that you 'do not really distinguish between drama, novels, or film'; you select the source material for its 'quality and its thematic interest'. I'm interested that you don't differentiate between these but also in what it is that particularly draws you to film.

Grzegorz Jarzyna: For me, as for Krystian Lupa, it is to do with a way of working with the actor and their appearance onstage, their inner world, their behaviour, what they think and feel. Lupa helped me to express this. At the same time, I'm looking for ways to stage a subject that can be found anywhere, in news reports, films, a novel, wherever. It could even be a picture – I made some small pieces based on Rembrandt. Then I try to find the story in it. But the form of expression, the language of the theatre, is of interest to me. That's why I often change performance genres as well as sources. Film is a genre that is very rich for the theatre because, for me, it's almost as though there was first the theatre and then film came out of it. Now I feel that the theatre should be inspired by films, their way of telling a story, their montage, their focus. I think that they are a perfect support for the theatre.

PA: Let's take *Festen.* The film is the story of a family celebrating Helge, the patriarch figure's 60th birthday. Gradually it reveals what's going on underneath in the family especially in relation to child abuse. What attracted you to the film?

GJ: I chose it because of this subject. It was the 1990s and in Poland, after we had become independent and more democratic, many social issues were not being discussed – problems with drugs, child abuse, religion. We hadn't discussed them because under the Communist system we had been a 'new magnificent society', much better than Western countries and with no problems at all – that was the politics then. People weren't used to talking about such subjects. Even in the newspapers there were no articles about child abuse. That's why I did this performance. It provoked a lot of discussion initially because it was a time of change.

PA: So you're using the theatre to challenge taboos. Some people say you're a controversial figure.

GJ: I'm not controversial. When you look at the subject of this performance from your British perspective it's not controversial at all. But it was in Poland then. I was young and I wanted to speak out for my generation. Of course I saw many things that were not being talked about, which were being covered up. I felt that we had to discuss them. That's why I did *Festen*. And I decided to make it quite classical for me, concentrating very much on the actors. I used lighting and various devices to make some rapport with the film. I tried to zoom in or have close-ups with the lighting but focused mainly on the actors, on the people in this performance, and tried to intensify the emotions a bit, the truth. The truth was very important for us at that time.

PA: For the actors?

GJ: For the company. In their way of acting too, because our style is as close to life as possible. Of course it's not real, because we exaggerate the emotions somewhat. But we just want to be natural onstage, to be truthful.

PA: We can see structures from film in your works, in the montage, the way you use music almost as a soundtrack.

GJ: Yes we work with good sound engineers in the theatre and we try to make the theatre space a musical space as well. We use a lot of soundtracks, like in films.

PA: You've spoken elsewhere about how the theatre building itself, TR Warszawa, almost forces you to make filmic work or forces certain artistic decisions.

GJ: After the changes in Poland, theatres stayed empty because the repertoire didn't fit in with what was going on in society. The Romantic repertoire that had once been very political was useless. City authorities had problems with what to do with these theatres. They also didn't have any money of course: whatever you might say about the Communist system, they really cared about culture, and they constantly supported it. After 1989 the theatres' budgets were cut a lot. The authorities had the idea of giving this particular theatre to young people so they approached me. I was the youngest Artistic Director in Poland at that time, straight out of drama school. In fact my first performance there, Stanislaw Ignacy Witkiewicz's *Tropical Madness* (1997), was when I was in my third year. The theatre had opened in May 1939 just before the Second World War. Because they were anticipating the war, permission had been given to build a theatre there as long as it doubled up as a bunker. It's very strong, it's underground and it's not so big. I soon realized that the small distance between the stage and the audience, this intimacy in the theatre was a privilege, and we started to use it. You can really feel the emotion. We always produce our performances on a small scale first and later expand them. When you get the emotion right, you're natural on stage, and then it's easier to enlarge the performance for a bigger space; but it is very difficult to do this the other way round.

PA: Can I ask you about *T.E.O.R.E.M.A.T.* which was based on Pier Paolo Pasolini's 1968 film and novel? What was your relationship to these sources and why did you want to create this piece about his work?

GJ: Pasolini is very interesting for Poles because he was a Communist and dealt with religion. He was a kind of prophet who spoke a lot about how society was changing and what we were losing because of our development. Such a process is very evident in Poland. In an interview he had said that he was a writer first but then he decided to make films because they're much quicker to do. What I like about him is that he's not focused on film as an art form or on the art of novels, he just wants to express his thoughts on as large a canvas as possible, to tell a story in pictures. It was quite difficult to write a drama without words, so he changed his mind and started to write a novel. But he didn't finish it, so he started to shoot the film. When he had shot the film he finished the novel. He put into the novel what, from his perspective, was missing in the film. It was interesting for me to start with this material and analyse what he had done with the film tools and what he had done in the book. At first they seemed completely different but when you thought about it, you realized it's the same idea. He simply has an idea and explores it. For me, he's a real artist.

PA: But the theatre is very different, isn't it? You can't montage so quickly, you have a lot less control over the story, you can't use all these devices.

GJ: It's a problem, yes. There are alot of technical issues but, on the other hand, the theatre has charm.

PA: It's a live event. In your *2007: Macbeth* you use a lot of film within the performance, huge projections. You don't use film as a starting point but within the performance. Why use film?

GJ: *2007: Macbeth* was like a site-specific project on a vast scale. The Iraq War was the first time that the Polish army had joined an open conflict since the Second World War. We had always been the victims and suffered and everybody had betrayed us. That was the atmosphere I grew up in. Now, suddenly the army had quite good equipment from the United States and were going to war. All the newspapers were talking about oil and energy and about how it was economically good for us to have such an alliance.

That was embarrassing and I thought that maybe I should express this in the play, which is why I decided to do *Macbeth*. And then I realized that this whole war is channelled through the media, through television, through images, through slogans. This media stuff was very important for me in that performance, which is why I wanted to make it as close as possible to television or a film and use these technologies.

PA: Is it a criticism then, to make people aware of how media control our viewing?

GJ: Exactly. And I wanted to make it in as contemporary a style as possible because the subject was very current.

PA: Do you need Shakespeare or *Macbeth* for this though? Why stay with a classic? What value does it add or is it just a pretext?

GJ: First, it's quite important to show that Shakespeare, his ideas, his thoughts are still current, still actual. Second, people don't change so much. Then, they chopped heads off and put them on London Bridge to show people how a rebellion would end, to frighten society. And then people would say that they didn't want that.

PA: Like a kind of media show.

GJ: Exactly.

PA: You have directed *Medea* as well and have said that the form of the ancient Greek play stops contemporary audiences understanding the heart of the story. You only actually use one line or so from the original dramatic text.

GJ: Yes, I use the last line at the end of the performance.

PA: So why use classical texts?

GJ: I strongly believe that the stories which our ancestors wrote down are still valuable for us, that there's something like DNA, a genetic code, some emotional code in our bodies. We think that we have changed greatly but in fact we haven't. We have just changed our clothes and the set up around us – that's all.

PA: So you're really using the story or the essence of the myth …

GJ: … to tell the story, the core of the story. In ancient Greek theatre, they focused on a single subject and went a very long way with it, for instance in *Medea* or *Orestes*. I'm amazed that they discovered how sick we human beings are. They knew how to tell stories.

PA: Some of these pieces you write yourself, as author. You take out the essence, the heart of the story, and then you dramatize it. Is that how you work? Or do you work more with the actors, collaborating to create the scenario?

GJ: It depends. First I write and then I work with the actors on their feet to make the dialogue more fluent and live, more natural. My process is always like this: first I talk, then we read, and then for a couple of days I talk about what I would like to express and why I'm doing it and so on, what I imagine the characters and the performance to be like. I ask them to learn the text and then we improvise. Improvisation is the most important part of the process. Two weeks or so before the opening we fix everything and stage it.

PA: So roughly how long is your rehearsal period?

GJ: The shortest was two weeks and the longest was six months, for *T.E.O.R.E.M.A.T.*

PA: You also are quite free with play texts. With a play like Sarah Kane's *4.48 Psychosis* you added characters and developed the piece in different ways. What did you want to get across with this production?

GJ: At first I was moved that someone who was going to die was leaving us a kind of testimony and wanted to describe certain moments from the end of her life. In order to make a performance from this I started to research who she was, her relationships, her brother. I wanted to be honest to the text and to know everything about her. I discovered in the text that there's some sentences probably spoken to a girlfriend or a brother. The text is not structured at all, it's just put on the page. I took these chapters and tried to make them chronological. My idea was to rearrange the text.

PA: Magdalena Cielecka was almost playing Sarah Kane. Were the actors involved in developing the structure or was this something with which you came to the rehearsals?

GJ: No. We just worked. She wanted to be very close to the character and try to think like she did, behave like she did – it was quite difficult for her.

PA: We've seen you like the classics, such as Dostoevsky, ancient Greek plays, Shakespeare. Have you worked with new writers? Are there any emerging playwrights or is this something that Poland still lacks? Is this something you see developing in the future?

GJ: I made a new piece with Dorota Masłowska called *No Matter How Hard We Tried*, a comedy about Poles. What I liked about it was that she really made fun of the Poles wanting to be European – with all our history and self-images, thinking how noble, emotional, and patriotic we are. I liked the piece because she turned everything inside out. She always put negatives in – if a character wanted water then she said she didn't want any water.

PA: Is this a new phenomenon, Poles being able to laugh at themselves?

GJ: It's very new. The new generation is really creating another image of Poles – they're sick of the old one. I'm in the middle. I remember the Communist past and yet I can also understand younger people.

PA: I want to ask you about opera and your *Giovanni* where you used actors with pre-recorded music and mixed opera, film and theatre. What were you trying to do with this hybridization?

GJ: My first opera in Poland, *Così Fan Tutte* (2005), where I treated the singers like actors, wasn't very successful. I wasn't satisfied with their acting. Later I understood that it was not theatre but opera, and it's the music that's most important and that as directors we have to support that. We don't create; the composer creates and the conductor creates, and we support them. So I thought that I would like to do an opera but with actors from my troupe. *Giovanni*'s libretto was based on Molière's *Dom Juan* and Da Ponte's libretto with Mozart's music. We hired the Polish National Orchestra and recorded the voices and music. Then we taught the actors to sing in a two-month opera-singing course. They sang very well but behind the loudspeakers, though you had the illusion they were singing. When we opened, people from opera came and some people from theatre. They weren't sure what was going on and were clapping after every aria. Some of them didn't realize that the actors were faking. The music is so dramatic and there is so much emotion in it that I wanted to express with the actors, their bodies.

PA: You've said elsewhere that because technology is changing so fast your performances can quite quickly become out of date. I was wondering what is next for you, particularly in this new theatre building that you are planning?[6] Do you worry that you'll lose touch with contemporary technologies, or will your style change?

GJ: They allowed us to sketch a space so we designed an empty box without audience seating, just a huge empty box. If we get this space we'll think about the new language and use some more media, but for the time being I feel somehow that we are a bit ruled by all this media projection. In *Nosferatu* I wanted to be more classical, a bit more old-fashioned.

PA: Do you not use so much technology in this piece?

GJ: No. It's also like a tribute to film. For me, in the cinema vampires are quite an old subject, but they are a way of analysing something contemporary in our society. In the past, in the south of Poland, as a child you would hear stories about vampires and in the villages they would really be scared of them. We always put everything we fear onto vampires. They come from abroad, strangers, anti-gods.

And what is most important is that they're still alive, they don't die. It also relates to our fear of dying. I find that nowadays we have so much and we can do so much and we can express ourselves so easily and quickly. We materialize our desires and in this we are very vampiric. We suck the energy out of other people. It's a bit like that in this performance for me. Each character represents some sort of profession or belief, like Seward represents science. The vampire is a man who doesn't desire anything but to die, fall in love, be human. Nothing changes in his life, it just repeats itself. That is why I made this piece. We want to be young, to run away from death, we don't want to face this truth. I think that's why we invented vampires, this fear.

PA: We're now going to open the floor to questions.

Audience member 1: What do you think the role of media technologies is in performance? You mentioned that now you're moving away from them, that perhaps they are corrupting the liveness of the event. From your *2007: Macbeth* it seems that your concept of theatre is that it is a hybrid medium in which film, the internet, live performance and singing can interact perfectly with each other. So where do you place the theatre in contemporary media networks? Do you think it's a hybrid medium that can accommodate all kinds of technology in a productive way?

GJ: I wasn't saying that using media is wrong. I think they can be very useful tools for the theatre; but not always. In *2007: Macbeth* there are a lot of media and technologies but they have a purpose. It depends on the subject. Since *2007: Macbeth* the actors always use radio microphones so that they can speak more naturally. They don't have to shout.

PA: It seems that the actors are still at the heart of what you're doing, even though your designers create very beautiful *mises en scène*. Is the fact that you have a stable company important for you?

GJ: Yes absolutely. I work with a company because we share things together, we influence each other, and we make progress in our work. The actor is the most important thing in the theatre, its defining characteristic. I think the living human is what attracts people to the theatre. If you can combine new techniques with acting, that's a good mix.

Audience member 2: I was interested in hearing you talk about the fact that when you directed *T.E.O.R.E.M.A.T.* you worked with the novel and the film. *Nosferatu* is a novel and a film, and with *Giovanni* you had the Da Ponte libretto and the Molière play. What is it that grabs you in stories that are available to you in many forms? Is there something about your process that is helped by having the same story told by several people?

GJ: I'm not interested so much in the form as in what is behind the form. When I'm watching the film and reading the novel I'm trying to catch what it's about. Then I create my own form. For me it's quite good to mix two things, because then I am not slave to either. When watching a film, I get fixated on it because, for example, the way you are drinking that water, Paul, is brilliant and somehow the image will stay in my mind. I would like to repeat it but when I do, I don't add anything new. I can't repeat it so I have to find something for myself. When that's not possible, I read another novel or watch a film. I mix them at my desk, just to be inspired by the film, for instance, the idea. I make three performances every two years and spend a lot of that time at my desk with my computer, first of all reading. I decide what I want to do, then I make a selection of music for the subject. I listen to this a lot and I write. This first musical choice is never in the performance, but music brings me closer to the feelings, the atmosphere, to understanding the characters or plot. Then I watch a lot of films that are close to the subject, and later look at pictures. That's when I start to talk to the set designer.

Audience member 3: I went to see *Macbeth* in Edinburgh and the message that came across was about how war and brutality can dehumanize us. That made the whole thing very alive. I just wanted to say thank you.

GJ: Thank you. That was what I intended, so that's great.

Audience member 3: As Peter Brook would say, the meaning has passed.

Link

TR Warszawa: http://www.trwarszawa.pl/en (accessed 18 January 2014).

Selected bibliography

Kopciński, Jacek. (2005). 'Directors' Solos: Grzegorz Jarzyna and Krzysztof Warlikowski', trans. and ed. by Paul Allain and Grzegorz Ziółkovski, *Contemporary Theatre Review*, 15.1, pp. 84–92.

Sellar, Tom. (2003). 'Copernican Discoveries: Zbigniew Brzoza, Agnieszka Glińska, Grzegorz Jarzyna, Jarosław Kilian, Krzysztof Warlikowski', *Theater*, 33.3, pp. 20–35.

Tuszyńska, Agnieszka and Dorota Wyżyńska (eds). (2009). *Jarzyna: Teatr/ Theatre*. Warsaw: TR Warszawa.

Notes

1 This interview, advertised as 'Paul Allain in conversation with Grzegorz Jarzyna of TR Warszawa', was part of the series entitled Leverhulme Olympic Talks on Theatre and Adaptation. It was presented by Queen Mary University of London in partnership with the Barbican and the University of Kent. It took place at the Barbican Centre on 1 November 2012 before a performance of Jarzyna's *Nosferatu*.

2 Now known as the Państwowa Wyższa Szkoła Teatralna im Ludwika Solskiego (The Ludwik Solski State Drama School).

3 Adam Mickiewicz, Juliusz Słowacki, and Zygmunt Krasiński are the main examples of such writers.

4 Krystian Lupa, born in 1943, is a celebrated director who was a key mentor and teacher for Jarzyna amongst other Polish theatre directors.

5 Including actress Magdalena Cielecka and designers Magdalena Maciejewska and Małgorzata Szczęśniak.

6 This plan is mentioned on the TR Warszawa website but is still not definite at the time of writing.

3

Creating X-Rays of the Text to Dissect the Present: Ivo van Hove of Toneelgroep Amsterdam in Conversation with Peter M. Boenisch

Introduction

When Flemish director Ivo van Hove graduated from the RITS Theatre School in Brussels in 1983, the European capital had become a second home for Robert Wilson, the Wooster Group and other US artists who had found their financial support cut stateside. Belgian venues eagerly co-produced their work, above all the Kaaitheater, founded in 1977 by Hugo De Greef to bring international theatre to Belgium in order to stimulate new developments there. Along came some curious American critics to sample the local scene, and so it happens that van Hove's very first performance experiment, *Geruchten* (*Rumours*, 1981), was prominently reviewed in *The Drama Review*, the central organ of the New York performance scene around Richard Schechner.[1] The director's early imagistic performance collages were staged in empty buildings in van Hove's home town of Antwerp, with his first company, AKT, the Antwerps Kollektief voor Teaterprojekten. They already featured the bare architectural spaces by stage designer Jan Versweyfeld, van Hove's creative partner ever since. When, a decade and a half or so later, this inseparable couple staged the first of their productions with the New York Theatre Workshop, Eugene O'Neill's *More Stately Mansions* (1997), they had been directing texts from the Western repertoire for some time: first in Flanders (Euripides's *Bacchae* and Shakespeare's *Macbeth* in 1987, Schiller's *Don Carlos* in 1988), before moving to the Netherlands, where van Hove was appointed

Artistic Director of Het Zuidelijk Toneel, a major Dutch repertoire company, in 1990. This permeation of experimental performance and classical drama is characteristic for an entire generation of directors who emerged in Flanders and the Netherlands at the time, such as Luc Perceval, Guy Cassiers (who played the lead in the 1981 *Geruchten*), Johan Simons, and Jan Lauwers. For overseas audiences, however, the blended aesthetics of this 'performance theatre', a far cry from the stage realism that dominates the Anglo-American theatre world, remained foreign, outrageous, and hugely controversial. Yet, van Hove's work received frequent awards, too, at home as well as in New York (Obie Awards in 1998 and 2005) and Edinburgh (Angel awards in 1998 and 1999).

In 2001, van Hove then took over, as Artistic Director, the largest Dutch ensemble company, Toneelgroep Amsterdam (TA), a position he still holds successfully in 2014. Many of his TA productions have toured as far away as Canada and Cairo, and van Hove regularly works at major theatres and opera houses around Europe (including Lyon Opera and Schaubühne Berlin), while also returning to New York Theatre Workshop, for instance directing Lillian Hellman's 1939 play *Little Foxes* (2010). It took, however, until 2009 before London audiences got their first chance to see his work, when the seven-hour *Roman Tragedies* (2007), a non-stop performance of Shakespeare's *Coriolanus, Julius Caesar*, and *Antony and Cleopatra,* visited the Barbican. In addition to his enduring penchant for American drama of the twentieth century, in particular Tennessee Williams and Eugene O'Neill, van Hove also created over the last decade stage versions of movies by Ingmar Bergman, Pier Paolo Pasolini, Michelangelo Antonioni, and John Cassavetes. In 2014, he will adapt *The Fountainhead* by controversial American novelist Ayn Rand for TA. In the following conversation, which took place at the company's home, the Stadsschouwburg on Amsterdam's Leidseplein, I explored van Hove's work on these film adaptations as well as his directorial strategies for adapting well-known classics in a new and often surprising *mise en scène.*

Interview

Peter M. Boenisch: Adaptation – is this a term you use at all when you think about your work as theatre director?

Ivo van Hove: To be honest, not really. Here for us the culture is different because we don't have a Shakespeare, a Molière, Kleist, or O'Neill: we are used to working with plays that are written in different languages, so we have to start with a translation anyway. This is then my first choice as a director. For instance, for Shakespeare, I used a lot the translations by a famous Flemish poet, Hugo Claus. Even though his texts are very near to Shakespeare's, he has his own language – you recognize it as a Hugo Claus text immediately. But for *Roman Tragedies,* I chose a professional translator. That was a real choice: you decide what kind of language you will work with by choosing the translator. We then always study the text closely, and out of that comes something that you perhaps call adaptation: how to adapt this play to today, how to make it work today.

PMB: When you stage a film and start from a different medium, do you then think more in terms of adaptation?

IvH: I never look at the movie. I don't make an adaptation from the movie – I make a theatrical event out of the film script. So for me, it is the same process: I have a script and I'm trying to figure out how it can work on stage. Of course, the challenge is much bigger with screenplays, because they're not meant to be put on stage. But when you read *Antony and Cleopatra*, there are 40 different locations – that's almost like a movie script, it moves from Rome to Egypt within a second. How do you make that work?

PMB: What attracted you to directing cinematic scripts?

IvH: I was searching for themes that I couldn't find in plays, for example immigration. *Rocco and His Brothers* by Luchino Visconti [which van Hove directed in 2008] is a family drama, but you also see in these four brothers and their mother five attitudes towards immigration, from sticking to your roots to total assimilation to a new city and a new life. Those were themes I couldn't find in a play. *Cries and Whispers* by Ingmar Bergman [2011], to give another example, is about dying, and I wanted to make the audience feel what the pain of dying really is about. Again I don't know a play that deals with that. So that's themes. But at the same time, it's also a world premiere, because usually nobody has done it before us. So it's as if you get *Hamlet* in the post, and you have to do the play for the first time.

PMB: Could you elaborate more on this challenge of putting on a script? I'm interested to hear how you would describe the task of the director.

IvH: I have to bring it together. Theatre is a unity of place and a unity of time: we are together for two hours, and there is only one proscenium. Most film scripts have no such unity of time and place, they are totally broken up. So you have to find a theatrical world for what the script is dealing with. For instance, in *Rocco and His Brothers*, the guys move from Southern Italian countryside to Milan, a big city in the North. Some of them are lost, they cannot find any connection with the city, with the people there, or cannot find jobs. But they go together to a boxing club and there they become a family again. But it also means beating each other up: it's a destructive behaviour that lets frustration get out. In the movie, this is just a few scenes, but we made boxing the central metaphor, and the family was always around this boxing ring. At the same time, the story happens in a big city, which we created by a soundscape. In *Opening Night* [from John Cassavetes, 2009], there are a lot of scenes in the film where they rehearse or perform. We played these scenes towards a group of spectators seated in the wings on the side of the stage. The other parts were played towards the normal auditorium, where most of the audience were. And we filmed everything and showed everything so that everybody could see everything all the time.

PMB: How do you prepare, and how long does it take?

IvH: Of course it's not me alone: it's me with the dramaturg, the set-designer, perhaps the video or sound designer, and we talk together and out of that develops a concept, slowly. With a big production, like *Roman Tragedies,* it's two years – not full time of course, because I'm directing other things in-between. For a normal production, it's about a year. I like to prepare long before, so that I can digest it – so that like wine, it can lay, settle and then refresh. This way it keeps improving and, I hope, it becomes richer.

PMB: Your principal partner is of course Jan Versweyfeld with whom you have worked for more than 30 years. How does your collaboration work?

IvH: Well, it goes on day and night. Sometimes we go for a drink and we suddenly come up with ideas, and then this happens, I can show you *[shows pages from a notebook]*. This is a production that's not even concretely planned, but we were discussing the play, and then we started making up something. So our work is like a continuous conversation where sometimes we talk for half an hour about a production we will do in three years from now, and then it switches to what is currently in rehearsal, because all productions are also one big work. They are not disconnected; they are about us, about me. You can see a little bit who I am in my productions.

PMB: So these conversations are also about making links between the plays and your own lives, and by extension the lives of today's audience?

IvH: Yes of course! Because I live today, I read a text with the knowledge of today: of what I've read, what I've seen, my personal experience and what happens in society. Of course, as a director you have to understand a text from its time, but to simply restore and try to make a text work in the way that it worked in the nineteenth or even in the twentieth century is useless, I think. Theatre has the capacity of talking about today, and that's the only sense theatre makes for me. I can only direct a text when I believe

180 per cent that this text should be staged *now* because it matters for us *now*. That doesn't mean that my theatre is political, or only about current events. Not at all, actually. I think that this never works in theatre. In the theatre, we should reflect, but that's a much slower process than what happens every day in newspapers, magazines, or television shows. Of course, the current war in Syria is terrible. You can say this on stage and we all agree, but we all agree anyway. So it's much better to stage, for example, *Troilus and Cressida*, and show the consequences of war, and allow us to reflect. That's what theatre is for, and not to represent reality. I like to quote the line by Harold Pinter from his lecture for the Nobel-prize that the theatre should look *behind* the mirror, and not *into* the mirror.

PMB: You already mentioned the importance of time and space for what you describe as your 'concept', but what other guidelines do you follow when you approach a play? For instance, when you staged Tennessee Williams's *Streetcar* in New York in 1999, it was very controversially received, as the set consisted solely of a bathtub …

IvH: But it's in the text! She's always going to the bathroom and locks herself into the bathroom! As I said, it always starts from a close analysis of the text. So for me it was so clear that this was the place where she went to hide, where she was finally alone and found peace so that she could rest and escape the struggle. It's her one place of 'splendid isolation'. For us that became very important, and it was something that was never shown on stage before in this way. But it comes from the text, from reading the text very carefully. So we reduce, we try to find the core of a play, as I always say. I try to X-ray a text, and from there we start. Realism doesn't interest me that much. I prefer Rothko paintings. That's what I like in the theatre: reduction. That's not minimalism, but going to the core of things. I think I am a servant of the text, but not in a way that when an author writes, 'He enters through the garden', you simply see someone coming in through a door. I do take stage directions as seriously as text, but I try to understand what the author is trying to express with them. I try to see the poetry of a text, and equally the poetry of a stage direction rather than the naturalistic side of it. When Tennessee Williams wrote his stage directions in the 1940s, they were really progressive, but if you reproduce them on stage today, it would not work in the way he wanted it to work. I'm really sure about this! So as a director you have to understand what the author wanted. His stage directions, for instance, are full of sounds: there are always cats screaming, radios playing, and so on. And that idea I used in *Streetcar* for the soundscape that was there for this violent, aggressive jungle of New Orleans, which is what I think he expressed through these stage directions.

PMB: So you consider your work as 'true to the text', in the sense of the German notion of *Werktreue*?

IvH: Yes, that's what I think, because the text is the only thing that I have, nothing else. That's the material. But it's *material* – like when you have a car. You need to put in petrol, and only then you can start. Without petrol, nothing happens. A text in itself is not alive. I have to make it alive. I think that's the big misunderstanding of being 'true to the text': Shakespeare has been done over 100s of years in totally different styles, totally different attitudes, so what's the problem? The text of *Hamlet* will always be there, everybody can read it, but even then, ask three people what it is about, and you will get three different interpretations. There are always only interpretations of a text, there is not one objective truth about it. Directing opera, I learnt that even when there is the instruction of 'fffortissimo' with the three f's, even there you have different stages of 'very loud loudness', and that's what the director can influence. That's what I do.

PMB: When you discuss some of your productions, you tend to start by talking about the setting. In my opinion, this points to what I see as a key characteristic of your work: you create, above all, a spatial solution, a spatial interpretation, or perhaps one could even say, a spatial adaptation of the play that isn't an illustration …

IvH: [interrupts] … no, not an illustration, never an illustration! Well – space defines everything. It's a very basic and most important decision you have to take about making a production. But I rather call it a 'world': we create the world where this production will live. We try to find the right house for the characters to live in, and give a lot of attention to it, because it's their home. Of course we think that this world is the best world this play can be represented in. Sometimes we're right, sometimes we're wrong. But the actors often say that in Jan's designs they can feel immediately what you can do and what you cannot do – and that is what's important for me.

PMB: This non-illusionistic use of space in your work is maybe most evident in your staging of movies. There is this tradition in film criticism to read films as imaginary stagings of the mind, and I wonder whether something similar is the case here – whether your sets help the audience getting into your mind. Perhaps parts of the audience will not have grown up watching the same European art-cinema movies that you stage, but it appears that you facilitate the entrance into that world of thinking through space, even more so than through characters and identification.

IvH: Of course, yes, because the first thing you see on stage is space, even if it is empty. The space makes a text accessible, and it makes you understand why the characters are saying what they are saying, why they behave the way they behave. Take the two screenplays by Ingmar Bergman we recently did, *After the Rehearsal* and *Persona* [both 2012, as a double bill]. The first is a television movie in a rehearsal space, and *Persona* deals with two basic spaces – that's what Jan and I analysed. So for bringing those two plays together, I saw three spaces: the rehearsal space, the hospital, and a lake. That's how we started, and so Jan builds a space like this *[draws in his notebook]* – there was a table, because there is always a director sitting behind a table, and some props. For the hospital, my inspirations did not come from the movie, but from the work of Flemish artist Berlinde de Bruyckere. She makes these sculptures of corpses, of pieces of bodies that you cannot recognize any more. They are all scarred, you can see they are in pain. So, Jan empties the space totally for the second part, the lights are changed, but it's still the same space. And then to go to the lake, we dropped down all the walls and there was water, and suddenly you were almost on an island in the middle of water. Now water is of course about purification, it is a healing force, and the person who was in the hospital goes to this lake – but I did not want to push that metaphorically too much. For me, a space never becomes a metaphor. That doesn't interest me. It's always a real surrounding, a real environment. But it can have different layers you can fantasize about.

PMB: You keep your stage worlds usually very sparse and empty, emphasizing a rigid clarity and focus.

IvH: Some of Jan's sets are like this room here [*points around his office*]. I can put it full of furniture; it would be the same space, but I decided to keep it quite empty for a director's office. It opens my mind and there are a lot of people sitting here all the time who fill this space with their thoughts, with their criticisms, with their questions. That's enough for me. And sometimes that's how it is in the productions as well. For instance, you will barely see props. I use chairs only when it's really necessary. Or, only chairs and nothing else. We could say it's as simple as that, but of course to find this simplicity you really have to know, and you really have to analyse what's there in the text. So it's again about reducing, and about finding a right balance. It's like a sauce; you don't make a good sauce by adding things together just hoping it will work. You have to find the right balance. And then sometimes it has to cook for a long time, and sometimes it's done within a second and then you have to stop. It's the same balancing act that you have to make in rehearsing and creating a production.

PMB: Another prominent aspect of your work is of course your use of media and of audio-visual technology: you use live-feed video projections, and also sound as an aural medium in its own right.

IvH: I first used live video for *Caligula* by Camus [1996]. The play is about the crisis of an emperor, something we would witness today through the media. After that, I didn't use live video for a long time, in fact. I now use it more and more because it has become a device that is accessible for us. You can express things in a way that cannot be expressed without video. For me, video is like a Greek mask: it enlarges things, it allows us to come nearer to the emotional dimension and to make it more visible, so that you can empathize more with that emotion. It's the same with the sound and with the microphones. The microphone gives us opportunities that you really wouldn't have without it. The Greeks had masks, and as theatre tools developed over the centuries, we now have video and microphones, so why not use them?

PMB: The sound often seems to furnish the empty spaces of your sets, contributing to the atmosphere we talked about.

IVH: Yes, the space is always there first, but sounds come also pretty quickly to my mind. I use sound in basically three different ways. Sometimes we have, like in *Persona*, a soundscape that goes on all the time and that becomes almost like a space in itself. In other productions, I work with a composer who creates his or her own music. That is a different working method. And then, sometimes I do music myself: I choose one or two songs to stress or give accents here and there. When I read a play, most of the time I hear something immediately. For instance, with *Long Day's Journey Into Night* [2013], I thought almost immediately of Randy Newman. He composed some cynical political songs, which I won't use, but he also did these very tender loving songs about family, about brothers and sisters, about the difficulties of living together and losing somebody. They came to my mind when I read this play. This is of course very intuitive. It works or it doesn't. You cannot argue about it. But in *Long Day's Journey*, there is no video; it wouldn't make sense for me for this very gentle play. So I don't have a formula. I always consider with every production what I should do. I'm not Bob Wilson who has a style.

PMB: Well, I'm not so sure. First, there is the major role of the space as one rather distinctive aspect of your work. Another central aspect which the live media bring in, as you use them in *The Roman Tragedies* or *The Antonioni Project* [2009], is that as you just said, you can zoom in on the characters, you get the big image, but at the very same time, there's an emphasis on the theatricality, on the fact that this is not an illusion but actually happening here in front of us in the live moment …

IvH: Yes, but again this has to do with what Antonioni wants to tell us: the alienation of individuals in a larger cosmos or society. My idea to express this on stage was by making a movie out of what you see, but you also see that the movie is being made. When I directed a movie myself in 2007, I found it a strange experience that on the set two characters were talking to each other very intimately or making love, but there was a camera and a lot of people standing around behind it, also people who were not looking and who didn't care at all. This was a perfect metaphor for the alienation that is in Antonioni. And he did that in his movies by always filming individual people against huge architectural buildings so that they were small people with a small shadow that looks like a halo almost – that's what I remember from his movies, but you have to find a way to express this on stage, it would make no sense to do it that way and simply replicate it.

PMB: So is this sense for the live moment that goes beyond the plot, this awareness that we are watching a play that is made right in front of our eyes, important for you?

IvH: In this case, in the Antonioni Project, it was. I guess, sometimes the illusion is important and sometimes the breaking of the illusion is important. As I said, I don't have a set formula. But basically you're right: illusion is not my thing. When I create an illusion, I make it also clear that we are watching people who are playing. That came to me when I saw Kurt Cobain on *MTV Unplugged* a long time ago. He was singing very intensely, and then, when the song was over, he just took a glass of water and smoked his cigarette, he was very relaxed – but when the first note was played, he was totally into the next song again. That's exactly the way that I like theatre the most. I like organic acting. This means it has to start from the actors themselves. I don't like actors who only play a character: no, they *are* the character and have to find their connection with the character. And I like to show that process a little bit without making it too clear. In theatre we have the tendency to represent a character as if personality is just one thing. But in real life, we're not just depressed all the time, but our personality consists of 30 different elements or more. That is what I want to bring on stage. A person is not one thing. He's many different things and he can behave in the next scene in a way that makes you think this cannot be the same person. That's what happens in real life all the time.

PMB: And probably similarly, in the texts you stage, especially in the well-known plays, you bring out these elements, so that we meet another, a different aspect of the text.

IvH: I was really inspired by performance art when I was very young. In a performance, everything is what it is, and that stayed with me: I want to go as near to reality as possible. It's like the blue paintings by Paul Klee: there is always a tiny little red spot, and because the red spot is there, you can really appreciate the blue. I also need that other little thing, this performance element that is this red spot in my theatre – the one moment in a production when something is just what it is: when it is real. I always search for that moment. Perhaps this is what surprises a lot of people when they see a production by us, and they say, 'It is as if we saw this play for the first time'. I take that as the greatest compliment.

Link

Toneelgroep Amsterdam: http://www.tga.nl/en (accessed 18 January 2014).

Selected bibliography

Billing, Christian M. (2010). 'The Roman Tragedies', *Shakespeare Quarterly*, 61.3, pp. 415–39.

McNulty, Charles. (2000). 'Commuting Beyond the Stereotypes: The Dangerous Trek of Ivo van Hove's *A Streetcar Named Desire*', *Theater*, 30.2, pp. 155–9.

Thielemans, Johan. (2010). 'Ivo van Hove's Passionate Quest for a Necessary Theatre', *Contemporary Theatre Review*, 20.4, pp. 455–60.

Note

1 David Willinger, 'Van Hove's *Geruchten*', *The Drama Review*, 25.2 (1981), pp. 116–18.

4

'Something New Is Sure to Happen': Daniel Veronese in Conversation with Jean Graham-Jones[1]

Introduction

Director-playwright Daniel Veronese (b. 1955) is arguably Argentina's most successful theatre artist, both home and abroad. Toggling fluently between Buenos Aires's independent (experimental) and commercial theatre scenes, he has introduced recent plays by Lindsay-Abbaire and LaBute to mainstream audiences throughout the Spanish-speaking world and produced his own stripped-down texts and radically re-envisioned versions of Chekhov and Ibsen. One of the leading artists to emerge in post-dictatorship Argentina, Veronese achieved early international recognition through his participation in object-theatre troupe Periférico de Objetos, which he and fellow puppetry students co-founded in 1989. The 'Periféricos' – working collaboratively from a self-declared periphery separating actors and objects – radically reworked texts, created their own, and constructed textual tableaux in productions incorporating myriad objects, all manipulated in the audience's full view. Best known abroad for their brilliantly violent version of Heiner Müller's *Hamletmachine*, the company was renowned for performances in which words were separated from image and puppets from puppeteers, themselves in turn split into manipulators and actors.

In addition to an early apprenticeship in carpentry and preparation as a puppeteer, Veronese studied acting with director Ricardo Bartís and playwriting with dramatists Mauricio Kartun and Roberto Mario

Cossa. While still working in El Periférico, Veronese began writing plays for actors, his first premiering in 1992. Twenty-one of his plays have been published in two Spanish-language collections.[2] Like many of his generation and its successors, Veronese grants himself complete aesthetic freedom to mix genres, registers, forms and even political positions in service to what he has called 'bastard theatre'. Veronese's theatre multiplies, contradicts, and makes us rethink everything we have taken for granted, inside and outside the theatre.

Recent productions reflect the dramatist-director's intensely intimate writing, design, and directing style in stagings stripped to the most elemental of human interactions with thoughtfully constructed environments and actors bringing their all to onstage encounters. Veronese says he writes 'thinking about the stage'; unsurprisingly, he has become not only an accomplished playwright but the favourite director of some of Buenos Aires's most talented actors, who clearly respond to his deceptively minimalist approach.

Veronese has had the greatest impact on the recent international performance scene with his radical 'versions' of Chekhov and Ibsen. *Un hombre que se ahoga* (2004) distils *Three Sisters* to 90 minutes and inverts gender roles without any cross-dressing on a bare-bones set under natural light; *Espía a una mujer que se mata* (2006) weaves texts from *The Seagull* and Genet's *Maids* into a condensed *Uncle Vanya.* In *Los hijos se han dormido* (2011), *The Seagull*'s concern with theatrical realism takes centre stage, in a home that is clearly a set and actors cast without regard for verisimilitude. 2009's *Todos los grandes gobiernos han evitado el teatro íntimo* finds an older Hedda living in a theatrical set created for *El desarrollo de la civilización venidera*, a version that crosses Ibsen with Bergman as Nora and Helmer remain caught in the web of an incomplete liberation. In the conversation that follows, we discuss these adaptations, individually and within the larger context of Veronese's sustained career.

Interview

Jean Graham-Jones: You've adapted many works for the stage: you've staged your own versions of texts by Chekhov and Ibsen, which have toured internationally, and for the commercial theatre – in cities like Buenos Aires, Barcelona, and Mexico City – you've also directed plays by Mamet, LaBute and Williams, always lending them your own singular touch. But your first experience in theatrical adaptation was with the group El Periférico de Objetos. How did those early experiences in adapting Müller's *Hamletmachine* [*Máquina Hamlet*, 1995] or Hofmann's *The Sandman* [*El hombre de arena*, 1992] influence your later work? Could you tell us a bit about the adaptations you did with El Periférico?

Daniel Veronese: With El Periférico de Objetos, since it was an object-theatre company, our versions had to patrol an especially visual terrain. The adaptations were to a large degree situated within a field of expression dominated by the force of images, light, and music. The spoken word, as enunciated by the actors, remained almost outside our perimeters. If there was a text, generally it ended up framed within sonic processes of amplification or distortion. We also used a mode of projecting [the text] so it could be read. You asked me about *Máquina Hamlet*: there we relied on the important contributions of Dieter Welke, a dramaturg that Buenos Aires's Goethe Institute had made available to us. His presence was really enriching for all of us, as we spent two weeks on table work, during which he opened our minds in various ways. This allowed us to make the version we as Argentines wanted to present. With *El hombre de arena* the process was very different. We wanted to work on the idea of the automaton. It was our subject and in Hoffman's text this, for us, very lovely theme was touched upon, but as we went deeper into the short story it became simply impossible for us to move beyond the idea. In some desperate – but necessary – attempts we arrived at Freud and his work on this subject. There we forgot about everything and just allowed our instinct of the sinister to run free. There's a very strange fact [related to the production]: anyone who saw the finished piece could not help relating it to the period of the military dictatorship. But the truth is that when we were working on the version and then performed it, we never mentioned those tragic Argentine events; nevertheless, it was obviously there in our subconscious. It's impossible for us to talk about the sinister and not have that part of Argentina's dark and brutal history appear. I also want to point out that in El Periférico we worked as a group. Even if I stepped outside in order to make final decisions [about the staging], the road leading to a work that all of us found convincing was always one of complete consensus.

JGJ: Almost all your versions come from texts that have been translated from other languages into Spanish. In other words, they are already in a sense adaptations. How do you work with the written text? Do you consult multiple translations? Do you always grant yourself the same amount of creative freedom in modifying the original (or translated) text? In other words, what is your adaptation process?

DV: I start off consulting various translations, but there's a point at which I begin to work with the text as if it were one of my own. This means that I modify what I need to without keeping the original too much in mind. I ought to mention that these versions are created because I have every intention of staging the text, but then I very quickly stop thinking about literature and decide with my mind focused on the stage. I write while I'm directing, because during rehearsals I will modify texts the actors have already learnt, but I also direct the play in my head while I adapt and write.

JGJ: I think your dual training and practice as a playwright and director is very important. It's certainly influenced the versions you've staged. What about the other way around? Has the experience of staging versions of others' texts affected your creative process when writing your own original plays?

DV: What caused all this was a decline in my own dramatic output. I used to be able to write various plays at the same time, and I did so, but since I really got into adapting for the stage, I cut back considerably on writing plays that originate from me. For a time, because of the pleasure I found in this new way of working or simply maybe because it was a new phase, I stopped producing my own texts in any significant way.

JGJ: If I remember correctly, with the exception of a couple of Periférico projects, you've always worked with dramatic-theatrical texts. Did you ever consider working with another genre to adapt it for the theatre?

DV: Yes, that's what I'm doing now. I was inspired after seeing Krystian Lupa's stage adaptation of a work by Thomas Bernhard.[3] I want to adapt novels, and I'm currently looking for novels that captivate me.

JGJ: What does this captivation consist of? Do you have specific criteria for selecting a text?

DV: I don't have any criteria other than my instinct at the moment of selection. When reading I also hope to find something that motivates me and makes me choose that piece of literature. It can be its subject or its structure, but if it doesn't produce any magical spell, then obviously I don't go for it.

JGJ: These days everyone talks about your 'Chekhov Project'. You first took on the Russian writer with a version of *Three Sisters*: *Un hombre que se ahoga* [*A drowning man*]. Why Chekhov? Why that particular play? Did you have in mind from the start a 'Chekhov Project'? If so, what was that project for you?

DV: If you connect the titles of the versions of *Three Sisters* and *Uncle Vanya*, it creates a sentence: 'Un hombre que se ahoga espía a una mujer que se mata' [A drowning man spies a woman killing herself]. I carried this line by Urs Graf [discovered in a book by Jacques Prévert] around with me for years. I allowed myself to use it as a trigger each time I found myself stuck or detained by some problem. Twenty years later I discovered that Graf wrote in a very poetic and forceful way about Chekhovian behaviours. I got into Chekhov because he's very emotionally close and readable to me. He's a contemporary author. He speaks of us. The name 'Proyecto Chéjov' was invented by a producer who needed to publicize the plays as if they belonged to some aesthetic plan. I simply created one after the other, with some space between them. I did not plan to make a trilogy either. I don't think that these plays dialogue with one another any more or less than they dialogue with the rest of my work.

JGJ: And of course in all your plays there's a prevailing emotional and physical intensity, a style of acting that I would describe as centripetal and that has always attracted me as a spectator. Nevertheless, it's difficult not to connect your first two adaptations of Chekhov: the conjoined titles, similar adaptive strategies, same theatre [Buenos Aires's Camarín de las Musas], minimalist aesthetic, shared casts. For example, I think about the actor Osmar Núñez, who played Olga and then Vanya. How can we not see a little of Olga in Osmar's Vanya? Neither married, both sacrificed on the family altar … For me, the connection between the two productions goes beyond Graf's unifying phrase. I also think about the recycling of the set that bonds one of the Chekhovs to your previous original play, *Mujeres soñaron caballos* [*Women dreamt of horses*]. When the actor Fernando Llosa originated the role of Serebriakov, he'd already appeared earlier in *Mujeres* as the eldest brother, Iván. So when I saw Fernando-Serebriakov seated with his daughter holding a gun at the very same table he'd occupied five years earlier with the same actress [María Figueras], who had before been pointing the gun at him, Chekhov became, at least in my spectator's experience, haunted by Veronese. In fact, the three productions – the two Chekhovs and *Mujeres* – might be seen as a kind of triptych that underscores a social disharmony that is both Argentine and global. I'm finally getting to my question and ask you to rethink your earlier answer: don't your adaptations dialogue with your other plays?

DV: I would like to have the distance necessary in order to see this and be able to respond to you and so many others. In looking at the work of a creator, there's an overriding need to create families and sets. What one generally does alone is think, select, and make. One procreates and shows. But people need to agree or disagree over whether this last creation was better or worse than the one before, or if it is similar to or different from another one by the same author, or if it is a summation that conforms to a strategic plan of production. I'm exaggerating a bit, I know, but most of us create with enough difficulty without additionally trying to create a collection that dialogues intertextually with itself. Obviously, if I use the same actors, something coincidental is going to be noticed, especially because I do not introduce the actor into the character but rather try to place the character inside the actor. The actor onstage is a very powerful sign for me. As far as the situation with the shared set for *Mujeres soñaron caballos* and *Espía a una mujer que se mata* (my version of *Uncle Vanya*), it got me thinking about some issues regarding theatrical space. I think the opening of *Espía* is a good example. This opening is totally different from Chekhov's *Uncle Vanya*. Taking advantage of *Mujeres*, where Iván and Lucera [his much younger wife] end the play at a table with her pointing the revolver at him, I concocted something similar for the opening of my version [of *Vanya*]: the same two actors played Serebriakov and Sonia, and I had them seated with the revolver – the same one Vanya would use later, at the end – on the table between them as they talked about the theatre. I thought about performing *Mujeres* and then *Espía*, one after the other. The first play would end, the actors take their bows, and without too much change the next play could begin. That's why [I created] this opening for my version of *Vanya*. I know that this is not gratuitous, but in reality I don't think about what people are going to think about it, what sign I'm developing – I think about playful, ludic issues. I trust these practices and I put them into play.

JGJ: Not all your adaptations are equal. For example, in your version of *Vanya*, you interpolate scenes from Genet's *The Maids*. These scenes are rehearsed by Vanya and Astrov when they're not doing something else. What does Genet have to do with Chekhov? Was Genet always present in your version of *Vanya*?

DV: I simply wanted to do Chekhov's play but inserting at the beginning a short but emblematic piece of contemporary thinking about the theatre. I considered deploying a speech about contemporary theatre and from the start annulling *Uncle Vanya*, something I didn't end up doing. I'd already obviously thought about having the play talk about theatre and that Serebriakov would be the one to give the speech at the beginning. But we had a problem with getting the rights to the work I'd chosen for this insertion. So I simply began to rehearse and modify the first scene, in some way, in the direction of my initial idea. That's how in the first scene Serebriakov [ends up] explaining to his daughter why it's a mistake to follow those new theatrical forms – forms that in some way her Uncle Vanya takes on, and especially Astrov, with whom she's in love. As we advanced in rehearsals, I noticed that the inclusion of short acting exercises into the original play produced the effect I was seeking. That's why there are various moments in which they use Genet's lines, inserted within the Chekhovian structure.

JGJ: You've spoken of your creative process and rehearsing, both of which obviously have a lot to do with your approach to adaptation. You tend to work with the same actors in your own productions and we've already spoken about certain overlaps in casting that can affect the work's reception (at least mine with, say, the double casting of Osmar Núñez). What role do these trusted, experienced actors play in your process of adapting a text? On various occasions you've had to recast for tours, for subsequent seasons, etc. When you recast, do you find yourself making further modifications to the version?

DV: The actors are the beginning of everything in my work. I brought together a group of actors and then resolved [the problem] of what we were going to do together. Without them obviously nothing of what I've done would exist. They have a lot of freedom to create and propose. I trust them and I need to have this trust reciprocated in order to work. I believe the actor is a powerful mechanism who does surprising things, and I continuously let myself be surprised. Yes, I've had to recast actors for tours or other things, but bearing in mind this last precept, I'm able to end up casting in the same role an actor diametrically opposed to the one I had before. Something new is sure to happen. In general, my actors and I are open to that new universe that is opened up in the play. I have to say without any shame that at times it's more interesting to me for something extraordinary to happen on stage than for something to happen that's determined by the literary work. So, versions can end up being modified, but the theatre stays alive; that's what matters to me.

JGJ: Your *Seagull*, *Los hijos se han dormido* [*The children have gone to bed*], struck me as perhaps less of a 'version' than your other two versions of Chekhov. How does this third project figure into the reflection that lurks in the other Chekhovs, in your own words, 'God, Stanislavski, Genet'?

DV: I think I've already justified Genet. Stanislavski appears as a reference to a method of expression of a kind of theatricality that should be respected. When it's an actor who says, let's stop talking about God and Stanislavski, because we're talking about important subjects, evidently the idea is to distance oneself and not examine this staging from a scholarly position, but rather accept it as it is. And not expect religious miracles. We're human beings. God is a punctured life-preserver in a space lacking love or compassion and tremendously flooded with pain and the impossibility of truly projecting a happy life. Obviously I'm talking about the play.

JGJ: In your two versions of Ibsen, *Todos los grandes gobiernos han evitado el teatro íntimo* [*All the great governments have avoided intimate theatre, Hedda Gabler*] and *El desarrollo de la civilización venidera* [*The development of the future civilization, A Doll's*

House], the overarching theme is the theatre. Indeed, I'd say the major shift in your Ibsen adaptations is taking his famous naturalistic living room to the theatre (or is it the theatre to the living room?). In both versions, the theatre becomes the set, and the characters make almost constant references to performing. Both versions further benefit from some striking casting choices that make us rethink the original plays entirely. What place do such extratextual elements like casting and scenography have in these two particular versions?

DV: Once again, the ideas appear a priori. I let them appear but with the almost certain intuition that at the moment I begin to make theatre they'll move to the side. In this case, the idea was to consider Nora, from *Doll's House*, as if she were Hedda Gabler but a few years earlier. I had two actresses that easily could be seen as the projection of each other. I wanted to use the same actor as the husband in both plays, so he would not age. Ideas, ideas. None of this worked out favourably. Yes, I had the two actresses, but at the time of adapting each play separately, I became involved in such an intricate task that it became impossible to create two successive plays out of it. Yet the need to have the two versions in dialogue with each other ended up expressed with Hedda living in a set mounted in a municipal theatre. That is, she used the set as if it were her own home, and the characters declared it as such. And it just so happened that the play they talked about was my version of *Doll's House* – *El desarrollo de la civilización venidera*. Which in *Hedda Gabler* is the title Ibsen gives to Lövborg's impressive manuscript. What impact does this have in the mind of the Ibsen spectator? I'll never know. But what's certain is that for his time Ibsen wrote in a devastating way. His plays in his era exploded on the stages. But today some of these issues have been, if not resolved, apparently overcome. That's the difference with Chekhov, who I think wrote for posterity.

JGJ: I'm interested in the emphasis you place on the theatre as a place of action. At the beginning of *Espía a una mujer que se mata*, you interject some pieces of dialogue from the first act of

Seagull, but in your version it's Serebriakov who complains about the modern theatre. Hedda lives in a set that's then used for Nora's play. Your actors wear costumes that look like their own, as if they've just arrived for rehearsal. How do you handle onstage the *place* of the theatre? What does the theatre mean to you, as Hedda's home, as a possible doll's house? And why does all this happen in a municipal theatre?

DV: The place where we make theatre is a privileged place from which we can offer to audiences emotions, illusions, discoveries that they can't find in another space, that representativity is impossible to find elsewhere, not even in everyday life. I don't want to assess the theatrical space as better, but as different, distinct. People leave their home, they travel, buy their ticket, spend an important portion of their time, then you need to offer them something that they can't find somewhere else. That is in general the respect I have for the audience. I should surprise myself with my creation. And so there's the possibility that the audience can, too. And I always make references to that unique and privileged place we occupy. I always try to talk about the theatre in my plays. It's a mania. If I made films, I'd definitely talk a lot about the cinema in my movies. It's a way to feel secure. I don't wish to explain it case by case, because I'd disappoint you, the initial idea will surely seem inferior to you in comparison to the final product. The first is raw while in the production I'm serving you the other is fully baked.

JGJ: For you, is there any difference between your independent [experimental] projects and your commercial productions? I'm struck by how in the commercial theatre you've tended to direct relatively recent and not 'classical' plays, whereas in your independent projects, you've often worked with texts from the theatrical canon. Why the difference in the selection of plays?

DV: They differ principally in that with the commercial theatre I'm contracted to create, to direct a product that satisfies already-determined needs. In the independent theatre I'm the owner of all these issues. But at the moment of starting to work, I don't have different strategies or ways for approaching the material or the actors.

JGJ: El Periférico's version of *Hamletmachine*, with which we began our conversation, relocated a text with strong references to Nazi Germany to an Argentina that had recently emerged from its own dictatorship. You spoke earlier of the impossibility of talking about the sinister without this history appearing. How do you react to the idea some critics have that your versions must always be Argentine? Or are they, for you, already part of a culture that for better or worse we might call globalized?

DV: When I referred to the Argentine unconscious that surfaced in *Hombre de arena*, I was referring to how it can end up approaching a theatre with political resonances without passing through propaganda. I'm Argentine, with everything good and bad that implies; obviously my work is going to reflect who I am. But there are many ways of being Argentine. I don't know what would be an Argentine result in some other way. I direct a lot abroad, and my work can end up standing out because it's different from others', but no one can say that I have an Argentine way of directing; here [in Buenos Aires] there is a considerable variety of aesthetics and poetics. Perhaps what's operating here is the unnecessary pre-judgement often made of a play: if the artist is from a certain country, then he is read in a certain way. You can't fight against that.

JGJ: Daniel, a final question that's somewhat related to the previous one: what's your opinion of the idea of theatrical adaptation as 'intercultural'?

DV: I believe that an intercultural result might be produced when a director directs actors from another country or when one takes a foreign work and stages it trying to retain the essence of the original. I take on versions generally because it's a territory in which I feel best. In the same way that I introduce the character into the actor – what it would mean for the actor to work with the possibilities that he already has for confronting that character – I perform a process of drawing this material to my private level, a place I can potentially reach to produce more organic theatre. I don't know if that's interesting to other cultural views, to those seeking a geographic map of theatre, but it's interesting to me. And obviously for the audience.

Selected bibliography

Graham-Jones, Jean. (2013). 'Daniel Veronese's "Proyecto Chéjov": Translation in Performance as Radical Relationality' in J. Douglas Clayton and Yana Meerzon (eds), *Re-Writing Chekhov: The Text and Its Mutations*. London and New York: Routledge, pp. 203–16.

Veronese, Daniel. (1997). *Cuerpo de prueba: textos teatrales* (Body of proof: theatre texts]. Buenos Aires: Centro Cultural Ricardo Rojas, 1997; re-ed. (2005) by Jorge Dubatti, Buenos Aires: Atuel.

—(2000). *La deriva* (Drift), ed. by Jorge Dubatti. Buenos Aires: Adriana Hidalgo.

Notes

1 This conversation was carried out in Spanish over a series of emails between February and June 2013. The original has been translated into English by the author.
2 See Veronese (1997, 2000).
3 This was Krystian Lupa's *Kalkwerk* (2009), based on the homonymous novel by Bernhard.

5

Conservative Adaptation in Japanese Noh Theatre: Udaka Michishige in Conversation with Diego Pellecchia

Introduction

How does the notion of 'adaptation' apply to a classical theatre genre where language, dramatic structure, music, and *mise en scène* are prescribed by a canon? Can this English word be used invariably to describe works belonging to any cultural area? This interview will explore the concept of adaptation in the context of one of the world's oldest existing performance traditions, Japanese Noh theatre, filtered by the experience of Kongō School *shite* actor Udaka Michishige.

Following Linda Hutcheon's definition,[1] a first understanding of the term 'adaptation' implies the acknowledgement of two distinct entities: a pre-existing source, whatever is 'already there', and a 'new' work, separated from the first and chronologically 'second'. Whatever the pre-existing sources may be, by utilizing something that previously existed in order to create a new work of art, adaptation draws a line between the 'old' and the 'new', or the 'existing' and the 'not-yet-existing', and then crosses it. This crossing movement is not linear but circular: Hutcheon stresses the importance of looking at adaptation as being 'second without being secondary'.[2] However, the idea that no art is born from nothing, but is in fact the re-elaboration of pre-existing art, has emerged in relatively recent times. The nineteenth-century Romantic image of the individual genius, whose inspired gesture breaks from the past and creates something new, was challenged by early twentieth-century modernist authors, who advocated a return to tradition. T. S. Eliot refuted the conception of the artist as an isolated entity, and called for a repositioning of art within the track of tradition as collective past.[3] Later, poststructuralist and postmodernist thinking stressed the deceptive nature of originality, with Roland Barthes proclaiming the 'death of the author' and the birth of the reader in 1967, hence stripping the author of the exclusive right to authorship.[4]

This progressive dismantling of authorship in art production and reception by Western critical thinkers did not 'trickle down' to popular Western understanding of creativity and originality, usually still regarded as merits in aesthetic judgement. 'Trite', 'banal', 'cliché', 'stock', 'stale' – English has a wide range of derogatory adjectives to describe what is *not* 'original', 'imaginative', 'innovative', 'inventive', or 'fresh'. In line with nineteenth-century approaches, 'originality', understood as both 'novelty' and 'authenticity', is still perceived as a universal merit in contemporary Western discourses. But how does this discursive framework, which is also valid in Eastern cultures like Japan, apply to traditional genres like Noh theatre? Here, artistic 'perfection' is achieved by polishing a pre-established technique, rather than through innovation as an act of distancing from pre-existing forms.

George William Aston and Basil Hall Chamberlain were among the first Western intellectuals to attend Noh performances during the early Meiji period (1868–1912), when Japan opened its borders to the outside world and foreigners started visiting its shores. Early appreciations of Noh were often uncomplimentary because of the difficulty of untrained audiences to accept a different view of art and tradition: Aston considered Noh to be literarily insubstantial because it was based on systematic plagiarism of pre-existing sources,[5] while Chamberlain noted that hardly anything in Japan that was praised in the West for its originality was, in fact, 'original'.[6]

Both comments, which perpetuated a stereotypical view of the Japanese as a people of imitators, respond to the very nature of Noh text composition. Noh verse typically draws from a variety of pre-existing sources, including folk-tales, classic literature, epic poetry and Buddhist scriptures. Often proceeding by superimposition of images and coordination rather than logic causality, entire sections of Noh plays can be successions of quotes from other texts. Noh theatre's sophisticated intertextual quality makes allusion and reference one of the most important features of this genre. Noh scholar Sanari Kentarō wrote that 'Noh verse is like tapestry', comparing it to interweaving fabric patterns that do not have clearly defined narratives, yet contribute to the overall tightly-knit beauty of the composition.[7]

Kan'ami Kiyotsugu (1333–85) and his son Zeami Motokiyo (1363–1442), the creators of Noh, were able to combine various elements of pre-existing traditions, such as *dengaku* field rituals, *kagura* religious dances, and *kusemai* dance-song into a new harmonious genre. The result of such fusion was a performing art containing dance, mimetic movement, music, chant, poetry and masks. When Noh started being patronized by the aristocrats, passing from countryside to court entertainment during Zeami's lifetime, both text and performance style gradually adapted to suit the taste of new sophisticated audiences: movements slowed down considerably and became more abstract.

Though many famous Noh plays are written by Zeami, his name did not rise to popularity until his 'treatises' on the art of Noh were rediscovered in the early twentieth century. In the Noh tradition, emphasis is not placed on single authors, but on the flux of knowledge transmitted by the five *shite* (main actor role) schools. The notion of the author as the proprietor of the work of art did not exist in the Muromachi period (1336–1573), when most Noh plays of the current repertoire were composed. Steven Brown points out that 'Medieval practices of authorship and revision meant that Noh plays were open to the contingencies of restaging and re-writing that divided the singularity of the play's initial performance and created room for future innovations'.[8] Eric Rath explained how in Japan the notion of authorship emerged in the seventeenth century with the advent of the print industry, a technology that 'facilitated the identification and idealization of the "authors" of writings as great patriarchs of ways of knowledge'.[9] While during the initial phases of Noh history performers were comparatively freer to modify repertory and stage techniques, later the many traditions comprised within the Noh spectrum were categorized into defined stylistic schools (in Japanese, *ryū*: 'flow').

Each school is led by an *iemoto* (literally, 'origin of the house'), a leader who has power over all actors belonging to the school. With the establishment of the *iemoto* system during the seventeenth century, all aspects of Noh were crystallized into orthodoxy: text, movement, music, costumes and so on. Since then, relatively little changed until the Meiji period, when the country entered a vast process of modernization through contact with Western civilization. Unlike opera, a traditional genre which is no longer rigidly dictated by conventions in the twenty-first century, in Noh every aspect of performance is still prescribed by a canon, and eventual variations proposed by actors must be approved by the *iemoto*. The Noh environment is therefore characterized by two contrasting features: on the one hand, the artistic predilection towards adaptation of pre-existing material into Noh plays, a practice that is inscribed in tradition and prescribed by canon. On the other hand, the same canon imposes a formal rigidity, both aesthetic and political, that might be seen to limit the performers' freedom to modify established conventions.

Despite the rigidity of tradition, new plays usually referred to as *shinsaku Noh* ('newly written Noh') are produced every year. In his survey 'One Hundred Years of Shinsaku Noh', scholar Nishino Haruo defines the canonical repertoire as the group of 300 plays written until the end of the Nanbokuchō period (1334–92), while *shinsaku Noh* are those 100s of plays written from the beginning of the Meiji period until today.[10] A number of these are adaptations of stories or works of art of both local and foreign origin, ranging from adaptations of Shakespeare's plays to depictions of historical characters such as Joan of Arc or Albert Einstein. However, in order to be considered *shinsaku Noh*, these new plays must abide by traditional aesthetic rules. For scholar Yamanaka Reiko, in order 'to be called nō, a performance should consist of the traditional, well-known, existing units. Even if the actors wear nō-style costumes and nō-style masks, and perform with the concentrated posture and the unique walking style of nō, a performance cannot be called "nō" if the music is completely new, or if the actors' movements on stage are not based on traditional kinetic units'.[11] For Nishino, an ideal *shinsaku Noh* should, among other things, be 'enrooted in tradition but allow the audience to feel novelty, it should not depart from classic Noh, but should have the freedom and be able to transcend rules'.[12] Such definitions of *shinsaku Noh* reflect a Japanese tendency to innovate in a conservative way, remoulding tradition without necessarily obliterating the old with the new.[13]

It is possible to articulate such a definition of '*shinsaku*' because Noh is a *genre* in which rules govern composition and performance. For example, Nishino points out how Mishima Yukio's *Modern Noh Plays*, adaptations of canonical Noh, cannot be considered as Noh. They are, in fact, adaptations into another dramatic form that is broadly termed *engeki* ('theatre'), or *shibai* ('play'). Judging from the way in which scholars in the field discuss where to draw the line between Noh and other forms of theatre, adaptation in Noh emerges as a one-way process, where it has the ability to absorb external influences and adapt non-canonical material to its aesthetic conventions while maintaining its brand, whereas adaptations of Noh outside the limits of what are considered to be its essential features cannot be considered as Noh.

In order to explore the notion of adaptation in Noh I have interviewed *shite* actor Udaka Michishige. Udaka (b. 1947) is both a professional Noh actor and a Noh mask carver, and was designated as representative of a National Intangible Cultural Asset by the Japanese government in 1991. His commitment to the art of Noh is total: after graduation from elementary school Udaka entered the household of Kongō Iwao II, the 25th *iemoto* of the Kongō School as a live-in apprentice. In 1970 he gained his independence as a fully trained actor and began his teaching and performing career in Japan, with numerous experiences abroad. In 1984 Udaka founded the International Noh Institute, aimed at opening the knowledge of Noh to the non-Japanese. Though his artistic endeavour is strongly enrooted in the tradition of the Kongō school, Udaka has composed three *shinsaku Noh*: *Shiki* (2001), *Ryōma* (2003), and *Genshigumo* (2003). In the interview below,

I discuss with Udaka the role of adaptation in the creation of new Noh, and, more broadly, in the development of the individual technique of an actor.

Interview

Diego Pellecchia: The English word 'adaptation' signifies a process of utilizing pre-existing material in the creation of a new work. Usually this is translated in Japanese as *hon'an* or *kaisaku*. Is the notion of adaptation familiar to a Noh actor?

Udaka Michishige: I can only speak for myself, but I think that 'adaptation' [*hon'an*] is not a term Noh actors use as frequently as practitioners of other art forms would. We Noh actors spend most of our artistic life learning the classic repertoire, with little time for activities such as adaptation of non-canonical texts that diverge from tradition. So far I have written and performed three Noh plays: *Shiki* (2001), *Ryōma* (2003) and *Genshigumo* (2003). I suppose they could be described as adaptations. However, I am more familiar with 'adaptation' as 'remodelling' [*kaizou*], a term which describes the development and polishing of one's technique over the years.

DP: I would like to hear about both meanings of 'adaptation'. Would you like to start from your *shinsaku Noh*?

UM: In 2001 I wrote *Shiki*, about the Meiji period poet Masaoka Shiki (1867–1902) as part of the celebration for the centenary of his death. Shiki's hometown is Matsuyama, on the island of Shikoku, where the Udaka clan also originates. I therefore feel connected with him in various ways. Although it is newly written, *Shiki* follows the conventions of the Noh tradition in terms of dramaturgy, verse, and *mise en scène*. A poet from the capital (the *waki* side-actor) is hurrying to Matsuyama after he learnt of the death of Masaoka Shiki. During his journey he sees sceneries reminding him of poems. Reaching the city he meets an old man (the *shite* main actor) who quotes Shiki's poems and is very knowledgeable about his life. He in fact is the ghost of Shiki in disguise, who will appear in the second half of the play, describing the art of poetry as a way to Buddhahood. Shiki had a fan-base in Kyoto during his days. I am from Kyoto, and I am a fan of Shiki's, which is the reason why I decided to put myself into the story – I identify myself as the *waki* character. Shiki was born on 17 September and died on 19 September, while I was born on 18 September. I thought this was a sign!

DP: How did you approach the adaptation of Shiki's poems into a Noh play?

UM: The Noh is inspired by the life of Shiki, hence the whole play is pervaded by his poetry. Classical Noh plays contain numerous quotations of Japanese poetry, so I also included Shiki's poems in the play. It could be said that I 'used' Shiki's work in order to create my original work: I put together various *uta*, *haiku* and *tanka* and created my story.[14] Though many expect Noh actors to read Zeami's treatises on Noh, I didn't make much use of his suggestions: the techniques I used in creating *Shiki* came mostly from my experience of acting many Noh plays.

DP: How is it possible to convert classical poetry such as *waka* or *haiku* into Noh verse?

UM: Noh verse uses a meter similar to that of *waka* or *haiku* (alternating verses of five or seven syllables), hence it is very easy to integrate classical poetry into Noh. Basically any *waka* could be sung in a Noh style. It was all very natural. In the Noh *Shiki* I used *waka* in order to describe the feelings of the characters. For example when the ghost of Shiki enters the stage, he sings one of his *haiku* (five-seven-five metre): 'Yesterday's gourd water, not collected', a reference to the remedy made from the juice of the *hechima* gourd which was helpful in relieving the pain of coughing and phlegm.[15]

DP: In this play there is mention of Shiki as being *kabu bosatsu* (bodhisattva of song/poetry and dance). This reminds me of the poet Ariwara no Narihira (825–80) described as *kabu bosatsu* in the Noh play *Kakitsubata* [*The irises*]. Were you inspired by this play?

UM: I never thought of *Kakitsubata*. I wrote *Shiki* in one night, as 'in a trance', jotting down verses as they surfaced in my mind. Apart from this there was no intellectualization in the creation of the play. I think that Noh permeates so much my mind and body now that other sources flow naturally through me: I become one with Noh.

DP: Shiki lived in the early Meiji period. Did you include any sign of the modern historical setting in the *mise en scène*?

UM: There was no such thing as historical adaptation in *Shiki*. Noh is a classical performance tradition: although many of its performance elements such as its costumes originate in medieval Japan, its stories often refer to myths and legends of even older times. In addition, Noh changed very much since its creation until today, and each historical phase left its mark. This is why I think one of the most important features of Noh is being atemporal: it does not simply represent a specific period of time. Likewise, I didn't want to limit *Shiki* to a particular period: I think that this play, as other plays of the canon, could be performed anytime without any need of further adaptation.

DP: I would like to talk about another *shinsaku Noh* you wrote and performed, *Genshigumo* [*The atomic cloud*]. While *Shiki* is a rather traditional theme, the bombing of Hiroshima and Nagasaki is less 'usual' in Noh. How did you tell the horror of the atomic bombing through Noh?

UM: Noh focuses on a single emotion embodied by the *shite*. While in *Shiki* I explored the power of poetry to help us reach enlightenment, in *Genshigumo* I focused on the feelings of a mother who loses her child to the atomic bomb; the mother is later led to where her daughter's soul resides after death, only to find her reborn as a willow tree. This play is like a requiem, acknowledging the victims of the bombs who did not even know they were about to die. How to portray this? I don't think that violence, blood, or explosions are effective on stage. Noh is an art of restraint: I chose not to focus on extreme images. The spiritual world impresses me more than realistic portrayal. I did research on Hiroshima, Nagasaki, and also other nuclear tragedies such as Chernobyl and Three Mile Island, but decided to focus on the feelings of a single actor, as I was worried about losing consistency.

DP: *Genshigumo* shares similarities with *Sumidagawa* [*The Sumida River*], another Noh about a woman who travels looking for her lost child, finding him reborn as a tree.

UM: I never thought of *Sumidagawa* when writing *Genshigumo* [*laughs*]. Maybe it is similar. You might think of *Sumidagawa* as if it were my inspiration but the truth is, I had no other choice. It is normal for me to think of the soul of a dead person as inhabiting a tree. This is the language we have in the Noh tradition. I think that real Noh is created by Noh actors, who have a deep knowledge of the dramaturgy and who master its staging. If we want to call this 'Noh' we need to refer to the canon we know. It is a very difficult task: many have tried to adapt new stories to Noh but only imitated the appearance. Others have diverged from the shape of Noh, and have created some other kinds of drama which we cannot call Noh, because it lacks its characteristic features. Finding the middle way is most difficult.

DP: Does *Genshigumo* follow Noh conventions like *Shiki*?

UM: In *Genshigumo* I experimented with various new things, for example I did not employ a *waki* actor but two *Kyogen* who interact with the *shite*.[16] This is not conventional, but still part of the traditional Noh elements. I also carved new masks for the three main characters, and for a group of figures clad in black and wearing masks, representing the spirits of the victims.

DP: Could you explain the process of creation of the new masks?

UM: For these I used masks that I was carving, but stopped because I was not satisfied with how they were coming about. They were 'sleeping' in my studio. I then decided to 'resuscitate' them: starting from classical Noh masks, I distorted their features, took out teeth, scarred their skin, made the eyes bulge. Later though I decided to simplify the performance and not have such presence on further stagings of the play – they distracted from the character of the mother, the real fulcrum of the story.

DP: You seem to have taken various liberties in the creation of *Genshigumo*. To what extent can Noh actors develop their own style, express their individual creativity?

UM: I would like to reply with a metaphor. There is only one mountain to climb, but there are many ways to climb it. I think that all Noh actors have an ideal of artistic achievement, but there are many trails that lead to the top. Even though Noh is understood as a rigid art form, every actor has his way of understanding the technique, and of transmitting it to the audience. For example, the day after tomorrow I will perform the Noh *Fuji* [*Wisteria*], where the *shite* main actor is the spirit of the wisteria flower. Obviously no one has ever seen how this character looks like, so each actor necessarily has to make an effort to imagine how to interpret it, which naturally leads to a creative effort to dance what is otherwise impossible to portray on stage. The choreography is fixed, but that will not come alive unless the actor puts a spark in it, which is, adapting it to one's understanding. Of course, not all Noh actors are equally capable of such effort.

DP: Could you make an example of such alteration?

UM: I think that, generally speaking, all changes tend to simplification. Most of such alterations are invisible to the untrained eye, for example taking a step less in a sequence of steps. Noh is an art of refinement: we perform the same movements, sing the same melodies all our life. For us, and for the expert audience, even a slight alteration can be revolutionary.

DP: Since when did you achieve the freedom to perform such alterations, adapting what you learnt to your own sensibility?

UM: I did the best I could to copy my teacher's style until I turned 50. Then I had enough confidence to start putting my personality and aesthetic sense into my performance, changing the dance and chant style. However, even now I don't feel entirely independent. Although my teacher passed away 15 years ago, he still is my model: when I make some alterations I always think about how he would have done it.

DP: Earlier you mentioned changes to the staging of *Genshigumo*. Do you adapt your style to different audiences?

UM: Naturally so. For *Fuji* I decided to shorten part of the instrumental slow dance in order to adapt it to the season: even seasoned theatregoers would fall asleep during such a slow dance if performed in the summer! [*Laughs*]. In Noh, each play has a set of variations [*kogaki*] which comprise changes of costume, mask, dance, verses and so on. It might be said that each play comes with a range of possible prescribed adaptations. On top of these it is possible to cut or substitute bits and pieces. These changes are often decided last minute, keeping the audience in mind. Lastly, there are decisions that an actor will take directly on stage: in this case if the *shite* main actor, *jiutai* chorus, and *hayashi* musicians are performing on the same level, it is possible for the *shite* to linger on a meaningful pause, or to accelerate emphasizing a dramatic dance sequence. The *shite* decides this depending on the audience's response.

DP: In the treatise *Sandō*, Zeami said that 'depending on the varying taste in different periods, words are slightly altered, the music is renewed, and a new flower is created in response to changing times. In the future as well the same principle will continue to apply.'[17] Do you think Zeami's suggestion is followed by Noh actors today?

UM: Frankly speaking, I think that to an actor's effort to adapt to the audience should correspond an equal effort from the audience's side. I don't think that in theatre 'the customer is always right'. Rather than acceding to the general audience, I think it is my responsibility to take them by the hand and show them the beauty of something that is not necessarily familiar to their eyes and ears.

DP: What do you think of the recent attempts at modernization of Noh, trying to change Noh medieval language into modern Japanese, as in Umehara Takeshi's *Super Noh*?

UM: The classic poetry of Noh has the power to take us beyond time. Noh uses classical Japanese, which is very hard to understand today. However, I made an effort to use simpler language in various parts of my Noh, in order for everyone to understand. For example in *Shiki*, after the *haiku* I talked about before, the ghost explains how reading or composing simple poetic verses can lead anyone to an understanding of the essence of man and nature. I also think that everyone should enjoy the beauty of Noh and I believe that experiments done now will have a great impact in the future, even though contemporary spectators may be sceptical. Noh is a wonderful art form and could take many shapes in the future. Many claim that endurance is the most important quality of Noh actors, which is a way of saying that tradition should not be touched, but I think it is necessary to have someone who breaks the dam and lets water gush in, allowing new, fresh currents of change to flow in the great tradition of Noh. However, it is necessary not to forget the 'essence' of Noh, which does not lie in realism, but in the ability to let the audience's imagination fly.

Link

International Noh Institute: http://www.noh-udaka.com/en/ (accessed 19 January 2014).

Selected bibliography

Pellecchia, Diego. (2013). 'Traditional Theatre: The Case of Japanese Noh' in *The Cambridge Companion to Theatre History*. Cambridge: Cambridge University Press, pp. 136–48.

Rath, Eric. (2004). *The Ethos of Noh: Actors and Their Art*. Cambridge, MA: Harvard University Press.

Yamanaka, Reiko. (2008). 'What Features Distinguish Nō from Other Performing Arts?' in Stanca Scholz-Cionca and Christopher Balme (eds), *Nō Theatre Transversal*. Munich: Iudicium, pp. 78–85.

Notes

1 Hutcheon (2006), p. 8. Quoted in this book on p. 5.

2 Hutcheon, p. 9.

3 T. S. Eliot, 'Tradition and the Individual Talent', *The Egoist*, 6.4/5, (1919), pp. 54–5 and pp. 72–3.

4 Roland Barthes, 'The Death of the Author' in *Image Music Text*, London: Fontana Press, 1993, pp. 142–8.

5 William Aston, *A History of Japanese Literature*. London: Heinemann, 1899, pp. 202–4.

6 Basil Hall Chamberlain, *The Classical Poetry of the Japanese*. London: Trübner, 1880, p. 1.

7 Kentarō Sanari, *Yōkyoku taikan* [Complete collection of Noh plays], 7 vols. Tokyo: Meiji Shoin, 1930, I, p. 11.

8 Steven Brown, *Theatricalities of Power: The Cultural Politics of Noh*. Stanford, CA: Stanford University Press, 2001, p. 18.

9 Rath (2004), p. 161.

10 Nishino, 'Shinsaku nō no hyakunen (2)' [One hundred years of *Shinsaku Noh*], *Nōgaku kenkyū* [Noh research], 2005, pp. 1–34 (p. 1).

11 Yamanaka (2008), p. 84.

12 Nishino (2005), p. 3.

13 See Pellecchia (2013).

14 *Uta*, *haiku*, and *tanka* are forms of classical Japanese verse.

15 Shiki died of tuberculosis.

16 Kyogen is the traditional farce, performed either between two acts of a Noh play, or as independent skit between two plays.

17 Zeami, Motokiyo, *On the Art of the Nō Drama*, ed. Masakazu Yamazaki, trans. Thomas Rimer. Princeton, NJ: Princeton University Press, 1984, p. 161.

Part Two

Defusing Tradition

6

On Literality and Limits: Romeo Castellucci of Socìetas Raffaello Sanzio in Conversation with Nicholas Ridout[1]

Introduction

I'm sure many of you already know a lot about Romeo's work with Socìetas Raffaello Sanzio, the company of which he was a co-founder back in 1981, and for whom he has directed and created a quite extraordinary range of work, predominantly in theatre but also in installation and sculpture. I will keep my introduction fairly brief. While I was preparing a few thoughts for this evening and choosing some material that we'll show you, I was taken back to the occasion in June 1999 when I went to see some work by an Italian theatre company of whom I knew nothing. It was a production of *Giulio Cesare* [1997], a version of Shakespeare's *Julius Caesar* in the Queen Elizabeth Hall – a rather strange venue for such an event – and I found myself confronted with a theatre the likes of which I had not previously encountered. I quite simply didn't know what my response to it was when I first saw that piece. And so I did what only those people with time on their hands are able to do: I went back the next evening to see a second performance of *Giulio Cesare*. It remains for me one of those moments in my theatre spectatorship that I think of as extraordinarily important to the way I think about theatre. It led me to engage with Romeo's work and that of his collaborators over a period of some time, and it's been a huge joy to do so.

Romeo has been invited to this event not least because, in the body of his work over the last 30 years, there have surfaced from time to time various projects that we might think of as adaptations, ranging from work that addresses mythical materials such as a theatrical engagement with *Gilgamesh* [1990], to versions of two Shakespeare plays, *Hamlet* [*Amleto. La veemente esteriorità della morte di un mollusco*; *Hamlet. The vehement exteriority of the death of a mollusc*, 1992] and *Julius Caesar*, through to work on other texts such as *Genesi. From the Museum of Sleep* [1999], which was derived from the first book of the Pentateuch. Recently, people in London may well have had the opportunity to see some or all of Romeo's trilogy freely inspired by Dante, *La Divina Commedia* [*Inferno, Purgatorio,* and *Paradiso,* 2008]. Romeo is currently continuing to work on material in relation to Nathaniel Hawthorne's *The Minister's Black Veil* [*Il velo nero del pastore*, 2011], which is I think what's preoccupying him at the moment. These are all things we may touch upon.

The form I thought we'd have for this evening is that Romeo and I will begin a conversation around an opening question, after which I think we might show a little bit of material on video, so that we then have something in common which we might then talk about between us. Before we go any further I need also to acknowledge and express my gratitude to our interpreter Flora Pitrolo who is very kindly bringing her expertise not just in the languages of Italian and English which Romeo and I share in strangely unbalanced degrees, but also her own expertise in contemporary performance, both in Italy and beyond, which means that she is *au fait* not just with the languages we're speaking but also the intellectual and artistic material that we're engaged in.

Interview

Nicholas Ridout: I thought I'd start, Romeo, by asking you if you might talk a little about how and why you choose certain material to work with, to enter into a relationship with, whether perhaps you do choose it, or whether it chooses you, how that works and whether it works differently in different situations?

Romeo Castellucci: To answer this question I have to first briefly talk about how I work, because the choice of a title or the choice of a subject or a script isn't the first thing that comes. The choice of a title comes towards the end of the creative process. The process is mostly organized around a notebook, a series of notes, which is quite a common, normal way to go about things. It's a notebook that mostly assembles things: it's notes, sensations, feelings and images that I put together day after day. It's feelings and suggestions that I receive from reality. At a certain point when there's an accumulation of these images and feelings and suggestions, it's about tracing lines, about tracing a constellation between all of these various elements. These lines, these traces, constitute the primitive version, the primitive form of what may happen later, and at this point, I meet a title. So before even knowing the material the title comes from, the title has to resonate with the material from the notes. It's a tuning of the two, of the title and the material. There needs to be a consonance, a vibration that makes it possible for one to be contained by the other. To remain with the example of *Giulio Cesare*, the title is an intuition. It might seem a provocation but I'm not an expert on theatre, I'm not an expert on literature and theatre, I've never studied any of that. The title of *Julius Caesar* came from a series of notes that had to do with voice, that had to do with power, the power of the voice, the power of words and with rhetoric. It was intuition that led me to believe that that was interesting material to put together and that's when I began to study *Julius Caesar*. That's the phase of attack. It's a question of life or death, it's a very exciting moment which leads to beautiful discoveries. Naturally the problem lies in stereotypes. Western dramaturgy in general and Shakespeare in particular is so filled with stereotypes that are very dangerous, in my view, so it's about reawakening that material. But as you said, in a way, the opposite is also true, it is the titles that come and find me, in a certain sense it is like this. I have never chosen a title as a first movement in the process.

NR: When you said that's a question of life and death, is that the life or death of this project, does that encounter, that attack, sometimes not work? Does that meeting sometimes *not* produce something?

RC: Yes, it's a danger, it happens, it's an exposure to something that is irreparable. Of course it's not automatic, there are times when nothing happens, when there's no blood running through the veins, and then it becomes intellectual material. But, if I may say that, I don't think culture has anything to do with theatre and the first degree of the encounter with theatre has to do with the cortex. It's maybe a physically cerebral encounter; it's about the reptilian brain … The idea of heat, the idea of temperature, the idea of danger, that's where the first encounter takes place. The first degree of language is how the body of the spectator is exposed to an environment, that's what really interests me. Because when we're talking about the body it's clear that we're not talking about the body of the actor. Naturally I refer to the body of the spectator, which is the only interesting body. And that's why I find that what I have to figure out is a strategy in order to occupy a text, and this kind of struggle is ultimately happening at the heart of the text, because the text can't ultimately be there; there can be no text if there's theatre. It would be a contradiction in terms. Carmelo Bene used to speak about the text-testicle, the testicle of the author, because he saw it as a domination over the theatre of the author. And yet the authors are dead, so it's a sort of power of death, and so what happens if you pursue a text, the text-testicle, is that you end up in the sort of funerary cult by celebrating the dead. Whereas, as we know, theatre is a carnal art, an art that more than any other art doubles life and substitutes itself for it. So for this reason there can't be a text, but what there can be are words. Another thing that's fundamental to me is the idea of *fabula*, the Latin idea of *fabula*, of what happens, the bare bones of a plot, actions.

NR: Shall we look at a very famous bit of *fabula*, and some very famous words and look at a short sequence? This will be about eight minutes, from Romeo's *Giulio Cesare*. For those of you familiar with the play, we are about to see Mark Antony's speech after Caesar's death.

[A video clip from *Giulio Cesare* is played.]

NR: So I wonder if we could continue where we were but maybe try to talk very specifically about what happened in the case of *Giulio Cesare* after the encounter between the constellation of notes and the title *Giulio Cesare*, and what you then had to do in order to inhabit that, and to make a world to inhabit to which you expose the spectators' body.

RC: As an example it's probably best to stay close to what we just saw. The whole show was made following the same kind of philosophy. It was a question of defusing Shakespeare's text as if it were a bomb because I was interested in the heart of the material and the system of power of words. So one strategy was, in the place of literature, literality. Mark Antony's speech is extraordinary and rhetorical, because at the end of this first act there's a sort of race, almost a standoff, between Brutus's rhetoric and Mark Antony's. So Mark Antony's discourse is organized upon the wounds on the body of Julius Caesar, and it speaks about those wounds on Julius Caesar's body as 'povere povere bocche mute' ['poor poor dumb mouths'].[2] The sentence for me was a key for the penetration of this character, and I thought I would ask someone who had had a laryngectomy, who really and actually projected his voice from a wound. So evidently, rhetorically speaking, his was a victory, a factual victory that the spectator could hear and experience in that moment. The actor in that moment was a victorious triumphant character; it wasn't about pity. His illness was in the background, because at that moment he was exercising the true power of words. So this corresponded to the reassembled nucleus of Mark Antony's speech about the wounds on Julius Caesar's body, which actually came from a wound. It was literal. And there was a continuous return to the idea of rhetoric, so there was an actual reference to Cicero's *De Oratore*, and the idea of pausing, gesturing, and to Roman statuary art and to sculpture. And towards the end when he's backlit, there was this base as if for a statue and, he actually does look like a statue, but these are statues that these days we normally see amputated, and this is their romantic beauty if you like. And this statue had been 'amputated' of its voice. So I found that this voice resonated through this lack, through this nostalgia, through this new strength, a new beauty.

NR: The question of literality or literalness is, for me a particularly interesting one in relation to your engagement with other material. We might say in English, that you, in your theatrical work, take the material very literally. And this seems to be clearly the case in *Julius Caesar* with this project of literality in relation to the wound, but it's there elsewhere, I think; there are things in *La Divina Commedia* that seem suddenly to appear as 'I'm going to do literally what it says I should do.' And this seemed very much the case with *Giulio Cesare* and *Amleto*, and in a way the scandal of those pieces is that they literally did what the play set out in ways that, it suddenly occurred to me, theatre avoids. Most theatre does not do this literal thing.

RC: Exactly.

NR: Can you talk a bit about what happens when you do that, when you take things so literally. For an audience. For example, Marco Antonio points to 'ARS', which is slightly funnier in English than it is in Latin. So someone's just very literally pointing out that this is art. Or later in this production when a character is dead a plaque is lowered onto their body with written on it – in cursive script that we're familiar with because of René Magritte – 'Ceci n'est pas un acteur'. I'm interested in the relation between that blunt, direct literality, and what you talked about in terms of substitution, what an audience experiences there.

RC: It's about moving the frame, about making the container not coincide with what is contained. Excuse me if I quote Artaud. Normally I don't like to quote Artaud, in any case Artaud says that you have to '*forsennare il supporto*' in Italian, to madden the structure of the fundamental laws of theatre, somehow, by taking them outside themselves. You have to make the theatre vibrate, to make it resound, and then put it into crisis. And this vibration, this taking it outside itself creates space, a gap between what is contained and its container, which is a deliberate and formal space. And this is the space that the spectator inhabits, the private space of the spectator. This gap creates a space of indeterminacy, an interrogative space; it's the space in which there's a question for each audience member. It's the chance for a spectator to be alone. For the spectator to be alone is really necessary. I say that as a spectator, I want to be alone, I want to feel alone. And if anything, to share my solitude with the solitude of other spectators. Whereas text confirms the dimension of the group, it confirms knowledge, it confirms culture, a certain being at ease with knowledge, a certain being at ease with each other in our knowledge. This 'derangement of the structure' penetrates into the body of the spectator. In terms of what the spectator feels, I can talk for myself as a spectator but it is not for me to direct the feelings of the spectator, to decide what the spectator feels.

NR: I wanted to just open up another area of questions which might lead us towards looking at *Inferno*. With *Giulio Cesare* you arrived via the encounter with the title as material that was conceived for the theatre, and had a sort of shape and set of relations in it. One might say it is a certain kind of creature, an organism that has already existed in the theatre. And I wonder whether you feel that there is a big difference between those occasions dealing with material that is already a creature of the theatre, and when you're dealing with material that is not, as for example with Dante or Céline? And does that create different kinds of opportunities and questions for you as you make the work?

RC: Yes it's completely different. The texts that aren't made for the theatre are somehow more available, and simpler if it's possible to use that word, because they're a desert. Because *The Divine Comedy* is a desert that's made up of a completely filled space, it's a completely saturated space, saturated with imagination. The saturation necessarily becomes a sort of field in which everything is possible. I'm not really interested in a kind of freedom of manoeuvre, a freedom to move around as I wish, I'm not interested in that. The desert isn't a free space; it's not a space of freedom. On the contrary, the desert is a space that makes a lot of demands on you. I don't believe at all in freedom in art, or freedom of creation, because the experience of the limit is much more interesting. Because it's in the limit that you can be heretical. I don't think there's another possibility in Western art. Otherwise you become an illustrator, and illustration is the worst spectre you can imagine. So the strategy changes depending on whether it's a theatrical text or a non-theatrical text. For example in *Julius Caesar* there is a series of characters, of which some remained, others were absorbed. You have to reckon with ready-formed characters. In *The Divine Comedy* what I looked at first was the geometric structure of the poem as a whole. First of all it's a trilogy, and so I started by figuring out from a geometric point of view the fundamental movements of each part. I tried to understand also what the main substances at play are in *The Divine Comedy* and the fundamental substance of it is theological, and that opens another river. These are opportunities that these books can offer.

NR: Shall we look at the beginning of *Inferno*, and think about that and particularly I think this question of the limit and the un-freedom of the theatre maker?

[A video clip from *Inferno* is played.]

NR: So we could talk more about literality in relation to this and we could talk about geometry. Maybe both of them will come up. I actually wanted to put into play the word 'tradition' and to ask you about your relationship with it, maybe particularly within this piece, how the tradition that one may associate with Dante comes into relation with a certain theatrical tradition of Avignon, with this particular venue as a theatrical venue but also as a Pope's palace, and how those constraints might function as chains for you as a theatre maker.

RC: It's true. Tradition is very interesting. I don't think I make avant-garde work. I prefer to think of my work as inscribed in the problem of classical representation. From this point of view *The*

Divine Comedy offers an extraordinary example because Dante is the first person to put the figure of the artist at the centre of representation, in that work. From that moment onwards the artist becomes an autonomous figure who comes and adds him or herself to the frame of classical representation. The artist in the centre of representation has obviously been developed over the course of the centuries, but Dante is the first person to put himself at the centre of his work and to face the fundamental problem of doing so, as it is not a simple gesture. The beginning of *The Divine Comedy* is the beginning of a journey, the journey of the artist, and it is terrifying, in the literal sense, because there are three animals that he encounters, three ferocious beasts, who are the ones who push him into the *inferno*, into hell. In a certain sense he would prefer not to write *The Divine Comedy;* he would prefer to escape but he's forced into hell. And he does it at a very high price. And this is a traditional figure that I wanted to confront.

The space of the Pope's palace is a very complex space. It's stratified in tradition, layered in tradition. First of all it's a place of tourism. It's a historical space. It's a historical place that has quite incredible coincidences with Dante's time and the time that he was writing his work. Clement V, the Pope who built that palace is in Dante's hell. And of course there is also the stratification of the festival of Avignon itself, which was born in that space. So there are all these condensations of tradition that are necessarily part of the dramaturgical material that I am working with. The first danger to avoid was to let it slip into scenography. In the scene you just saw, I was trying to interpret the idea of falling into the abyss, and falling into the *inferno* through a similar movement, but the other way around. Rising to hell. So once again the body of the spectator was implicated with a sense of vertigo. That was a way for me to work with the traditional aspect of that space.

NR: This maybe takes the conversation slightly to one side of the particular question of adaptation but this seems relevant to me because it seems that the kinds of problems and circumstances that you describe in relation to tradition are not simply the case when you are making theatre that adapts from other works. It's something you're dealing with in a very fundamental way in *Tragedia Endogonidia* [2002–4], for example, or in relation to the space of the theatre itself. I know you've talked before about the way in which certain kinds of architectural forms of theatre are something that is given to you, and against which, or with which in some way, your work has to struggle. So I'm interested in this relationship that arises between someone, like yourself, who, as you say, has not studied dramatic literature or that tradition, but who finds himself in a set of institutions that incarnate that tradition. Has that always been the stance of your work, that you're in a sense always put in a place where you are not the boss?

RC: Yes absolutely, because the space of the Court of Honour of the Pope's Palace is the equivalent to the space offered by *Julius Caesar*. It's something already given. There is a sense of being given limits. In one case because there are the limits of architecture, and on the other there's the architecture of the text. So you don't feel like you're a guest in this space. There's no sense of hospitality in this space: what this space gives is a sense of conflict. But a necessary conflict. There isn't a comfortable space; there can't be a comfortable space, or at least I don't know of one, perhaps because I am not interested in knowing. Improvisation, spontaneity, these are words I don't understand. I admit that people can work with that sort of vocabulary, but I find it very difficult. The most interesting thing is the search for limits, trying to build oneself a prison. A prison into which you can then try and sculpt some spaces and gaps. But what was the question?

NR: I think the question was, and you've just actually answered it, do you always live in prison?

RC: This prison in effect mirrors reality and that's why the first words in *Inferno* are 'My name is Romeo Castellucci'. Because this is a name and a surname, it's not a question of ego. It's a question of things I've been given that aren't my own. They're things that someone else has given me. It's an anti-biographical sentence because as soon as I say my name, my name is immediately devoured by these beasts, again, very literally. From a certain point of view I need to disappear, I need to set myself aside, and that is an attitude which is also very much part of our tradition. Dante is conducted like a child through his journey, by Virgil. Apart from the fact that there's a child that appears soon after I do, there's a sense of being alone, and a world that we don't know, that's unknown, and which you have to discover. So the artist in a certain sense is intermittent. He or she has to disappear, has to make him or herself transparent. Here's another example: *Las Meninas,* in which Velázquez is in the centre of the painting but he's in a moment in which he's about to disappear. And that's another way of confronting tradition, classical representation and the laws of classical representation.

NR: Shall we invite other people to join our conversation?

RC: With pleasure.

Audience member 1: One way of thinking about the question of adaptation might be as an act of giving shape or visibility to things that are difficult to shape or visualize, especially in the theatre which is an art that has its own very strong constraints. So I wanted to ask you if you could talk about the relationship between what can be shown and what can't be shown. In the back of my mind is a question about *Purgatorio.*

RC: The strange thing is that it's a question of fighting against freedom, in a certain sense, but within this fight against freedom anything can happen. For me a very important word is structure, which is a discipline. It is possible to find a limit within a structure, and then find parallels with the structure of a given material, for instance you have mentioned *Purgatorio* but we could mention any other title. There are structures that express different bodies and different ideas but that can be superimposed. These might be structures in different worlds, but which mirror one another. This is one of the wonderful discoveries of structuralist anthropology. For instance, you can find a correlation between the main moments of the development of an organism and Mark Antony's speech. Or the structure of a mask as studied by Lévi-Strauss can mirror the kinship system in a given culture. These are completely different worlds but they deeply reflect one another. So it's about finding a resonance, almost in a musical sense, between two structures, without there being an apparent conflict. I think the structure, the invisible skeleton of form, which holds it together, is what actually touches the spectator, because everyone is capable of recognizing a structure at a basic level, not in an intellectual way. Intellect can be involved but at a second or third degree. A structure by definition is something in which one abandons one's self. Structure is a guarantee. One can rest in it. These are the structures that we then find in language, and they are those that give us the certainty of belonging to a human community. I think that 'structure' is a very important word for those that work with words, texts and adaptations.

Audience member 2: You talked a lot about classical representation, I wonder what classical means to you?

RC: For me the classical is when there's *un quadro* which in Italian is both the painting and the space around a painting, the frame. So the frame in the sense of the frame of a painting or the frame of a proscenium arch, the frame of the space around the sculpture. This frame has developed over time and was born and developed on this side of the world. I'm not interested in Oriental theatre. I like it but I cannot interact with it; it's not my space. There are limits. Cultural limits which are also religious limits. It's impossible to separate the experience of art from the experience of religion, because they were born together in a cave. It's not possible. So for me classical representation starts in the classical age and it starts with tragedy. And tragedy begins with a lack of something, the death of the gods, something which is no longer there, so theatre is constantly the twilight of the gods. And this is our given; this is something that belongs to us. It's in the fibre of us. It's there. It's ours. Classical representation also lies in the position of the saint, and so the idea of a painting and the idea of what the vectors are and what the distribution of weight is, and what the lines are that hold together a representation in painting. This is just to give an idea of what I mean by classical representation, which we could also call tradition. It's a problematic relationship.

Link

Socìetas Raffaello Sanzio: http://www.raffaellosanzio.org (accessed 19 January 2014).

Selected bibliography

Castellucci, Claudia, Romeo Castellucci, Chiara Guidi, Joe Kelleher and Nicholas Ridout. (2007). *The Theatre of Socìetas Raffaello Sanzio*. London and New York: Routledge.

Kear, Adrian. (2013). 'Falling into History: Romeo Castellucci and Socìetas Raffaello Sanzio's *Tragedia Endogonidia* and *Divina Commedia*', in *Theatre and Event: Staging the European Century*. Basingstoke: Palgrave Macmillan, pp. 119–49.

Ridout, Nicholas. (2006). 'Make-believe: Socìetas Raffaello Sanzio Do Theatre', in Nicholas Ridout and Joe Kelleher (eds), *Contemporary Theatres in Europe*. London and New York: Routledge, pp. 175–87.

Notes

1 This interview was part of the Leverhulme Olympic Talks on Theatre and Adaptation. It took place on 24 April 2012 at Queen Mary, University of London.

2 Shakespeare, *Julius Caesar*, Act 3, Scene II, v. 1769.

7

The Subtle Aggressors: Julia Bardsley and Simon Vincenzi in Conversation with Dominic Johnson[1]

Introduction

At the fertile peripheries of theatrical practice, artists draw from a complex network of diverse and potentially remote disciplinary traditions, including the visual arts and dance. In the visual arts, particularly, the term 'adaptation' might seem limiting, problematic, or even alien. Artists regularly have used found objects in art works since Marcel Duchamp's invention of the 'readymades' around the time of his iconic sculpture *Fountain* (1917), an upturned porcelain urinal signed by the fictional artist 'R. Mutt', which was submitted to (and rejected by) an open exhibition of the Society of Independent Artists in New York in the same year. It was later shown at Alfred Stieglitz' studio, photographed, and has since become a touchstone of avant-garde art, securing the place of appropriation among crucial techniques in modern and contemporary art over the forthcoming decade.

For Peter Bürger, Duchamp's innovation signalled the 'sublation' or merging of art and the everyday, which may open onto a newly reinvigorated conception of the politics of artistic production. 'When art and the praxis of life are one,' he writes, 'when the praxis is aesthetic and art is practical, art's purpose can no longer be discovered, because the existence of two distinct spheres (art and the praxis of life) that is constitutive of the concept of purpose or intended use has come to an end.'[2] Bürger stipulates that the provocation 'cannot be repeated indefinitely,' without blunting the teeth of appropriation as a tool for critiquing the autonomy of art and its markets: 'If an artist today signs a stove pipe and exhibits it, that artist certainly does not denounce the art market but adapts to it.'[3] The 'adaptation' in Bürger's critique is the way in which formerly radical acts are disarmed by repetition, and by the containment of the market, which adapts itself to find marketable relations to artistic provocations. Despite or because of 'the failure of the avant-gardist intent to sublate art,' in Bürger's damning reading of the neo-avant-garde, appropriation has evolved to be a common or traditional technique in post-war visual arts practice.[4] For Rosalind Krauss, appropriation in 'pirated' photographs by Sherrie Levine does not wishfully reinvent avant-garde strategies, but facilitates a 'break,' a 'critical attack' on the tradition that precedes it, and a form of 'demythologizing criticism'.[5] For example, Levine appropriated the modernist masterworks of the photographer Edward Weston, by re-photographing his portraits of agrarian life from an exhibition catalogue and exhibiting them as works of appropriation. These works from the 1980s are now lauded as landmark instances of postmodernist art, a critical refusal of the modernist myths of artistic genius and the paradigmatic and singular masterwork. 'It is thus,' Krauss writes, 'from a strange new perspective that we look back on the modernist origin and watch it splintering into endless replication.'[6] Yet the 'endless replication' of Levine – and other seminal appropriation artists such as Richard Prince, Andy Warhol, Sturtevant, Jeff Koons, or Mike Bidlo – does not clearly escape the critical endgame that Bürger foresaw in 1974, especially considering the ubiquitous position these artists occupy within the corporate economy of museum and commercial gallery culture.

Appropriation is now a tool in the repertoires of a wide range of artists. In some of its more interesting manifestations, appropriation is used among a range of other techniques, to tease out new insights – 'another opportunity to glean knowledge,' as Julia Bardsley puts it, below – in the course of an artist's engagement with the wider culture. In the following interview, I discuss adaptation, appropriation, and other contingent techniques and strategies, with two compelling artists working in the intersections between theatre and visual art: Julia Bardsley and Simon Vincenzi.

Julia Bardsley has worked as a director, solo artist, and collaborator since the early 1980s. Between 1985 and 1989, her earliest works included devised productions for dereck, dereck, the theatre company she co-founded with Phelim McDermott. Bardsley served as Joint Artistic Director of the Haymarket Theatre, Leicester (1991–3) and at the Young Vic Theatre, London (1993–4); at both venues Bardsley directed highly experimental versions of canonical plays. At the Haymarket, these included adaptations of T. S. Eliot's *The Family Reunion*, Federico García Lorca's *Blood Wedding*, Dylan Thomas' *Under Milk Wood* (1992), and *Macbeth* (1993). At the Young Vic, Bardsley remounted her own adaptation of Emile Zola's novel *Thérèse Raquin* (1993) and directed a controversial production of *Hamlet* (1994). Abandoning direction and institutional spaces of theatre, Bardsley became an independent artist, and has since made spectacular pieces, often in collaboration with the sonic artist Andrew Poppy. Her recent works use sculpture, installation, movement, costume, and elements of performance art, most notably in her *Divine Trilogy*, consisting of the pieces *Trans-Acts* (2003), *Almost the Same: Feral Rehearsals for Violent Acts of Culture* (2008), and *Aftermaths: A Tear in the Meat of Vision* (2009).

Simon Vincenzi is a director, choreographer and designer. He co-founded Bock and Vincenzi with Frank Bock, and between 1996 and 2007 made works for both adult and child audiences that include *Three Forest Dances*, *In A Room Of Wood*, *Being Barely There I Saw You Too* and *Breathtaking*. In 1999, Bock and Vincenzi began a seven-year research period culminating in both *Invisible Dances ... From Afar* (a work made to be heard on the telephone) and the live performance *The Invisible Dances* (2004–6). Vincenzi's current project *Operation Infinity* began in 2007 and involves a series of theatre works performed by a fictional theatre company called Troupe Mabuse. His current project *King Real Against the Guidelines* appropriates *King Lear* as an installation for theatre spaces.

Bardsley and Vincenzi are widely presented in galleries, theatres, and festivals in the United Kingdom, Europe and farther afield, yet their works have rarely been addressed in scholarly writing, partly because they exceed the conventional parameters of cultural production, but also, strikingly, unsettle the newer paradigms that have evolved to contain experimental practice, including the genres of Live Art and Performance Art. Below, we approach the different techniques and terminologies of adaptation and appropriation in theatre and visual art, through a series of themes including the visibility and invisibility of source material, the technique of stripping authorship as a 'hostile' or irreverent strategy, and the relationship that adaptation or appropriation can set up between artists, performers and audiences.

Interview

Dominic Johnson: If we define adaptation as using existing source material in the service of a new work, how has this strategy been important for you? How is existing material useful in the production of a new work?

Julia Bardsley: Existing source materials come with a body of history and connections. Sometimes that can be problematic and sometimes it's useful, because audiences already have some kind of connection with the material. If you're using classic works from the canon, which have a particular strength and robustness, they can take quite a lot of being mucked about with, and it's their classic status that allows them to be pillaged and plundered in a particular way. But they exist as objects in themselves. The process you go through is assessing the degree to which you allow the base material to be buried or shown.

Simon Vincenzi: *The Infinite Pleasures of the Great Unknown* was the first production in what evolved to become a project called *Operation Infinity.* This project is based on Doctor Mabuse, a fictional character in three Fritz Lang films, who wants to destroy civilization through various different modes of control. We took this as the context for the new work and the idea of him presenting some form of entertainment – an entertainment of terror. Because he's from a film, it made sense that he would communicate through another film. In this show the performers work with the second Fritz Lang film, *The Testament of Dr. Mabuse* [1933]. They re-transcribe it live, from a monitor, to recreate the film. The other text that we used was a version of *King Lear*. The reason we chose *King Lear*, in part, was that it was a very famous play, and, in theory, if you put it on lots of people would come and see it, and again this relates partly to what Julia was saying about the associations of canonical works.

DJ: Are there other differences between using a very recognizable text, and something that's perhaps less well known, potentially marginal? Does one allow more freedom than the other? Julia, you suggested that well-known texts allow you to be more aggressive.

JB: I think the degree of freedom allowed is up to the artist dealing with the material. I would say that on the whole I use well-known, established, mythical texts, like the Medea myth in my current project *Medea: Dark Matter Events*. Medea is a fictional character, manifest in many different ways throughout history, including a number of plays. Before I started to work with the Medea myth I hadn't read any plays about Medea. I just thought the idea was quite interesting. The plays themselves are irrelevant. The plays are receptacles, in which you can start to explore things you're interested in. In *Medea* I was interested in the idea of performance as a force – the idea of collision, combustion, and energy forces. I started thinking about the idea of sexual and erotic energies, and the idea of orgasm and electricity, and this led to the question of how to make electricity visible. I began using violet wands, then connected the themes of chemistries and magnetism between people in terms of sexual attraction. This relates to the relationship between Jason and Medea. When the idea starts rolling I can move away from the base because the piece leads into other territories that are tangential. The source text is just an excuse for research, a holding point or base line. If you're lost you can always refer back to it. So the source material is like a structural security blanket.

DJ: Simon, how important is it for you that the source material is visible or recognizable?

SV: It's not terribly important. If people want to see it, then nothing's really hidden. Literally, if people want to see the monitor the performers are responding to behind the screen, then they can go round and have a look. I think partly some of Julia's interest in *Medea* is somehow to do with the historical narrative. Within *Operation Infinity* the progression of the work becomes a meta-narrative, rather than dealing *with* a narrative – the narrative of the source materials is not crucial in itself, but instead functions as a prompt. I am interested in the narrative of *King Lear* but it's not necessarily what I'm working with. We don't work with the narrative of *The Testament of Dr. Mabuse*, we work with the presentation of *The Testament of Dr. Mabuse.* They are different things that will hopefully add up to another, new narrative.

DJ: Adaptation strikes me as a literary term, whereas appropriation seems potentially more tied to the visual arts, especially looking at late twentieth-century art history and its ties to photography. I'm thinking of Richard Prince re-photographing billboards of the Marlboro Man, or Sherrie Levine re-photographing Edward Weston's images – there's a blatant form of adaptation in those examples of appropriation in conceptual art of the 1980s, where the approach overtly and happily approaches visual forms of plagiarism. Is the difference between adaptation and appropriation important to you? Are you invested in the differing legacies of theatre, literature, and visual arts?

JB: In the early days when I was doing things with dereck, dereck, our productions were definitely adaptations – of texts that weren't original theatre sources. They were adaptations of poems or short stories, so in those cases 'adaptation' seems the right term to use, because you're taking something that exists in one form and adapting it into another. Appropriation is more aggressive, more robust.

SV: I never talked about adaptation. In terms of appropriation there was something in *Operation Infinity* that I wanted to be quite cheap. *Invisible Dances*, a previous work, became something that was quite pure and very self-reflective, and I wanted something that was dirtier or cruder. I think that was one of the reasons that I chose its source materials quite impulsively. I work much more with the idea of translation because it has a slightly more brutal relationship with the material. There is a long training period for the performers within *Operation Infinity*. Half of that training is aimed at removing them from their relationship to the source material, so it only becomes about either seeing the words or seeing the image. Part of that process involves making sure that the performers don't make any choices – or as few choices as possible. When I think of adaptation, I feel that means there are things I can make conscious choices about. I've never really been interested in that. I'm much more interested in finding situations in which the performers are literally translating what they are seeing or what they're being fed – in that moment, in the moment of it happening. People ask if it involves improvisation, but there is no space for performers to improvise. The performers are doing what they need to do to communicate that moment.

DJ: That's very interesting, because removing some level of the agency or subjectivity of the performer, or of the maker, relates quite closely to the reading of appropriation in postmodern visual art. Instead of expressing your own artistic subjectivity, the artist using appropriation duplicates, mimics, or approximates someone else's expression. The artist can revel in the deskilling and re-skilling that appropriation often involves.

JB: I think it's a strange tension between having such incredible structure and discipline, technique, and training, and at the same time wanting a state where you kind of relinquish control. I think that state of relinquishing control is something I've become more and more interested in.

DJ: You've both touched on the idea that appropriation involves taking an object or a source and stripping away its authorship. To my ear this is something quite hostile. I think there is something positively alienating in the work both of you make. Could you talk about the aggressive or hostile qualities of appropriation or adaptation? Do your relationships to source material celebrate a certain kind of irreverence?

JB: I don't see it as irreverent or hostile. I just think of the source material as stuff that is up for grabs at the moment that you're working with it. Simon never gives an audience what it thinks it wants and I find that really exciting because he doesn't make any concessions towards an audience – in that sense he respects the spectator.

SV: In the *King Real*, we re-translated the storm scene from the third act of *King Lear* through Babel Fish, an online translating system. We translated the text into German, then back into English, then back into German, and repeated this process several times, and a new translation was made of this text. It wasn't a hostile or violent act. I just wanted to see what would happen. There's something about the internet that allows that to take place. Once that text arrived I personally found it very thrilling because it retained a lot of the experience or process of these quite odd worlds being thrown together, so it became a sort of talk between different periods of time. We worked with that text with utter respect. However the work is perceived, for me there is never hostility towards the materials I'm working with. I'm only interested in what the audience brings to its experience of the work.

DJ: I would reiterate that I don't think what either of you do is hostile to audiences. I think you're both very generous to audiences. Yet I'd like us to pursue this idea of maintaining difficult relations with source materials, not least because texts

– including and perhaps even especially canonical texts – don't need to be respected. There's traditionally so much respect that circulates around texts that a different orientation is quite useful. The mechanically translated text that you produced, Simon, is a text that doesn't have an author – certainly not an author in the traditional sense – so it brings us back to this idea of hostility (for want of a better word), partly by way of the theoretical cliché of the 'death of the author'. Barthes writes that the birth of the reader is at the expense of the death of the author. There may be latent violence in doing something unexpected with a text. Possibilities emerge from this latency, not least because the artist does away with the mythical authority of the author.

JB: I think it depends what context you're presenting that work in. What might be acceptable in the visual art, live art, or performance worlds might not be acceptable in the more traditional theatre world. In a sense, there is a level of antagonism. Personally for me there is this struggle about this total love for theatre – the building, the mechanisms of it, the canon – but also frustration towards it. We are creatures of the theatre, both Simon and I. I don't think my antagonism is towards a specific text play, because some of these pieces have the most fantastic lines, like in *Macbeth*: 'where violent sorrow seems/ A modern ecstasy.'[7] To me that is a fantastic line, and I want to use phrases like that, but at the same time I don't want to have to be involved in the conventions, the protocols, the assumed sacredness of the text.

DJ: There is a difference between someone coming to see *King Real*, as I'm assuming audiences generally aren't expecting to see *King Lear* as a legible source material, whereas with your earlier pieces, Julia – *Hamlet* and *Macbeth* – audiences may have been expecting to see faithful productions of those texts. The effect must have been quite disconcerting for some audiences.

JB: Yes, well, that's why I'm not working in the theatre anymore. That context was incredibly problematic and one of the problems is that in theatre it's very difficult to be an artist. However, I still see everything I do as theatre, even if it's making a pinhole photograph – for me that's another kind of stage.

DJ: That's a kind of formal translation or adaptation: something might appear to be a certain form, yet take shape in disguise as another. Simon, I wondered about your relation to translations between theatre and other media, particularly dance.

SV: People saw *Invisible Dances* as a dance project, partly because I was working with Frank Bock who's a choreographer and worked as a dancer, but I also think that dance is more open to the idea of abstraction. We still have a very literary tradition of making theatre in this country.

JB: British theatre is still seen through the filter of literature, and in other countries it isn't necessarily. Having been brought up in the United Kingdom with this very heavy literary tradition, you don't realize that theatre could be something else. I do still love language, epic narratives, and the incredibly violent and extreme myths. But I don't want to be totally dominated by words.

DJ: Do you think you and your work have been freed up by circulating within the Live Art and Performance Art circuits you often tour in?

JB: I think for me it's been incredibly useful. In a pragmatic way it allows me to sneak in under the radar into a different world, because there are other contexts in which it is possible to experiment and make work in a particular way that isn't just about the three-week rehearsal and producing a product.

DJ: Let's open out to the audience.

Audience member 1: What mechanisms of appropriation and translation do you use in works that are not declaredly appropriation? I'm interested in the mechanisms that you describe specifically as appropriating moves. To what degree do you apply them to other works that are not specifically adaptations?

JB: In other works the source material is buried. The *Divine Trilogy* is loosely based on the Bible: *Trans-Acts* is based on the last few days of Christ and the crucifixion, the burial and the resurrection, and it's not explicit, but there are 12 spectators seated around a table, and references to wine and wounds. *Almost the Same*, the second part of the trilogy, is loosely based on the Nativity. Mary in this case gives birth to two hares, and also there are references to Noah's Ark, the idea of the doubles, the animals two by two. In the third part, *Aftermaths* is based on the book of Revelation. The sources are buried to different degrees, depending on where the emphasis needs to be laid. Sometimes the source material is more or less private and nobody needs to know about it. If you're lost it's like your map, and if you can't understand how to solve something you go back to the source material and it will give you an answer. It's like a thematic substructure.

Audience member 2: Thinking about the rigorous levels of research and the complexity of the methodologies, could you talk about the potential for your own works to be adapted or appropriated by others?

JB: I was asked to contribute to a Methuen anthology of texts.[8] One of the ideas for the anthology was to enable others to recreate the works. I couldn't envisage that happening.

I think a work exists in the moment, in the time that you're making it. It's not made for posterity. Nevertheless, the score of *Trans-Acts* was published in the anthology, so it'll be interesting if anybody tries to re-perform it. It might be an interesting exercise, as a reinterpretation of base material.

SV: I agree it's an interesting exercise with experimental theatre or performance. I think Beckett is one of the few people who wrote his theatricality into his writing and if you don't fulfil his stage directions the piece just doesn't work.

JB: I think there are interesting things about authentic reconstruction. But it would be much better to make something new.

DJ: You were saying earlier that you are a theatre animal, but this conviction against re-performance is counter to the traditional apparatus of the theatre. Performance art often embraces much more the cult of originality, but even that has been changing recently, with the spate of quite faithful re-enactments of other artists' works.

JB: Why do you think that is?

DJ: It's partly a theoretical enterprise I think. There are classic works that get re-performed quite frequently – Yoko Ono's *Cut Piece*, for example, has been repeatedly re-performed, either faithfully, or adapted with different bodies and actions, and so on. Personally I'm not sure it's terribly interesting. For me, there is little attraction in this kind of appropriation, beyond its function as a theoretical exercise, or as an archival practice.

SV: I think the reason we both balk slightly at the idea of our work being adapted or re-performed is that the work comes out of long personal processes, and the work is a result of that process. I would be fascinated, but it would be hard for me to imagine someone recreating that work, especially as my work is actually so much to do with rejecting the documented image, yet an artist re-performing the piece would necessarily have to work with images in order to reconstruct it.

DJ: So in a way if there is an anxiety it's about someone interpreting or adapting only the end result rather than the procedures that have led to them.

Audience Member 3: You both use the term 'research'. Can you say what you mean by this?

SV: In exploring the *King Real* script, we've taken various blocks of time to examine that text, outside the idea of presenting it. And over that two or three years I have been presented with a multiple view of the potential and energy contained within that text. For me that would be research.

DJ: One of the assumptions within the academy about how practice constitutes research is not just that traditional modes of research might lead up to a show. The performance itself produces a kind of knowledge that might not have been available by way of other methodologies. The relation between practice-based research and adaptation might be that the act of adaptation itself may function as a useful mode of research in and of itself, because adaptation teases out new kinds of knowledge from texts that may otherwise seem drained of novelty. How do you respond to the idea that live performance produces kinds of knowledge that can only be achieved through the act of performance itself, and not through traditional methods of research?

JB: I agree that the presentation of the work is – as you say – another opportunity to glean knowledge, and often you can't get to that knowledge until you put a performance in front of people. The sensation of that material when it's offered is not held back by the residues of old knowledges. It becomes a new thing.

Links

Simon Vincenzi: http://www.operationinfinity.org (accessed 19 Janaury 2014).

Julia Bardsley: http://www.juliabardsley.co.uk (accessed 19 January 2014).

Selected bibliography

Bardsley, Julia. (2011). 'Trans-Acts' in Anna Furse (ed.), *Theatre in Pieces: Politics, Poetics and Interdisciplinary Collaboration: An Anthology of Play Texts 1966–2010*. London: Methuen, pp. 155–98.

Johnson, Dominic. (2010). 'The Skin of the Theatre: An Interview with Julia Bardsley', *Contemporary Theatre Review*, 20.3, pp. 340–52.

Klein, Jennie. (2005). 'Genre-Bending Performance', *PAJ: A Journal of Performance and Art*, 28.1, PAJ 82, pp. 58–66.

Templeton, Fiona. (2004). *Bock and Vincenzi: Invisible Dances ... From Afar.* London: Artsadmin.

Welton, Martin. (2011). *Feeling Theatre.* Basingstoke: Palgrave Macmillan, pp. 159–62.

Notes

1 This interview was part of the Leverhulme Olympic Talks on Theatre and Adaptation. It took place at Queen Mary, University of London, on 3 April 2012.

2 Peter Bürger, *Theory of the Avant-Garde,* trans. Jochen Schulte-Sasse. Minneapolis, MN: University of Minnesota Press, [1974] 1984, p. 51.

3 Ibid., p. 52.

4 Ibid., pp. 52–3.

5 Rosalind E. Krauss, 'The Originality of the Avant-Garde' in *The Originality of the Avant-Garde and other Modernist Myths*. Cambridge, MA and London: MIT Press, 1986, pp. 151–70 (p. 168).

6 Ibid., p. 170.

7 *Macbeth*, Act IV, Scene III.

8 See Bardsley in Furse (2011), pp. 155–98.

8

Between Radical Adaptation and Strategic Adaptability: Ki Catur 'Benyek' Kuncoro in Conversation with Miguel Escobar[1]

Introduction

The *enfant terrible* of Javanese *Wayang Kulit* (shadow puppetry), Catur 'Benyek' Kuncoro is known for his unorthodox style and adaptations of traditional performance conventions. In order to grasp the audacity of Catur's work, it is crucial to appreciate the conservative cultural context in which they take place. *Wayang Kulit* is the oldest and most respected performance tradition in Java: performances of this art form conventionally last eight hours and are attended by people of all ages, usually within the context of highly ceremonial events. *Wayang* performances are defined by a set of strict principles called *pakem,* which could be thought of as a canon, a set of unspoken rules that dictate how every aspect of the performance should sound and look, ranging from the appearance of the puppets to the music and the movement that is appropriate to each character. Most performances draw their narrative material from the *purwa* story cycle, which corresponds to the Indian epics of the *Mahabharata* and *Ramayana*. There is no script for these stories, but the *dalang* (master puppeteer), should adhere to strict guidelines about the way the stories are to be broken down into scenes. The performances are always accompanied by a gamelan orchestra, but it is one person only, the *dalang*, who manipulates and gives voices to all the characters. He (rarely she) must possess great stamina and a variety of skills. He is at once a singer, storyteller, philosopher, stand-up comedian, and minister of religion. But Catur is not a conventional *dalang*, since he has subverted every convention that *Wayang Kulit* puppeteers are required to follow at one point or other in his career: for instance, he has changed the stories, the ways the mythical characters are supposed to be portrayed and, in *Wayang Hip Hop*, he has even replaced the gamelan orchestra with a DJ. His adaptations, however, refer strongly to the tradition and he has never changed *Wayang* beyond recognition, only shifted it enough to allow conservative spectators to disapprove of him and younger generations to hail him as an artist that speaks to their concerns. Catur's provocations, however, are not haphazard: a third-generation *dalang* from a reputed family of artists, he is as knowledgeable of the *pakem* as one would expect him to be. His careful and playful versions, therefore, are devised with deeply knowledgeable irreverence.

Along with other controversial Indonesian puppeteers, such as Slamet Gundono, Enthus Susmono, and Jlitheng Suparman, Catur has become one of the most prominent proponents of *Wayang kontemporer* (contemporary *Wayang*) and has developed several original pieces.[2] *Wayang Bocor* (2008), one of Catur's earlier works, is a series of collaborations with internationally renowned visual artist Eko Nugroho. This *Wayang* used the surrealist puppets created by Eko and experimental music from composer Yenu Ariendra to present narratives, characters, and situations that had little to do with the traditional Indian epics, drawing inspiration instead from contemporary urban life in Yogyakarta. This performance series was co-produced by the French government and was widely acclaimed by the visual arts circles of Indonesia. But Catur's most successful and polemic performance to date is *Wayang Hip Hop* (2010), which began as a collaboration with a group of young Hip Hop musicians. A shortened version of *Wayang* that combines *suluk* (a type of song used by *dalang*) and Hip Hop music, this piece explores traditional stories adapted to a modern context. The *dalang* here is accompanied by rappers who double up as actors. Another well-known performance is *Wayang Mitologi* (2010), which uses traditional myths from Yogyakarta that, despite being part of the oral tradition, had never been adapted to *Wayang*. In Catur's version, enough puns ensure that audiences understand that the gods in fact symbolize Jakartan politicians, viewed as a group of corrupt and reckless leaders. Another recent piece, *Wayang Republik* (2010), tells the story of the involvement of Yogyakarta in the struggle for Indonesian independence. When this performance was created, the status of the city as a semi-independent region was being revised by the central government in Jakarta. Through this historical narrative, Catur wanted to support the struggle of the city to maintain its special designation within the Indonesian Republic.

Polemic as these works are, there is another aspect to these adaptations that needs to be taken into account, that is, sponsorship. Performers in Java often need to 'adapt' their work to the needs of the market, or the needs of sponsors, as there is no public funding for the arts in Indonesia. Therefore, the performances need to suit particular situations, specifically following the needs of the sponsors. As a consequence, two understandings of the word 'adaptation' emerged during the interview, which was conducted in Indonesian. The English term can be translated into Indonesian as *adaptasi* or *penyesuaian*. The former suggests an assertive re-elaboration of rules, while the latter implies a degree of passivity: it is adaptation to external circumstances as self-renunciation. *Penyesuaian* is often used to describe the moments of familial or political life where a person resigns their own aspirations for the common good. In the context of Javanese ethics, achieving balance (*kerukunan*) by renouncing one's desires and focusing instead on the community as a whole is of utmost importance. This type of adaptation plays a strong part in traditional *Wayang* and, as it is clear from Catur's anecdotes, in *Wayang kontemporer* too.

Catur candidly retells of an episode where the sponsor asked him to shorten the duration of his play from one hour to 15 minutes. He did not interpret this interference as disrespectful and dismissed it as normal commissioner behaviour. On another occasion, I witnessed a more overtly disruptive intervention when, halfway through Catur's show, the sponsor approached the stage and whispered instructions to cut the performance short as quickly as possible. With a commendable disposition to irony and ability to improvise, he was able to wrap up the story and crack a joke about his sponsor in a matter of minutes. In a swift demonstration of virtuosity, he had managed to be both rebellious and compliant. This epitomizes perhaps the two aspects of adaptation he explains in the interview: *adaptasi* as a kind of radical and polemical intervention, and *penyesuaian* as strategic adaptability, a necessary skill used to comply with flimsy commissioners' demands and the circumstances for which the *Wayang* is being created.

Catur is deeply aware of the limitations imposed by the reliance on commercial sponsorship to continue developing his work. While it is in his character to be rebellious, he nonetheless chose to make a living as a *dalang* and he is greatly concerned with the future of this tradition. He believes that without adopting both strategies in order to reinterpret the work, the form will perish, unable to adapt to current times. In what follows, he discusses his adaptation strategies and describes how he manages to adapt his art to a complex cultural context.

Interview

Miguel Escobar: You have developed many performances which could be described as adaptations of *Wayang*. How did you first become interested in developing this kind of work?

Catur Kuncoro: I have always been curious and wanted to push *Wayang* to its limits, but working with friends that have a theatre and visual arts background opened my eyes to what can be done. Observing their process very much influenced me. For example, in theatre it was interesting to see how people almost got into fights about how to interpret a script and they all had very strong opinions that they defended in their arguments. This is something that does not exist in a traditional arts context where, even if I don't agree with other people's ideas, I still have to do what they say, even if in my heart I disagree. Whereas in a modern or theatre setting, or in the visual arts, people express their difference of opinion with regard to ideas they disapprove of. This helped me understand adaptation as a collaborative process.

ME: How has this affected the way you work with artists from other backgrounds in your own adaptation work?

CK: It depends. With Eko Nugroho, we usually begin by looking at a 'treatment' that has been prepared by Cindil.[3] Then we start working from that treatment or framework, and we discuss it together. The perspectives of visual artists are different from those of the theatre-makers and that is when things become interesting. I am always surprised by these differences! But when I talk to them I usually position myself as a traditional artist. If I positioned myself as a modern artist in that context, our ideas would overlap, so I use my traditional credentials and speak about the work in ways that they would not have thought of. In my eyes, these differences are what make the creative process interesting.

ME: How is this different from working with the artists of *Wayang Hip Hop*?

CK: It is extremely different. But let me tell you more about *Bocor* first. In *Wayang Bocor* I worked with people with different disciplinary backgrounds. Eko Nugroho tends to be funny and he likes introducing absurd ideas as a way to challenge the work. Then there's Cindil who is a rather religious person and brings his religiosity in a very serious way into the collaborative process. When we work on developing the stories, there is always an interesting discussion because we are very different in our approaches. But we try to combine this and 'mix' it [English word in the original]. Therefore, what comes out will certainly be interesting. And then we would work on the music, which was made by Yenu [Ariendra]. The first time I worked with Yenu was in the Yogyakarta Arts Festival in 2009, for something called *Wayang Pixel*, and it was not easy. The first time I heard his experimental music, my ears hurt and it was hard for me to adapt to those sounds. But then that feeling disappeared because I wanted to learn and understand that language. So for example, there is a specific kind of music that you use for fights in *Wayang*. But Yenu wanted to use recorded voices from people in the markets mixed with a sharp distortion, and he had me sing on top of that. I used a Javanese melody with Indonesian words. That process really allowed me to expand my views and to liberate my mind. So I had to be able to enter Yenu's dimension, his world, as it were. I tried this because I wanted to free up my thoughts. I tried to find a moment in the music that I could hold on to, however clumsily. I found that spot and it became my *gendèr*.[4] So I could hold on to that and I began to enjoy the music. And then our creation had its own kind of harmony. But when it comes to the *Wayang* puppets themselves, that is another story. Eko Nugroho's puppets have a lot of hinges which make them harder to manoeuvre than conventional *Wayang* puppets. They are also much bigger and have different configurations. So they constitute a challenge, and the creative process was quite tiring. *Wayang Hip Hop* required a different kind of process. My role in *Wayang Bocor* is more focused on the language of movements, but in *Wayang Hip Hop* I have more control over the actual words being said. So it requires a more verbal kind of adaptation. And I enjoyed this process more.

ME: What was the most difficult part of that process?

CK: Making the lyrics is perhaps the hardest part. Sometimes it takes a long time to find the right inspiration and to turn it into words. I might have a great idea but when I get in front of the laptop, it disappears. Some days I can only write one verse and that is it. The inspiration is gone. Often I go for long motorbike rides and that is when the best inspiration comes. These might be ideas for songs or for stories, and I always have my phone at hand so I can use it as a voice recorder. I stop and record them and I often realize I don't know where I've driven to, because I was so absorbed in my thoughts. The problem is that I wrote all the lyrics and the scripts myself for *Wayang Hip Hop* and I was also more responsible for the overall result. Of course, I was collaborating with the rappers and the actors, but I was the one to direct them, whereas in *Wayang Bocor* it was a more collaborative adaptation process. For *Wayang Hip Hop*, I had to train the rappers to act as well, because they don't have a background in theatre, so I became a kind of director. Many of the difficulties of creating *Wayang Hip Hop* were technical.

ME: Butet Kartaredjasa once described *Wayang Hip Hop* as an 'adaptable *Wayang*'.[5]

CK: He did, but the word 'adaptable' is very complex and has many implications. My work is an adaptation of *Wayang*. But adaptable also means that it can be performed anywhere. For example, in a *pendopo* [traditional building], in a theatre or in a shopping centre. And the story is adaptable as well. It can change [*bisa disesuaikan*] as it is performed and we can adapt it to the particular situation and the people for whom we are performing.

ME: Is there a risk in this? How do you ensure that your work doesn't lose its essence when such an adaptation [*penyesuaian*] takes place?

CK: Well, the fact that it is 'adaptable' does not mean there are no limits to how much it can be adapted to a particular situation. We have a set of general principles, something that makes *Wayang Hip Hop* what it is. And that is not up for negotiation. We can adapt many aspects of the dialogues and the story to a particular situation, but we try to stay true to what *Wayang Hip Hop* means for us.

ME: I once saw a sponsor ask you to stop the performance halfway through. How did you manage to stay true to what is important to you about *Wayang Hip Hop* on that occasion?

CK: Maybe that is connected to my culture. In Indonesia, we know that we must quickly adapt to the requests of our sponsors. This is different from working with foreign funding, which gives you total artistic freedom to develop your work. When we are dealing with commercial sponsors here in Indonesia we must learn to deal swiftly with unexpected conditions. For instance, once we got to a venue that was much smaller than the space we needed to perform and we had to adapt to it. I have once worked with European artists and they couldn't stand those last minute changes. They were stiffer. Maybe in Europe, if you are promised one hour, that promise will be respected. But over here, sometimes they tell me, 'You will have an hour for your performance.' And I say, 'OK.' But when I arrive, they say, 'Oh, we are going to use 45 minutes for an advertisement, so you only get 15 minutes to perform.' That is normal here. Not many people respect the work of the artists. They feel that if they have paid for it, they own the work. But our challenge is to use whatever conditions we have, and find a way around them. To find a way to make fun of them and still deliver our message, and pour our souls into our 15 minutes of performance time.

ME: Have you ever received a request that you were not willing to comply with?

CK: Once a sponsor didn't want me to use *Wayang*, and I immediately rejected the idea. I can find my way around other things but I found that excessive! With *Wayang Hip Hop*, we have developed a way to work around limitations and still defend the essence of the work, which lies in our sense of humour, our interpretation of the stories and our musical combinations.[6]

ME: What is, in your mind, the relationship between adaptation and the future of tradition?

CK: In my view, it all has to do with relevance. Let me give you an example. When I was a kid, if I was still playing outside the house at night, my parents would yell, '*Candhik ala!*' to me. In Javanese, this is the time when day changes into night but, as kids, we thought this was a kind of demon that was approaching the house. The kids would be always afraid of this and go inside the house. But I cannot yell the same phrase to my own children; they wouldn't react the way I used to. I have to explain things to them. I have to tell them that it is already dark and they need to take a bath and get ready to sleep. So things change and language changes accordingly. Maybe it is the same with *Wayang*. The methods have changed but the essence is the same. For example, in traditional *Wayang* sometimes the *dalang* uses a very refined *kawi* register, but it cannot be understood by young people or by those living in the city.[7] So it is not worth it. It's better to use another kind of language. Maybe even *bahasa ngoko* so that people can understand what is being said.[8] We still use aspects from the tradition, but we change them to suit the times we live in. That is how we adapt it to keep it alive.

ME: You once described your own work as a 'mischievous reinterpretation of *Wayang*'.

CK: Yes, I like to think of the *Wayang* characters as if they were normal people. For example Gatotkaca is one of the biggest and strongest characters, and he is always portrayed as strong and big. But for *Wayangku, Wayangmu* [*My Wayang, Your Wayang*], a TV series I did for a local television, I imagined Gatotkaca having flu. So this big guy is moaning and feeling sick at home. I also did the same once for Arjuna, who is supposed to be a ladies' man and is always well dressed, except when he has flu. For me, showing that weakness is a way to render them in their full human complexity.

ME: But many people consider that a transgression and you are often highly criticized for that. Sutadi, the director of the Surakarta Branch of the National Wayang Organization in Surakarta, spoke in a local paper against what you were doing to Werkudara and Gatotkaca in *Wayang Hip Hop*.[9]

CK: Yes, but it is precisely those kinds of adaptation that interest me. If I just used other characters for this, it would be boring. It is precisely in that combination, when a traditional character is presented in a mischievous manner that it highlights something new. But some people cannot laugh at it because they are too fixated on their conservatism, a traditional framework which is too solidified to change. But they should be able to realize that *Wayang* has always changed. They suggested I should only use the clown figures for these adaptions, but then everything would just be a joke.[10] If I depict Werkudara and Bima having a fight, it shows how disagreements happen inside the family.[11] And then it can make people think.

ME: Is this a form of social critique?

CK: In a way, it is. But I think some of my other work is more directly critical about society. Maybe even in a political way.

ME: This makes me think about *Wayang Mitologi*. There seem to be two types of adaptation in that show. On one hand, you stage a story which is not conventionally used for *Wayang*. On the other, the gods seem to represent well-known politicians.

CK: Yes, that is correct. In my country people's status is very important. So if someone gets into a position of power, they will do anything imaginable to retain that power. And if someone else says something truthful, they will make it appear as something made up. That is the context where the gods feel anxious about the actions of Rama and Permadi, two expert *keris* makers who are creating a weapon more powerful than any possessed by the gods.[12] They decide to make it because they read the situation in heaven and they know things are getting out of control. So they build this weapon to keep the gods in check, so to speak. But the most powerful will always win and exploit their power to find a way to remain in control. This is not different from what happens in my country. Here it is very easy to turn someone into a scapegoat. And people don't see that. I think that is the disease of power. What can the people do? Maybe as artists we can adapt our stories to talk about these things in indirect ways. We will not seek direct confrontation, but we will use our own knowledge to do our part.

ME: How is this different from the adaptation of *Wayang Republik*?

CK: That work was made in a particular period, when the special status of the city of Yogyakarta was being questioned. So I used *Wayang* to tell the story of the city and show scenes that many people didn't know about, like when Sukarno was captured.[13] This performance was inspired by a book by Umar Kayam which tells this little-known side of our history.[14]

ME: You have created quite a variety of adaptations, exploring different kinds of stories, music, puppets, and issues. What plans do you have for future adaptations?

CK: At the moment I am still busy developing *Wayang Hip Hop*. For the future, I would like to continue with my explorations. I think of myself as someone who *finds* things, rather than as someone who *creates* them. I try to find something that makes sense for *Wayang* today, in this time and in a city like Yogyakarta. I don't know what other generations will do with it, but I think adapting *Wayang* is a challenge and a responsibility. I feel a responsibility to be a *dalang* that makes work for today. This is my profession. Only the things that can be adapted will be strong enough to survive. And those which don't will be left behind. Maybe it is a bit like the disappearance of the dinosaurs. They were big and powerful animals. But they could not evolve with their times; they could not survive the challenges they faced. And then you have the ants, these tiny creatures. But they were able to adapt to the times and they have survived from the old ages all the way into the present. They were able to evolve under every condition. I think the *Wayang* I want to continue making is more like these ants. It may be something very small, but it is well adapted to these times.

Selected bibliography

Cohen, Matthew Isaac. (2007). 'Contemporary *Wayang* in Global Contexts', *Asian Theatre Journal*, 24.2, pp. 338–69.

—(2014). 'Traditional and Post-traditional *Wayang Kulit* in Java Today', in Dassia Posner, John Bell, and Claudia Orenstein (eds), *Material Performances: New Perspectives on Puppets and Performing Objects.* London and New York: Routledge.

Escobar Varela, Miguel. (2014). '*Wayang Hip Hop*: Java's Oldest Performance Tradition Meets Global Youth Culture', *Asian Theatre Journal*, 31.1, in press.

Mrázek, Jan (ed.). (2002). *Puppet Theater in Contemporary Indonesia: New Approaches to Performance Events*. Ann Arbor, MI: University of Michigan Centers for South and Southeast Asian Studies.

Notes

1 This interview was conducted in Indonesian, rather than Javanese, upon the artist's request, and was translated into English by the author. Indonesian naming practices vary greatly, but many Javanese people do not have a family name. Second names are not necessarily inherited ones and are rarely used to address individuals. In Java, Catur 'Benyek' Kuncoro is usually referred to as Catur, or Benyek (his nickname), and never as Kuncoro. In this interview, following the artist's wish, he is refered to as Catur. All other artists mentioned are referenced by their first of two names. The names between inverted commas correspond to their nicknames.

2 For an overview of contemporary *Wayang*, see Cohen (2007 and 2014) and Mrázek (2002). While other *dalang* are considered as provocative as Catur, many have now become more established. At the time of writing, Catur remains the most controversial provocateur. His adaptations continue to be received with a combination of criticism and admiration.

3 Gunawan 'Cindil' Maryanto (b. 1976) is a celebrated Indonesian playwright and director who works with Teater Garasi in Yogyakarta.

4 Musical accompaniment for traditional *Wayang* is always provided by a gamelan orchestra. The *dalang* will usually adapt his singing to the pitch of the *gendèr*, a metallophone consisting of tuned metal bars suspended over a bamboo resonator that are hit with a wooden mallet. This is why Catur likens a particular pattern of the experimental music to a *gendèr*, a sound to which he can adjust the pitch of his voice.

5 Butet Kartaredjasa (b. 1961) is an Indonesian actor who worked in theatre, film, and television.

6 *Wayang Hip Hop* changes drastically each time it is performed. This is why it is important for Catur to ascertain that the work does not lose its essence through its multiple versions.

7 A high register of old Javanese, closely linked to Sanskrit.

8 The Javanese language has several registers, each one with its own subset of verbs and nouns. The register a person chooses to address another in depends on the relative status and age of the two interlocutors. *Ngoko* is the lowest, everyday register of Javanese one reserves for people of one's own age or younger, with whom one has a close relationship. It is considered to be impolite in formal occasions. While this register is still actively used, more formal registers are being displaced by the less hierarchical Indonesian language (*Bahasa Indonesia*). A conventional *Wayang* show will relish in polite and uncommon words pertaining to the higher registers that few people can understand. This is why Catur's idea of using *ngoko* in performance is radical.

9 Gatotkaca and his father Werkudara are two of the most respected characters in *Wayang*. In Catur's performance, Gatotkaca challenges his father – an impossible transgression in a traditional context.

10 The clown figures, or *punokawan*, are Semar and his sons Petruk, Gareng, and Bagong. They are the servants of the warriors. In a traditional show, there is always a comic intermezzo called *gara-gara*, where the *punokawan* mock the story being presented thus far and make jokes about topical issues. Parodies in *gara-gara* are not considered radical or subversive. The critic of *Wayang Hip Hop* mentioned here is suggesting that Catur limit his reinterpretations of the *Wayang* characters to the *punokawan*, which is conventional when artists want to escape criticism.

11 Gatotkaca, the perfect son, is always portrayed as quiet and accepting of his fate, even when he is sent on a suicide mission to fight Karna, the only person who can kill him. By presenting Gatotkaca as a rebellious son, Catur's performance challenges established authority and family roles.

12 A type of mystical, short dagger.

13 Sukarno was the leader of the movement for the independence of Indonesia from the Netherlands and its first president, from 1945 to 1967. Months before independence was declared in 1945, he was allegedly captured by the *pemuda* (young revolutionary leaders), who wanted to accelerate the process. This kidnapping, which is omitted from official history, was re-enacted in *Wayang Republik*.

14 Umar Kayam, *Titipan Umar Kayam: Sekumpulan Kolom di Majalah Tempo* [*The legacy of Umar Kayam: a collection of columns from Tempo magazine*]. Jakarta: Pusat Data dan Analisa Tempo, 2002.

9

Beg, Borrow or Steal: Lois Weaver in Conversation with Jen Harvie[1]

Introduction

Lois Weaver was born and raised in Virginia, in the United States, in the Southern Baptist Bible belt. Via drama training at Radford University and early peace and social justice activist work in Baltimore, she arrived in New York in the 1970s, where her career in alternative, feminist and queer theatre, performance and activism took off. She has worked with Indigenous North American women's company Spiderwoman Theater and queer countercultural performance company Hot Peaches in the United States and Gay Sweatshop in the United Kingdom. She performs frequently at La Mama E.T.C. on New York's Lower East Side and at the Chelsea Theatre in London. In 1979/80, she co-founded both the women's theatre collective and venue WOW Café Theatre in New York's East Village and, with Peggy Shaw and Deb Margolin, the legendary feminist performance company Split Britches.[2] Split Britches' work adapts canonical texts such as *Beauty and the Beast* (1982), *Little Women: The Tragedy* (1988), and Tennessee Williams' *A Streetcar Named Desire* in *Belle Reprieve* (in collaboration with Bloolips, 1990), queering them and challenging their gender and sexual normativities. But Lois and Split Britches adapt other things besides texts, to challenge the effective exclusivity and heteronormativity of dominant forms and to extend address to a broader constituency excluded by sexuality but also class and simply a *sense* of not being welcome in particular places such as academic halls, or not being hailed by select modes of communication such as canonical texts. The range of things Lois adapts includes: pop cultural music, films and personae; academic forms of address and engagement; forms of activism; performance spaces; personal stories, dreams, desires, urban myths and anecdotes; costumes and props; and gender and gender roles. Since 1997, Lois has taught performance at Queen Mary, University of London. She continues to make performance work in collaboration and solo, for example as her alter ego Tammy Whynot, and to work as a director, writer, and activist. In 2012, Lois delivered her professorial inaugural lecture, 'What Tammy Found Out, a Front Line Report from the Back Porch, the Schoolyard and the Dinner Table'; Split Britches won the Edwin Booth Award 'in recognition of their outstanding contribution to the New York City/American Theatre and Performance Community';[3] and La Mama E.T.C. hosted *33 x 3*, a retrospective of Split Britches' 33 years of work.

Interview

Jen Harvie: One of your mottos is 'beg, borrow, or steal', which reveals a certain attitude to adaptation. Can you tell us how that motto informs your practice and attitude as a performance maker?

Lois Weaver: I came up with that phrase when people started asking me to define and write about *my* process. I thought to myself, 'How can I possibly write about a process that has been so much about a combination of so many other people's processes?' So much of what I do in the rehearsal room and on the stage is a combination of other people's work and other influences. I thought if I ever wrote a book it would have to be called *The Beg, Borrow and Steal Approach*, because I didn't feel like I could claim ownership to one particular methodology. It came up again when we [Split Britches] were asked to pull our scripts together to publish them.[4] At that point, 1996, we had seven scripts that had never really been written down; it was all pretty much oral and notebooks, and faulty memories and some old video tapes. That's how we would reconstruct the performances each time. So when we were asked to put that together it was terrifying, but one of the most terrifying things was that we had used so many other people's materials. We had literally used so many songs that didn't belong to us, so many popular cultural references that were not ours. So when it came time again to write it down, there was no way to claim ownership of that. We had to find a way of describing the fact that we used Perry Como's 'It's Impossible', or we sang 'I Want to be in America' in Yiddish. We had to find a way of describing that [process] without owning that [material]; we began to talk about our 'beg, borrow, steal approach' then.

I think the whole thing comes out of church. I was brought up as a Southern Baptist, and as far as I was concerned the Bible was a beg, borrow, and steal situation. These were stories that had been borrowed from other cultures and turned around, rewritten and handed on, and every time I saw a Bible story it seemed to be a different kind of adaptation of something I'd seen before. I think that's where I got the idea, 'Oh, there's all this material out there, let's just make use of it the way we want'. And then as I began working in the 1970s, in queer culture and working around Theatre of the Ridiculous and Hot Peaches, it was all about appropriating popular culture. So everything we did was begged, borrowed and stolen, including the spaces that we worked in at the time.

JH: I'd like to talk about pop culture stealing. Hot Peaches was doing that, Split Britches did that, you continue to do that, and presumably it's specifically *pop* culture that you want to ransack.

LW: Specifically, yes.

JH: Why that territory?

LW: I wanted to make work that challenged the norm, but I also wanted a route into that which was accessible for people, particularly when I started to work with Split Britches. We were working to challenge normative heterosexual images about what it means to be a man, what it means to be a woman, what it means to be two women together, and we really wanted to work with what it looked like to be heterosexual. So we took those images and those songs and those dances, you know, Barbra Streisand, Neil Diamond, George Jones and Tammy Wynette, Spencer Tracey and … Gertrude Stein, no, I mean Katharine Hepburn. But we took those combinations because they were recognizable and we wanted to start with something recognizable and just ever so slightly shift it so that people would come with us on that journey. This is actually a different approach to Hot Peaches, because Hot Peaches was very much in your face: 'We're queer, we're gay, everybody in the room that's gay raise your hand, smile if you're glad to be gay, all that, gay, gay, gay.' We [Split Britches] wanted to create images and characters where people would begin to like us and think they understood us and think they knew us. Then let them know that we were lesbians. We enjoyed that trick. Popular culture was the best way in to that. Besides, we loved it. I mean we just loved those songs; they were so tacky and you would never want to do them for real, but if you took them on as your material you could do with them what you wanted, and we did.

JH: A key word that's used about your work is 'subversive'. I would like to hear if that's a word that you want, and what's shifted over time in terms of what you want to subvert or problematize or screw up or whatever phrase you like best. Where have you put that political engagement that you've had across your career?

LW: I think the intention has always been *to subvert*, rather than to *be subversive*. I know that sounds a bit … but I don't think we've set out to be subversive. I think we set out to take the materials that we had at hand and to twist them slightly to tell a different kind of story. All three of us Split Britches, myself in particular, were interested in the eccentric, the unusual, the untold, the hidden, and the undiscovered, and I think that in order to get to that you have to twist the story slightly. In the beginning we were adapting normative heterosexual culture, and then as we became more established and we began to adapt within our own culture, we began to subvert ideas of what it meant to be a lesbian, even to lesbians. We began to work more consciously with eroticism on stage in a way which was slightly subversive to radical 1970s feminist ideas of what it meant to publicly display your lesbianism, let alone your feminism. And then we began to investigate the darker side of female sexuality, like in *Dress Suits to Hire* [1987]. And then with *Lust and Comfort* [1994] we began to look at our ideas about what it meant to be trans and the whole trans movement, and how that played out in popular culture with our adaptations of films like *The Servant* [1963, d. Joseph Losey], or [Rainer Werner] Fassbinder's *Bitter Tears of Petra von Kant* [1972]. We went in to look at how we could skew a community frame by slightly subverting the expectation of what that was supposed to be. And then I worked on the idea of what it meant to subvert the idea of being feminine and become the resistant femme by taking it on, and taking it on too big, by being femme but having hairy armpits and legs and dirty fingernails. We always have that little twist, or that little moment where we set up the picture, but there's just something not quite right with that picture.

JH: Could you talk about the work you're doing now which engages with femininity and sex and age?

LW: I have for some time been working on what it means to be a resistant femme. I know what it means for drag queens to resist being a male and how a butch lesbian resists being female in that normal way. So I wanted to find that place for myself where I could be feminine. I could be feminine without being post-feminist, I guess. I could be feminine and comment on it at the same time. There were lots of projects where I tried to work through that and failed, and only when I came to deal with it as Tammy Whynot have I been able to manage that. And so now I've shifted from wanting to represent femininity, to wanting to represent femininity as it ages. Because that's something that we don't see in very warm terms in this culture: how does femininity age? Masculinity ages brilliantly; people become more charming, they become debonair. But women just get old. And if you want to present as a feminine woman as you age, then you're constantly running up against – what is that phrase? – 'Mutton in lamb's clothes' or, you know, these terribly derogatory terms; so derogatory and so sort of internalized that you start to say it to yourself. I look in the mirror and I say, 'Ooh, is this too young for me? Is this just mutton in lamb's clothes?' It starts to really play out; how can I be the feminine fantasy and how can I play the feminine fantasy of myself and still be 62? And so I have been working on how to do that through performance. People don't talk about what women feel like, or what they need or what they want when they get to be a certain age. There's a lot of expectations but there's not a lot of dialogue around it, and I wanted to set up a dialogue where women in particular could talk about what it felt like to get old and have sex, or not have sex. So I used Tammy and I guess the adaptation of a talk-show in order to get people to talk about sex and age.

JH: I asked that partly to think about the ways that the political purpose of your work has shifted across your career. You said that Tammy worked as a way of doing a resistant femme. What is it that works about Tammy?

LW: I think Tammy's hyper-femininity is what allows me to go as far as I go with the other subjects, because she's so absolutely fake, everything about her is fake, and yet she's absolutely genuine and there's something for me about that combination that provides the split that I was looking for. I can wear the pushiest-up bra, the highest heels, the pinkest lipstick and the biggest hair, and it doesn't make me think about being 62, it makes me think about being Tammy. So it's somewhat ageless because it's so fake, I'm not attempting … it's clear what I'm attempting; you know what I'm going for there when I'm Tammy. And I call her my superhero because she allows me to fail, she allows me to still have a sense of wonder, she allows me to not worry about not knowing everything. That's the thing about Tammy: I can still, at this age, not know what things are and how they work and what it means, and she can ask those questions. There's something about that combination that's allowed me to find that place that I was looking for.

I've always worked with Peggy Shaw, and we always set up a butch-femme dynamic, and we worked that on purpose. But at a certain point there is a way that the butch kind of takes centre stage, so I become the straight man as it were to the butch's humour. Someone came up to me once and said, 'Ooh Peggy, the masculine Peggy *demands* attention, whereas you, the feminine, *commands* attention.' Always working in that dynamic I found it difficult to find the way the feminine can demand attention. I think Tammy demands attention.

JH: A lot of your work, with Split Britches particularly, adapts source texts, including classic plays. *Dress Suits to Hire* [1987] is a play written by Holly Hughes for you. How is that different from the kind of thing that *you* composed in the process of devising with colleagues and source texts?

LW: Well, we actually did devise that with Holly. Holly approached us and said she wanted to work with us, so we said fine. We were a little terrified and yet attracted to Holly because her use of language is amazing and her willingness to be so explicit sexually went further than we had gone at that point. We wanted to work with her language and her fearlessness really, her courage. There was a tuxedo shop in the Lower East Side, and there was a big rumour going around. It was the 1980s, and this was the only piece of real estate that had not been gentrified, because it belonged to this one woman. We didn't know her well but we knew her. And the place looked exactly the way it had looked in 1971. There was a sign in the window that said, 'Dress Suits to Hire', and it had always been there. We tried to rent it for the first WOW Café; we thought it would be a fantastic club for lesbians, 'Dress Suits to Hire', but she wouldn't have anything to do with us. She was a bit of an eccentric. Anyway, the story is that her sister had been murdered in the tuxedo shop, and that she had been murdered because there was a strip joint across the street – which I had actually gone to as a young person, just after I moved to New York. It was called 'Little Peters', and the sister supposedly had a voyeuristic relationship with someone at Little Peters, and well, one thing led to another and she got murdered. But it had never been solved. So we thought there was something very interesting about this myth, this rumour about the neighbourhood, and also this tuxedo rental shop. We liked the idea of a tuxedo going out to these major events in people's lives and then coming back full of stories of the events. So we said let's make a piece about that.

So Holly went away and wrote lots of text surrounding these two characters, Michigan and Deluxe, who could have been sisters, or lovers or twins, it was never explicit. That was her idea and she wrote loads and loads of text. And then we took that text back and we cut it and pasted it with some of our desires from different popular cultural numbers. And Holly had some of her desires – she was determined that Peggy was going to play Gilda, you know the title character in that film with Rita Hayworth?[5] She wanted to see Peggy in that Rita Hayworth-type dress. And she wanted Peggy to be, not the femme necessarily, but the butch in the dress who was also the prey, because we had a real interest in exploring this kind of feminine predatory sexual nature. The predator was my character, Michigan. And then underlying all of that was Holly's love of and inability to escape Michigan. So the piece was infused with all of this natural history of Michigan – the animal life and soil life and resources which are in Michigan but also were being taken from Michigan, and that became a real metaphor for the feminine. So yeah, it was written for us and yet we wrote it together. She wrote the text and we constructed it together, and we put it together in much the same way we put all of our shows together.

JH: You and Peggy did that show again almost 20 years later in 2005, which probably felt like adapting the original production.

LW: It was a bit.

JH: What did it feel like to do that show so many years later?

LW: Well, interestingly enough, we came back to it with the question, 'What does it feel like to go back to do something that's that sexual at the age we were then?' We wanted to look at age, and we wanted to look at change, and what's it like to return to something 17 years later. Also the community and reception had changed. We did that show in 1987, and loads of people walked out. Loads of women walked out. They were offended by it. It was right in the middle of the feminism and pornography debates. That's why we made *Little Women: The Tragedy* right after that. A lot of people had a lot of objections to our representations of lesbians in this way. So by the time we came back around to it not only were we older but the community had changed so we didn't have that kind of struggle.

The other thing we did was to do an adaptation of *Dress Suits to Hire* in Taiwan with 16 Taiwanese women. We took the piece that was built for two people and we broke it up into eight couples. We translated the piece into Taiwanese and translated also the popular cultural references into Taiwanese popular culture. So that was a great way to step back from the piece and look at it, particularly for me as a director. Then when we came to make it ourselves the second time around I think I was a lot less of an actor and much more of a performer and we both had much more distance.

JH: In *Anniversary Waltz* (1990), for example, you use a very literal form of adaptation, lip-synching. You lip-synch Paul Newman playing Brick in the 1958 film of the 1955 Tennessee Williams play *Cat on a Hot Tin Roof*. So there are all these layers of very literal adaptation. Could you tell us about the fun you have with that lip-synch sequence?

LW: Well, that was about 1990, and lip-synch was a big part of our culture, queer culture. The drag queens all lip-sanch, and we loved that. But I never actually thought it was quite enough, to sit through a three-and-a-half minute track of someone just singing a song. And it was then that I realized that I had to subvert something. Even in a lip-synch, we wanted to just slightly twist it. And we talked a lot about lip-synching [which] doesn't always synch or fit. The ice doesn't always go into the glass at the right time and there is that sort of distance from what you're doing live and what's being done in the recording. I love that distance, that split. So we've used lip-synching in Split Britches quite a bit. When we were putting together *Anniversary Waltz*, which was to celebrate mine and Peggy's tenth anniversary with Split Britches but also the tenth anniversary of our relationship, we did the whole piece as an anniversary wedding party. And we thought we'd really like to synch a [play] text because we hadn't tried that, and I'm obsessed with Tennessee Williams, and we were looking at the kind of failure of coupleness, and also the aspects of sexuality that are clearly in *Cat on a Hot Tin Roof*. We also wanted to re-feminize Peggy in the way she'd been feminized in some of the other pieces, like *Dress Suits to Hire*. Peggy had always had her desire to open her mouth and for Elizabeth Taylor's voice to come out. That was a real deep-rooted desire. That's how she got to be Elizabeth Taylor, and not me. I did a pretty good job as Brick.

JH: You are an activist and a teacher as well as a performance maker, and you have devised the idea of 'the long table' as a space and method of drawing people into discussion and working through ideas, which we could describe as an adaptation of conventional academic forms of debate. Why did you invent the long table and what do you think its future could be?

LW: I invented the long table because round about the millennium – remember that? – there were some projects that happened around the Small Acts at the Millennium that the Live Art Development Agency and a few other people supported, and I almost proposed a picnic in Trafalgar Square, because I had this desire to bring the domestic into the public. And then I started thinking, well maybe not a picnic, maybe a dinner. I said, 'Wouldn't it be great to have a big long table the length of Trafalgar Square?' And then after doing some prison work in Brazil with People's Palace Projects, we wanted to have an event that brought together some of the work that we had done with the women prisoners. We wanted to take some of the artworks and videos that we had made and make it an installation, but we also wanted to have a conversation in the context of that installation. I said to my collaborators, 'Can we try this idea of a long table?' I hadn't worked out what that would be or how it would work or anything. All I knew was I wanted it to be a long table surrounded by 12 chairs with some people watching and some people talking. I didn't want there to be a moderator: the conversation would move of its own accord, and we'd see what happened. I'd like to see it be as common as a panel discussion. Because the other thing for me is that it eliminates that fear I feel when I sit in a panel of people I think of as a whole lot smarter than me, and I have a few questions or something I'd like to say and my heart beats when it comes time to maybe even think about raising my hand. It really was sort of an antidote to that, to get away from that fear but also away from that posturing that goes on in those situations. Some people don't have that problem; they stand up and they have loads of things to say that aren't even that interesting. So I just wanted to get rid of that idea of expertise and to acknowledge that we're all experts in the room and put us all on the same level, and to give us all the ability to talk. And for me the success of the long table up 'til now has been that there's always at least one person who comes and shares in a way that they never would have done had it not been for this kind of set up. And I value that kind of exchange, the personal and the anecdotal, so I want it to be ubiquitous.

JH: You have recently performed your professorial inaugural lecture, had a retrospective of 33 years of Split Britches' work at La Mama E.T.C. and won the Edwin Booth Award. Can you tell us what you see from this point that's inviting you to reflect on the achievements of your career?

LW: I think that only when we get to a certain age, when we get to a certain point in our life we can say, 'Oh yeah I have this reservoir.'

Over the last month, all of the things that you mentioned, in particular the retrospective at La Mama, have been incredibly moving and nurturing to me. I could see not the amount of work I've done in a quantitative sense but a sort of fact that we began something that has meant something to a lot of people and that it wasn't a *piece* of work. It was *a way of making* work, a belief that everybody can do it; you just have to get up there and do it. It's a belief that desire is a force for making work; it's the belief that imagination can change things; it's a belief that you don't have to have a million dollars to make the thing you want to make. This is what we've got; what can we make together? And I just felt that that thing that we began with which felt like we were just doing it because we had to and because we could and it was fun, that it was a big thing. And it's had influence on other people, and that's enough man, that's plenty, that feels like a lot, and I feel really fed by that.

JH: Are there any questions from the audience?

Audience member 1: Can you tell us about how *Belle Reprieve* came about? It seems like an iconic adaptation of yours.

LW: *Belle Reprieve* came out of pure desire on every level, because Betty and Paul of Bloolips, and Peggy and I decided we wanted to make a piece together. We got together and said, 'What should we do?' And I am obsessed with Tennessee Williams, I always have been. When he died I carried a flask of Jack Daniels around in my pocket, as though I was him or something; I over-identified with that queer, Southern … sicko [*laughs*]. I said, 'Let's do *A Streetcar Named Desire*.' The moment I said that, I knew all I wanted to see was Peggy Shaw as Stanley Kowalski. I mean I had almost like an erotic desire to see her do that. And I knew that Betty and I were going to compete over who was going to do Blanche – Betty being the drag queen. Now of course what we did was we adapted the movie, not the play, because the movie was this iconic popular culture reference that we wanted to use, so we were looking at Marlon Brando and Vivien Leigh as opposed to the two characters. But the way we did it was that we took the play and the film and we looked at how our lives literally intersected with any of those moments and then we wrote our own individual stories into those particular moments. So it became a personal piece more than an adaptation to us.

Links

Hot Peaches: http://www.hotpeachesnyc.com/hotpeachesnyc/Home.html (accessed 19 January 2014).

La Mama E.T.C.: http://lamama.org (accessed 19 January 2014).

Spiderwoman Theater: http://www.spiderwomantheater.org (accessed 19 January 2014).

Split Britches: http://splitbritches.wordpress.com/ (accessed 19 January 2014).

Wow Café Theatre: http://www.wowcafe.org (accessed 19 January 2014).

Selected bibliography

Case, Sue-Ellen (ed.). (1996). *Split Britches: Lesbian Practice/Feminist Performance*. London and New York, Routledge.

Dolan, Jill. (2010). 'Belle Reprieve: LGBTQ Theory into Practice' in *Theatre and Sexuality*. Basingstoke: Palgrave Macmillan, pp. 59–80.

Martin, Carol (ed.). (1996). *A Sourcebook on Feminist Theatre and Performance: On and Beyond the Stage*. London and New York: Routledge.

Notes

1 This interview was part of the Leverhulme Olympic Talks on Theatre and Adaptation. It took place at Queen Mary, University of London, on 8 May 2012.

2 The archives of Gay Sweatshop Theatre Company (1974–97) are held by Royal Holloway, University of London, see http://www.aim25.ac.uk/

cgi-bin/vcdf/detail?coll_id=7091&inst_id=11. Split Britches' videos are archived on the Hemispheric Institute Digital Video Library at New York University, see http://hidvl.nyu.edu/search/?start=0&fq=collectionId%3ASplitBritchesvideocollection&q=&facets= (accessed 25 September 2013). The company's material archives (1978–2000) are kept by New York University's Fales Library and Special Collections, see http://dlib.nyu.edu/findingaids/html/fales/splitbritches/ (accessed 25 September 2013).

3 See Split Britches' website, http://splitbritches.wordpress.com/2012/03/27/edwin-booth-award-ceremony-honoring-split-britches/ (accessed 25 September 2013).

4 See Case (1996).

5 *Gilda* (1946), dir. by Charles Vidor.

Part Three

Intercultural Encounters

10

Shakespeare/Two Gents Productions: Denton Chikura, Tonderai Munyevu and Arne Pohlmeier of Two Gents Productions in Conversation with Penelope Woods[1]

Introduction

Two Gents Productions is a three-man theatre company founded in 2008. The programme for the Globe to Globe Festival at Shakespeare's Globe, in which Two Gents took part, lists the company as hailing from 'Harare/London'. The use of a solidus (or slash) here to describe the company's relationship to Harare and London is ambiguous.[2] We can read this as signifying that the company is from either Harare *or* London or that the company is from both Harare *and* London. But the multi-functional solidus might also propose – as m/h signifies miles per hour – that the company is in some way from Harare *per* London, or even from a Harare that is *divided* by London. Each of these may have an element of accuracy in its attempt to describe the complex geographic and cultural relationship of Two Gents Productions to the cities in question. Their production *Vakomana Vaviri ve Zimbabwe, or The Two Gentlemen of Verona* (2008 production in English; 2012 in Shona), an adaptation of Shakespeare's comedy, was performed on the Globe stage almost entirely in Shona, one of the three principal languages of Zimbabwe.[3] The production was rehearsed and developed in London for both a diaspora but also non-Shona-speaking audience, and has not yet been performed in Harare.[4] This permissively imprecise construction, 'Harare/London', gestures to the proliferation of possibilities and interpretations that arise through the abuttal of different approaches, aesthetics, languages, geographies and cultures in the work to date of Two Gents Productions.

Director, Arne Pohlmeier, is from Bielefeld in Germany; actors Tonderai Munyevu and Denton Chikura are from Harare, Zimbabwe. They met in London in 2008 when Pohlmeier arrived from a job in South Africa, signed up to the Young Vic Directors Programme and decided to make a two-man show based on South African protest theatre using Shakespeare. Pohlmeier chose *The Two Gentlemen of Verona* – an infrequently performed romantic comedy about two men whose friendship is tested while travelling away from home.[5] Pohlmeier chose this play 'simply' because of its titular congruity with the two-hander company dynamic he sought – this is one of many claims to simplicity in the Gents' work that has had complex performance outcomes.

The Gents' three productions to date, *Vakomana Vaviri ve Zimbabwe*, *Kupenga Kwa Hamlet* (an adaptation of the 'bad quarto' text of *Hamlet* translates as '*The Madness of Hamlet*', 2010) and *Magetsi* (a new-write by Denton Chikura about returning to Harare after living in London, 2011), are collaboratively devised by the small company.[6] These are non-naturalistic performances drawing on stylized physicality and gesture and indicative items of costume in order to effect character-changes. The productions are filled with dance, story-telling, and music, sung by the actors and accompanied by Chikura on the *mbira*, and they are self-consciously witty about the processes and conventions of theatre.[7] The productions speak about societies more than individuals and they are satirically funny in a way that parodies certain social practices, such as the hypocrisy of ceremony around death in *Hamlet*, the tedious complexity of letter-exchanges in *Two Gentlemen*, or even the cultural *cachet* accrued by the canonicity of the plays themselves in a reminder of the operations of cultural and colonial power.[8] Using a different source text to the canonical *Hamlet* text means that when Chikura says in 3.1: 'To be or not to be, ay there's the point', audiences laugh. So familiar is the canonical version and such is the cultural iconicity of this line: 'To be or not to be, that is the question', that there is surprise laughter at the change to it; however, the laughter also reveals a latent assumption by audiences that the Gents have got it 'wrong'. Using an Ur-version of the text, familiar to few but textual scholars, the Gents demonstrate a more knowledgeable and playful engagement with this cultural icon than those audiences who assume that this cultural object is somehow 'theirs'. The Gents break out of character to explain to audiences 'this is the 1603 version of the play,' and sometimes add wryly, 'but we know our lines'.

The porousness of this form and the invitation, or challenge, that this direct, unfinished theatre format makes to its audience to engage their imagination and reflect on assumptions produces a complex and rich experience. We might call it 'Shakespeare/Two Gents Productions', reflecting the divergent backgrounds, artistic influences and cultural and ethical concerns of the three company members in relation to their Shakespearean source texts.

Interview

Penelope Woods: Adaptation is intrinsic to the process and approaches of Two Gents Productions. A three-person company, each of you from different cultural and performance backgrounds have had to adapt to each other's styles as well as to the different audiences and theatre spaces you have performed for, throughout the United Kingdom, in South Africa, Zimbabwe, Germany, Poland, Australia and Italy over the past six years. Maybe we should start at the beginning to unpick how Two Gents Productions came about?

Arne Pohlmeier: I started looking for actors when I arrived in London and various people got in touch, including Tonderai (I met Denton later through a friend). I managed to get some rehearsal space through the Young Vic for a couple of hours one night and we worked on one of Launce's monologues from *Two Gentlemen*. I used a kind of spiral exercise, where you read the text, and then you put it aside and improvise it, and then you read it again, and then you put it aside and improvise it again. The idea is that when you come back to it each time it is informed by the associations and uses you have put it to in modern English. But it wasn't working, so I asked Tonderai to try doing the improvisation in Shona instead. And suddenly it seemed to open something up.

Language is important. It is such a topical and obvious form of culture, but it is part of a complex structure. I am aware that I am different in my behaviour, in speech patterns and mannerisms when I speak English and I am with English people, than when I speak German and I am with German people. There are a lot of codes around body language and behaviour that you are also reading, or decoding, simultaneously, through the lens of cultural context and habits that you have grown up with. Shona is a much more physical language, more rhythmical and musical in terms of its paralinguistic signs or signifiers, than German or English. That was a moment of discovery in that first rehearsal, switching into another language, which cracked something open.

PW: So once you thought you had something to work with, how did it take off, after that first evening at the Young Vic? Denton, can you say something about how you became involved with the company?

Denton Chikura: Arne got in touch with me through a mutual friend. He rang me one day and told me his idea and that he didn't have any funding for it or a space or anything. Despite that, I immediately saw the potential in it. I had worked with Tonderai before and thought the two of us would make a good duo.[9] I was unemployed at the time and living in the United Kingdom illegally, which meant it took me ages to actually *get* a job. It was either twiddle your thumbs job hunting or do this fun-looking project. The rest is history.

PW: Tonderai can I ask you about the start of the Two Gents. How did you see it?

Tonderai Munyevu: There's something important about our work with Two Gents that is about being international as opposed to just being Zimbabwean; it's almost a 'post-cultural' phenomenon. London is so culturally mixed and varied. Even from the beginning of the Two Gents this has been the case. I had already been living in London for a decade before the Two Gents started. Arne, on the other hand, is not African, and his influence on Two Gents was not limited to his work in South Africa and experience of protest theatre culture – it was also important that he had an American side as well.[10] I would call it the *Fresh Prince of Bel-Air* humour, which I think the three of us collectively shared.[11] Carlton Banks and Will Smith are a reference for us, the idea of expressionism is a reference, just as much as Grotowski and the Shona culture.

DC: It's all so very 1990s. That's our real reference point.

TM: It's about being young and growing up in the 1990s. But I think it's also about two middle-class people [Denton and Arne] and a working class person [me] on the stage together.

DC: Oh please! [*laughs*].

PW: So a sense of 'class' and upbringing, of differing styles and approaches informs the way you work together and the influences that shape the final production?

AP: Cross-cultural adaptation is always going to be complex and multi-layered. Take, for instance, *Two Gentlemen*: my original idea was to adapt a Shakespeare play in a South African protest theatre style. But then what happened, when the company came together once Denton and Tonderai were involved, was that further layers of language and cultural background began to fill the text and the scenes with meaning. Everything in yourself had to be brought into this text – cultural taste, background, physicality, and your make-up as a person is a crucial part of that.

Working collaboratively and physically enabled us to dig a little deeper, not to go for the obvious choices, but to try to find those elements that aren't part of the *status quo*.

TM: These days I find there is something rather French about us in *Two Gentlemen*, the kind of 'clowny', 'Frenchy' thing that Denton does so well. I remember when it first started happening I thought, 'We're past the Zimbabwean thing now', because that white glove [that signifies the character Silvia in *Two Gentlemen*] is no longer just the white glove, that cloth has now shifted into a theatrical tradition that is European and French and Clown. It's not possible to say it's just a Zimbabwean experience any more.

PW: It must have taken great discipline and creativity to work without the structures or support of money, rehearsal space, deadlines and so on. Do you think that those physical and material constraints informed the nature of the performances that you put together in the end?

AP: We definitely had to actively learn to take over larger spaces when we performed on tour; it was a real process of discovery in terms of expanding the piece each time after rehearsing in a living room. The experience of cramped conditions in the beginning informed the development of that kind of flexibility or virtuosity. Working within that poor theatre aesthetic and conditions glorifies that kind of making-do.

PW: There is a strong ethos informing your work about 'making-do'. This approach is all about stripping things back and minimalism, but the effect (and the pleasure) for the audience is actually about an invitation and the opening up of horizons and possibility.

DC: I'd actually attribute that to a specifically Zimbabwean characteristic. A common statement you'll hear a lot there is 'We'll make a plan.' Meaning, 'We'll improvise/make do.' In Zimbabwe nothing is thrown away – clothes, cars, shoes, electrical equipment. You just turn it into something else. I found this applied to the way we made theatre too. Theatre practitioners in Zimbabwe have to write, act, direct, light and stage manage their own shows. There is no, 'OK, now this is *your* job' – you just do it: a Shakespearean two-hander with few props and bits of costume – 'We'll make a plan.'

PW: On this literal and aesthetic journey over the years you have honed this production of *Two Gentlemen* and developed subsequent ones.

DC: It's rare to get five years to work on one show, to constantly develop it in front of different audiences and in different spaces. Having told the show over and over for so long now one feels like the rehearsal is over, and now each performance I can really go into the character and add in extra bits and pieces. It has got to the point where the characters have become like real people; they are like old friends. You come on stage and think, 'Why didn't I ever do this with Horatio? Yes, his hand is over here, but what if his hand is also a little bit like this?' So it has been a process of constantly building on it. Partly I think this is to keep your own mind present. You have to find something new each time so that you are present each time.

There is very little on stage in our shows which means that you constantly have to adapt the performance around what you had for lunch, for instance, how fit you feel, what has just happened off stage, whether you have had an argument with Tonderai, how the audience are responding in that moment, all of these things. Sometimes what I miss about being in a bigger play when everything is designated and pre-prepared. Instead, night after night, we rely on what is around us. This is why the show is so different each time and my Hamlet is so different and Valentine is so different from night to night, because you are having to create everything in your head and with the audience each night. You are not leaning on anything else because it's not there. As for the story, it's almost as if the structural form of using two people will always be foremost and what's second is the story. I think that the two-man form cannot support any of the classic plays with the depth and complexity and richness of story.

PW: But there *is* lots of depth and complexity in your performances.

DC: Perhaps there is, but not as much as you'd get with a bigger cast. With us I find I can sometimes be too busy thinking of other things. I'm thinking of being the next character. Tonderai is in a new place tonight, I am thinking, 'Where is he now? OK, you've done this now, and wait, this has suddenly happened. What do I do now?' All the time you are constantly adapting and re-adapting. It feels as if you're not actually telling a story, but just trying to maintain yourself within the structure. It is a huge amount of work.

PW: So let's talk about the experience of adapting to the audiences each night since they are co-creating the performance with you.

TM: At the beginning, because I always do the audience scenes, getting them up on stage and so on, I used to just loathe them, to the core of myself. Because I think innately I'm quite a reserved person. But then as time went on, I had to manufacture confidence; but it's also mixed with a sense of profound kindness, because what you need in those interactions with audiences is to be so courageous that you have more empathy for the person you are bringing up, than fear that they will say, 'No'. So you are projecting an invitation they can't refuse, effectively you are saying: 'You are going to have to come up here with me, getting up on stage is not something you usually do, but you are going to have to trust me and it is going to be fantastic and not only that, other people are going to enjoy it too.'

AP: This idea of opening out to the audience was something that was there from the outset. It makes sense in terms of workshop theatre and poor theatre ideas that have informed our practice, but then once we came to encounter the audience it then made *even* more sense. I think that's why there was this process for you, this initial resistance, and then once we encountered the audience we realized you can't actually do without it, because the delivery of the story is so flawed from the outset that we actually need to be complicit with the audience in order to just move the story forward.

PW: I suppose on the other hand it's also the case that the audiences are adapting themselves to you. With your productions they are adapting to those new rules of theatre that you offer them and trying to trust you, and trying to be generous but perhaps also feeling scared themselves.

TM: I don't know if they feel scared. I don't feel that they are. Most people just want to have a good time. I think what our style brings to people, really, is a vivid sense of theatre being live; that it can just change in a moment, and I think people are grateful for that and they enjoy it. But I also think that with our audience interaction, even though we ask them to do things they may not be expecting or are not used to, it is always clear that we respect them as audience members. We don't expect them to become the actors, the boundary between the actor and the spectator is always clear, and it has to be, I think that's crucial. I think with the outlaw scene in *Two Gentlemen* [4.1], for instance, they are going to be manipulated so really they are puppets. They are never really in the role of 'I have to go out and give something of myself in a way that I don't want to'.

DC: The other audience members are also a part of the joke. They want to see their friends go up on stage and they encourage them. They start taking their stuff, taking their bags off them and pushing them up. It's quite extraordinary.

PW: This is the ethical dimension of your performances: you address the audience, you use them, you break out of character and discuss things with them. It makes them (us) feel implicated in the performance and trusted by you but perhaps also a little more responsible for the performance than we might otherwise. It's a really special relationship that I think you fashion. But I also want to ask you about the politics of your work.

TM: It's not political; it's expressly not political. Of course people will always look into it and say, 'But the Duke [in *Two Gentlemen*] has a military beret on, is he meant to be Mugabe?' And we did discuss the analogies, but in the end there are other more interesting messages that we want to communicate.

DC: The actress Janet Suzman came to see us backstage one night in London. She was bewildered that we didn't seize the political possibilities of our work and style, but we didn't really know what she was talking about. What we are interested in telling are stories about our experiences of being Zimbabwean in London.

PW: So can we talk about the version of *Two Gentlemen* that you did in Shona as part of the Globe to Globe Festival at Shakespeare's Globe? How does this version fit into the journey of the production?

DC: We found out that we were going to be in the festival about a year beforehand. Tonderai found this lexicographer from the University of Harare, Noel Marerwa, who did the translation for us. It was amazing, he did it all in under a month and it provided us with a fantastic platform. We really learnt so much. We thought that we knew the play because we had been working on and performing our English version for five years, but what was apparent from the first time we read it was that this was going to be a completely different show.

PW: How did you manage working with an audience who, for the most part, could not speak Shona?

TM: We perform across Europe so we are used to having surtitles for our shows and we play with the fact that sometimes we don't know what the surtitles are saying to our audience because we don't speak Hungarian [for instance]. So we thought that was an element that we could play with here, so that the audience did not get a false sense of clarity from the surtitles which would undermine some of the subtleties *around* the action.[12] When the surtitles say, 'Julia is heartbroken', and the actor on stage is playing 'heartbroken' you just wonder what that is *doing*. So we make the convention playful rather than change it. It becomes a full theatrical experience when the elements of the performance that the audience have at their disposal are not always what they seem.

PW: The Zimbabwe Vigil group in London were invited to one of these performances and they wrote their experience up on-line.[13]

Did you get other feedback from the Shona-speaking members of the audience?

DC: Yes, they absolutely loved it. I think it's always great to see yourself represented on stage.

PW: My sense is that, since working on the Shona production for the Globe, the Shona aspects of both *Two Gentlemen* and *Kupenga Kwa Hamlet*, which are predominantly in English, are now more central to those productions.

TM: I think we are definitely more secure knowing that we can speak in our own language and it is still theatrically engaging in London or elsewhere.

DC: Working on the production for the Globe re-immersed us in Shona. We had both gone decades without having spoken Shona conversationally on an everyday basis.

TM: But it was a process that had started earlier, when we went back to Zimbabwe in 2009 [for the Harare International Festival of the Arts] and then working with Rahim Solomon, a choreographer and a dancer, on *Kupenga Kwa Hamlet* when we returned in 2010. While we were back in Zimbabwe we really developed some of the characters in *Two Gentlemen*. They had been devised almost through a kind of nostalgia. The play was about Zimbabwe, but we were both living in London. We were reliving memories through the production. Lucetta, for instance, is based on a real person; and when we were inventing Silvia we felt that she had to be the kind of girl who Denton always fancied but could never get at school. Back in Harare we were sitting in a café and we saw her! Our 'Silvia' was sitting with some friends, the queen bee of the group, eating a very large piece of chocolate cake.

PW: There was always lots of Zimbabwean music in the productions and some bits in Shona, but it feels more intrinsic to the productions, more political and more legible now. There is that great moment in *Hamlet*, Tonderai, where you address us in the audience as if we are the travelling players and expect us to begin the story as all good Shona *Ngano* stories begin.[14] When people don't know the call and response to start it off you are exasperated with us. You say: 'I thought you were the *best* players in Denmark?', and so we are put in a position of trying to assimilate, of feeling out of place, out of line because we don't know the lines that we 'ought' to know.

TM: I wonder what I would think about it if I could go to the theatre and see us performing. I hope that I would find it great, because I believe that with theatre audiences there is a bigger humanity available. This is why I find it very comfortable to be horrible to people on stage, because it seems so reductive to think that the words I'm saying as this character are going to harm someone. You have to think bigger of people; ask more of them. People know that we are in a theatre. We are playing a role and that is why they come. It might even be slightly pleasurable or exciting to be shouted at because nobody ever really shouts. With the Two Gents work I think we suggest a bigger humanity that we can commit to as theatregoers.

Link

Two Gents Productions: http://www.twogentsproductions.com (accessed 19 January 2014).

Selected bibliography

Gordon, Colette. (2011). 'Hamlet in England, Hamlet in Exile', *Shakespeare in Southern Africa*, 23, pp. 64–9.

Massai, Sonia. (2013). '*Two Gentlemen of Verona* for/by Zimbabwean Diasporic Communities' in Susan Bennett and Christie Carson (eds), *Shakespeare Beyond English*. Cambridge: Cambridge University Press, pp. 157–60.

Woods, Penelope. (2013). 'The Two Gentlemen of Zimbabwe and the Diaspora Audience at Shakespeare's Globe', *African Theatre*, 12, pp. 13–27.

Notes

1 This interview took place at the New Fortune Theatre in the University of Western Australia, Perth, on 2 March 2013.

2 The Globe to Globe Festival took place between April and June 2012 and was part of the Cultural Olympiad in London. A video recording of *Two Gentlemen of Verona* in Shona at Shakespeare's Globe (10 May 2012, evening performance) can be viewed at http://thespace.org/items/e000066w?t=cgmvw (accessed 27 August 2013).

3 See *2011 Census: Quick Statistics for England and Wales, March 2011*, Office for National Statistics, 30 January 2013, http://www.ons.gov.uk/ons/dcp171778_297002.pdf (accessed 10 April 2013).

4 A billing at the Harare International Festival of Arts in the same year was cancelled after sponsorship and funding difficulties.

5 *The Two Gentlemen of Verona* may be the earliest of Shakespeare's plays (c. 1590–1). It was also the first play to be performed at Shakespeare's Globe Theatre when it opened in 1996.

6 The first published version of *Hamlet* of 1603 is referred to as Quarto One (Q1). It is also known as the 'Bad Quarto', a term coined by early-twentieth-century scholar Alfred W. Pollard, because it was shorter and contained less verse than the standard version taken from *The First Folio Complete Works* (1623). For more on this production by Two Gents, see Gordon (2011).

7 The *mbira* is a traditional musical instrument of the Shona people. It is a lamellophone, with 22 to 28 metal 'tongues' which are played by depressing the free ends with the thumbs.

8 That their productions speak about society is true also of the Two Gents' adaptation of *Hamlet*. Given that Shakespeare's *Hamlet* has been essentialized in Western theatre traditions as *the* play of the individual, this is a notable adaptive approach.

9 Chikura and Munyevu first met in 2007 for a reading at Ovalhouse Theatre in London.

10 Pohlmeier spent much of his childhood in Bethesda, Maryland.

11 American NBC television, created by Andy Borowitz, which ran from 1990 to 1996, starring Will Smith as a street-wise teenager version of himself, Will 'The Fresh Prince' Smith, and his rich cousin Carlton Banks, played by Alfonso Ribeiro.

12 Globe to Globe productions used surtitles providing scene synopsis rather than line-by-line translations.

13 Zimbabwe Vigil Diary, 9 May 2012, http://nehandaradio.com/2013/01/07/a-bridge-too-far-zimbabwe-vigil-diary (accessed 21 August 2013).

14 The *Ngano* are the traditional folk-tales in Shona story-telling practice. It is standard for these to begin with the call, '*Kwaivepo*' (once upon a time) eliciting the response, '*dzepfunde*' (we are in agreement). For further discussion, see Gordon, pp. 64–9.

11

Being Affected: An Interview with Ong Keng Sen of TheatreWorks Singapore in Conversation with William Peterson

Introduction

Since the late 1990s, the intra-Asian intercultural work of Singaporean director Ong Keng Sen has toured to major festivals around the world, countering the dominance of well-known Western directors in assembling and fusing Asian cultural flows and placing them on the world's stages. Ong's multilingual productions, featuring actors from different performance traditions and cultures, have challenged existing models of intercultural theatre by highlighting rather than minimizing the discontinuities between individual Asian cultures, demonstrating the fiction of any vision of a monolithic Asia. As Artistic Director of Singapore's TheatreWorks, by the mid–1990s Ong had staged an impressive body of new works that reflected the history and multicultural complexity of his native land, collaborating with the country's leading theatre artists, including Kuo Pao Kun, Dick Lee, and Michael Chiang. Following a period of study at New York University under Richard Schechner, he returned to Singapore and conceived and created *Broken Birds* (1995), a vast piece of theatre about the Japanese *karayuke-san* [prostitutes] in Singapore. With its use of archival materials, intra-Asian style and content, and simultaneous staging that required audience members to choose how to assemble and interpret the event, it marked the beginning of a new mode of increasingly ambitious, intercultural, and international theatre-making. Of his subsequent touring work, *Lear* (1997) and *Desdemona* (2000) were the most discoursed internationally, with the latter being critiqued in many quarters for its opaqueness and intense self-referentiality.[1] Yet Ong, ever able and willing to defend his artistic choices, has been quite articulate about the ways in which this work staged the process of intercultural creation rather than a finished product.[2]

Ong's concern with process in an intra-Asian context both predates his international theatre work and fed into its development. In 1994 he started the Flying Circus Project, a laboratory that brings traditional and contemporary Asian artists together with international artists from the widest possible range of fields. As the interview that follows makes clear, the kinds of provocations and challenges that extended from these para-theatrical environments are present in some of his most ambitious theatre works, notably *Continuum: Beyond the Killing Fields* (2001), *Search: Hamlet* (2002), *The Global Soul* (2003), *Sandakan Threnody* (2003), and *Geisha* (2006).

By the time Ong curated and directed the *In Transit* festival for the House of World Cultures in Berlin in 2002 and 2003, it was clear that the cultural complexity of the work he was creating was no longer containable by the older models of interculturalism that had been circulating in the West. In the interview that follows, Ong speaks to the process of adaptation as it relates to reimagining Shakespeare in his *Lear* and *Desdemona,* and how being open to the continuous adaptations generated by the diverse Asian artists with whom he has worked necessitates a different working process for theatre-making that stands in contrast to that of Western auteur directors. This method, in which he allows performers to influence the creative process, led to a recent reinterpretation of his adaptation of *Lear*, entitled *Lear Dreaming* (2012). Ong's consistent need to constantly interrogate his working methods – sometimes in the context of the work itself – is one of his singular achievements as a theatre artist. His work and his career have served to shake up fixed cultural moorings in ways that require the constant repositioning of one's cultural coordinates.

Interview

William Peterson: Since the 1990s a range of terms has been used to apply to work that you and others do, from the intercultural to the transnational and the transcultural, along with concepts such as cultural syncretism and liquid modernity. How important is what we call performance work that crosses cultures?

Ong Keng Sen: When I first started doing this kind of work, it was very naive. I was really exploring my relationship as an urban Singaporean with Asian traditions and particularly my Chinese background. I saw it as a kind of reconnection to an emotional memory – being a kid watching street opera in Singapore with my mother, and then that whole experience disappearing. I was never able to engage that part of me while growing up. So theatre was a way for me to connect back to that. But as it grew bigger and bigger it started to *have* to be articulated and, I suppose, one often relates most to the paradigm one gets schooled in, and my paradigm then was the intercultural, the whole debate around Peter Brook's *Mahabharata* in the late 1980s and early 1990s. I've never identified with terms like 'transnational', which came into vogue in the new millennium, mainly because I never thought what I did was national. This transnational thing seems to be a kind of negative space in relation to the nation and I actually think that what I was doing was personal.

WP: In your keynote address at the 2010 Australasian Drama Studies Association conference, I was intrigued by the way you set out a model for looking at cultural exchange that didn't end with a homogenous globalized world. You prefaced your remarks by speaking to the distinction between globalization and Jean-Luc Nancy's concept of *mondialisation*.[3] Can you speak about this distinction, particularly as it relates to your own work? I'm especially interested in knowing who is doing the 'making' in the process of 'mondialization' or world making.

OKS: When I started reading Nancy I found that a lot of what he said was at the heart of what I was doing in the sense of 'world creating', which happens on so many different levels in my work. When we're making a production that circulates to festivals, the first thing you are making is, together with all the artists, a world you can inhabit as a group of ten people, 30 people or two people even, because you are basically creating a cultural, emotional, physical, spiritual world which you live in for however many weeks. This whole sense of creating a world has really been very side-tracked by a lot of this discussion around director-auteurs – such as Wilson, Foreman, perhaps Brook – where in a sense you basically move people around like chess pieces. This can never really happen in an intercultural process where you are trying to encourage everybody to participate as the first step, because in those auteur processes you really don't encourage participation. When we are in the process of creating a world in rehearsal, everybody is actually shaping it, even the nuts and bolts of deciding how they want to be positioned in that space. But if you are asking people to walk a slow walk from stage right to stage left and then you light them in a certain way and you limit what they're doing, *that's* when the auteur process starts and globalization can very easily seep into the process.

WP: You famously commented in a press interview around the time of *Desdemona* in 2000 that support for intercultural collaborations was as important as sewerage, and like sewerage, it was 'expensive but necessary'. Do you still hold that view?

OKS: I hold the view that the intercultural process very often creates 'nothing', something that, in a sense, looks like 'nothing' – but I am referring to Nancy's idea of 'nothing', where 'nothing' is everything. So in a way intercultural work resembles the sewerage systems. For example, someone I knew was building a house and I saw how it had sewerage containers buried in the land. This is something that you never see; you don't realize the process of planning that has to go into the quota of waste you can produce, the distribution of the organic waste, how that seeps slowly into the earth. That, for me, is the intercultural 'nothing', and that's why the transnational is something which I'm not so comfortable with, because I think that 'transnational performance' is very much linked to the final showing of the piece. It has a triumphal quality to it, because it seems to be transcending something, and transcending the nation which is itself so problematic and so powerful, while the intercultural – even though it's academically quite an old-fashioned term – seems to be more directly dealing with cultures. As individuals we *do* carry cultural traits which we constantly try to repress or erase, but they are so much a part of us.

WP: So similarly does 'transcultural' have that kind of baggage for you?

OKS: As for 'transcultural', at a certain time I was very fixated with that word, but in the end I just realized that maybe I had to move out of these terms which were within discourse. I was making work at a time when academia was very preoccupied with terminology and I just felt like I had to make something which was true for myself and that's why I reached out to Nancy, because it was closer to what we were actually experiencing day to day on the rehearsal floor.

WP: In many of your productions in the 1990s and early 2000s you used performers from a range of different performance traditions and training orthodoxies. When you did *Lear*, some critics wrote of the contained quality of the performers who stayed within their own traditions and training systems in the piece. What was or is the value of this kind of investigation, apart from the fact that it can be done with the aid of modern air travel and access to funding from foundations? I'm also curious if your time at New York University working on an MA under Richard Schechner might have contributed to this practice in your work.

OKS: My New York experience was really essential for me. It contributed to my interpretation of the aesthetic practice of juxtaposition, found objects, found cultures, assemblages. As a kind of practice it became natural for me to think in that way, that there was a validity and openness in these juxtapositions and assemblages. New York was really an aesthetic place for me, more than political, mainly because I was already very aware in Singapore, being gay, that everything you are doing is political. If I hadn't gone to New York I would have felt much more obliged to an aesthetic sensibility that would try to harmonize everybody together, as in the modern approach towards the intercultural when in China they were staging Ibsen plays, making everything natural or real or emotionally centred.[4] I wasn't so engaged with that kind of process, I was more interested in this aesthetic expansion coming from juxtaposition and assemblage. As an audience member you then have to make up your own mind about the value of what you see.

WP: *Desdemona* was one of your most controversial works, at least in Singapore. The story of the critic who stormed out of the theatre in the middle of the show hurling abuse at it is legendary.[5] Clearly this critic, as well as others, had difficulty understanding the structure of that piece. In a way you countered this potential criticism in *Desdemona* with a sequence in the work itself that suggested that the work was about the challenges of intercultural collaboration and should not be judged as a product. Has your thinking about *Desdemona* and what you set out to do shifted since that time?

OKS: Actually not much, because *Desdemona* was way ahead of its time and I think that it's one of the best works I've done, that it had a purity of intention and I really wish that I could be as pure now. Most people would like a seamless, fluid space where the intercultural *is* possible and unproblematic. But at that time I was quite relentless in trying to hold true to what I perceived as interculturalism, so I was involved with the opposite process of complicating and confounding that seamless fluidity. So this was for me the naivety of doing this kind of work; I was really in a minefield but I didn't really know it.

WP: You have a long history of staging Shakespearean adaptations, among them *Hamlet*, *Lear*, and *Desdemona*, which of course had a connection with *Othello.* In each instance, and particularly in *Desdemona,* as the title itself suggests, you departed radically from Shakespeare's text. Why were you attracted to these texts?

OKS: This is where the influence of the educational system of Singapore is very strong. I read my first Shakespeare text, *Twelfth Night*, when I was 14. At the age of ten, I had been introduced to *Macbeth* and *Midsummer's Night Dream* because my elder sisters were studying them in school and the books were lying around in the house. In Singapore's general education then, you would intensely study two Shakespeare texts by the age of 16 and that for me was ironically much more universal than Chinese opera, which I had to bury. Because of these three early works of mine from *Lear* to *Desdemona* and *Hamlet*, people think that I have a very strong relationship with Shakespeare. I actually don't have scholarly interest in Shakespeare, and you can see that I'm not using his language onstage. Shakespeare was part of growing up rather than theatre.

WP: One of your most iconic and controversial adaptations, the 1997 *Lear*, was based on a version of Shakespeare by Rio Kishida. You then directed a new version of the Kishida script again in 2012, *Lear Dreaming*. Can you tell us about the political landscape in which you situate these two shows? What was at stake politically, for you, in staging these two pieces? The two productions were done in two very different moments in your career and in two different geopolitical contexts.

OKS: I was hailed to return to *Lear* in 2012 mainly because I am intrigued by the question of who this father figure is that I have been critiquing, resisting, and rebelling against in different works. What is this monolithic figure and how do we go beyond its representation? What is his individual agency and his individual humanity? In 1997, when Kishida and I were story-boarding, we did not give much thought to him. We were ultimately not fascinated by him. We were more intent then on the narrative of youth who perpetuates heritage, legacy, and history. Kishida was interested in the male vs. female struggle and in appropriating men to perform as women, while I was interested in the fight between elders and youth. I was concerned primarily with symbols and representations of new Asia with all their ambivalences.

In 2012, my research as an artist and scholar has become more focused on individual agency and potentiality rather than on cultural shapes. I manifested my interest in individual agency in the latter production through an urgency to represent the dream time of Lear, the individual. At the end of the first half, the audience is 'swimming' in a laser atmosphere that suggests Lear's dreams of life and death. The father figure was redesigned in collaboration with Naohiko Umewaka, who played Lear in both 1997 and 2012. I no longer saw Umewaka as a Noh actor but more as an individual who also had specific skills in Noh theatre. In entering into the sensitivity and vulnerability of the dreams of the father figure, I hoped to tell a different story. The production was no longer an epic sweep of cultures but the tragedy of a human being. His final death as he remembers his wife is embedded in the narrative of a man caught at the crossroads of history, who ultimately decides to take his own life, perhaps the only action he has ever taken himself. In 1997, however, it was his daughter who killed him. In 2012, his daughter only lays the foundation for his self-immolation to occur. Perhaps in the 15 years that passed, I also matured from an impetuous young director into an older human being.

WP: Can you tell us about the significance of casting for these two projects? I am interested in the way you associate specific characters in the story with specific Asian art forms. How did casting and art forms change in the two versions and why? Some academics have criticized you for this practice of picking and choosing art forms in an almost consumeristic way, allegedly decontextualizing them and spectacularizing them in your shows.[6] But this practice of yours has a particular significance for you as an artist and I believe you are very attached to it.

OKS: In 2012, I became less interested in the conflation of art forms and cultures to represent characters. I was lucky to know Piterman (who in the 2012 production plays the Loyal Attendant, a Gloucester-like character) and Umewaka from our four years of intense work in the 1997 production. Piterman had been a central musician from that show and could suggest the colours of Lear's Loyal Attendant with his artistry. He is an expert in traditional music and Randai, a didactic song and dance form from the matrilineal Minangkabau culture of Sumatra. But unlike in 1997, this time I did not begin from matching Randai and Minang culture to the character. This time it was my belief that Piterman was the most appropriate individual to embody this man. I cannot imagine working with Wu Man (who played Lear's Daughter in 2012) and Kwon Soon Kang (who played the Mother in 2012) as cultural institutions. I treat them as individuals with their particular and strong sense of self. That's been the biggest fallacy from some academics, who think I treat traditional artists as clay to be exploited. Why do they think that? Because they cannot imagine traditional artists as being individuals like us who are ready to defend, attack, love, hate, lose and profit from our actions?

Finally, the making of transnational theatre or intercultural theatre, or however we call it, is about decontextualizing and recontextualizing to create a particular world onstage with different individuals. That's why I find Nancy very instructive in his approach to *mondialisation* as resistance to globalization. As a theatre maker who is committed to creating other worlds on stage in collaboration with individuals, decontextualization is inevitable. I believe in plurality and multiplicity. Hybridity occurs naturally in every field, and it constantly recontextualizes forms which have been rendered static and impermeable in our minds by the views of many scholars and their understanding of 'tradition'. Strangely enough, quite a few 'traditional' artists I have met are very porous in their practices, unlike the self-declared 'custodians of tradition', that is, scholars and historians.

WP: The staging and telling of the multiple stories contained in many of your large-scale intercultural or intra-Asian works is often heavily mediated, with multiple disruptions in the telling of the story. I'm thinking of the stories of the *karayuki-san* in Singapore in your play *Broken Birds,* the story of Australian prisoners-of-war in Borneo in 1945 in *Sandakan Threnody,* or the genocide and decimation of Cambodian classical dance in *The Continuum.* These works are also characterized by a high degree of self-referentiality, with the process itself deeply embedded in these works. Why do these extra layers interest you and why are they necessary?

OKS: When I say world creating, I mean that the world is created by the six people on stage. The world is created by them because they structure the first impulse. For example, when we were in Sandakan [in Borneo on a research trip] I asked everybody to visit the war cemetery. My directorial intervention was to ask Kabuki dancer Gojo [Masanosuke] to make a dance in response to this vast cemetery of the British soldiers killed in World War Two by the Japanese. And so he came back two days later and he danced and then the heavens opened during that time but he continued to dance. The world is created by all of us who are in it and this world is not necessarily the world which the audience may be interested in creating with us. So when a person's confronted with theatre, what happens? You as an audience member may choose to weave and to create the world with us but it is only an invitation from us the players, and in a way I see my relationship with Shakespeare like that. And that's where adaptation comes in. I'm actually trying to create a world with Shakespeare. Shakespeare is a proposition and, for me to inhabit his world, I have to re-make it into *my* world. So I create a world with his original narrative, even though that's not the first because he was re-writing from other sources. I am actively creating a world for me. In Gojo's response there were so many different moments where it could have just stopped. He could have said to me, 'No, I don't think this is interesting'. And when it rained he could have stopped. But he actively agreed to respond to my initial invitation to create a world for himself. On stage, it is important to allow these processes and these interventions if you are faithful to this idea of the assemblage, which is why I have never tried to smooth out all these rough edges. And that's one of the reasons why some critics and writers resist the work, not that they resist it wilfully, but there is just a kind of difficulty accepting that a rough edge is put there on purpose, because one thinks it should all be filed away or smoothed out so that it's a good table, rather than with all these bumps around it. So the work manifests all these knobbly complications and obstacles mainly because the world was created by all of us as we participated, with our different imaginations. And when the work is on stage it becomes a kind of invitation to the audience to create a world, to bring their personal imagination into this world creating activity for those two hours.

WP: From 2001 to 2003 you curated the House of World Cultures in Berlin, the first Asian to have undertaken such a role at an important European festival. As you moved into this role, was there any continuity between the processes you were engaged with as a director and what was required to curate an intercultural festival?

OKS: I have struggled in all the years of my work to find a way to create a world which would invite participants to engage without the need of 'directing' them and telling them how to engage. In Transit was a new festival and I was an outsider, non-resident Asian curating for European audiences; it was a potent mix of world creating forces. Perhaps we were all adapting to each other during In Transit. In some ways, adaptation for me is about active world creating, where you make sense of the world that you are suddenly in and you want to inhabit this world on your own terms. But at the same time there needs to be an engagement with the world that was there before you and then you are creating the world also in collaboration, which makes it quite different from the auteur model.

WP: In the last decade there has been an increasing preoccupation among performance scholars with the ethics governing practice. What ethical practices do you follow consciously or unconsciously when creating works, particularly when working with practitioners from a range of differing cultural backgrounds?

OKS: For me the ethics issue becomes more or less accentuated depending on the context you are in. For example, when we did The Flying Circus in Myanmar I had a caveat in the brochure about ethical responsibility, about what we were doing there as a group of international people arriving in that space. What should my ethical stance be? I feel it's very much bound to context. In working with artists who place themselves within the international art market, such as Maya Rao from India, there's already a kind of implicit agreement.[7] And that's very different from going to a village and taking a ritual Kathakali dancer and then putting that person on stage. I would like ethics to be *real* rather than some kind of breast-beating mechanism. So as a working artist I have to manage ethics in a very practical way.

WP: In your keynote at the 2010 ADSA conference, you spoke about how your more recent work with the Flying Circus Project seeks to 'move away from the market', lying adjacent to the dominant culture rather than offering a critique of it. Can you speak about the ways in which this work has done this?

OKS: I was quoting from Anurima Banerji's concept of 'paratopia' as a kind of adjacent space to the dominant discourse.[8] When artists agree to come into the Flying Circus, this adjacent space comes together like a flash mob and, as the group travels together, it becomes a kind of immersion programme in the context of the city, like in Ho Chi Minh City or recently Yangon. Artists are not under any obligation to discuss anything, to do a workshop or improvise together. The Flying Circus becomes a space where we are very aware that we are taking time out from our normal practice. That's the adjacent quality of it. It really is an all-expenses-paid thing where you don't have to present a conference paper or a showing for funders. You talk about your practice which could be about the past or the future or the present even, you spend time together.

WP: Unlike many directors, you have not discovered a singular style or process of working and stuck with it over your career as a theatre and performance maker. I'm wondering how you see the trajectory of your work over the last 30 years and what the connective tissue is that links this range of practices?

OKS: I suppose that one of the strongest drivers of my work is the question of how to remain affected by people that you work with and also how to affect them, so this recent revival of Deleuze and Guattari in American academic circles is for me quite fascinating because in going back to them we see that what they were talking about in those early writings is that you are a force that's affected by other forces and you are also affecting other forces as you're all in this space together.[9] The reason why I have not been singular in terms of the expression is mainly because in my collaborations I believe that we are all forces affecting and being affected by each other. And so I cannot really go into a Taiwanese opera rehearsal and say, 'OK I want you to be Orlando in this way', because I'm being affected by the artists and I am affecting them as well. This is also how I see adaptation. That old-fashioned idea of appropriation is something which seems to suggest that you are not affected by the original at all, by that first version, and I think that it cannot be possible, because there must have been a reason why you felt that it was necessary to adapt it. So in that way already you are reacting; you are being affected by that force of the work that came before you, which you are now adapting. So I don't consider anything that Robert Wilson does as adaptation because Robert Wilson for me is just re-casting. He is casting everything in his mould, so that is not an adaptation. Adaptation for me is about being open to what is there and to adapt *with* it rather than to re-cast it. Being affected keeps me going and I can see it continuing in my work.

Links

TheatreWorks Singapore: http://www.theatreworks.org.sg (accessed 19 January 2014).

Videos of Ong's productions can be accessed at: http://a-s-i-a-web.org (accessed 19 January 2014).

Selected bibliography

Grehan, Helena. (2001). 'TheatreWorks' *Desdemona:* Fusing Technology and Tradition', *The Drama Review*, 45.3, pp. 113–25.

Tan, Marcus Cheng Chye. (2012). 'Listening in/to Asia: Ong Keng Sen's *Desdemona* and the Polyphonies of Asia' in *Acoustic Interculturalism: Listening to Performance.* Basingstoke: Palgrave Macmillan, pp. 133–64.

Yong, Li Lan. (2010). 'Shakespeare Here and Elsewhere: Ong Keng Sen's Intercultural Shakespeare' in Dennis Kennedy and Yong Li Lan (eds), *Shakespeare in Asia: Contemporary Performance*, Cambridge: Cambridge University Press, pp. 188–218.

Notes

1 See Bharucha, 'Consumed in Singapore: The Intercultural Spectacle of *Lear*', *Theater*, 3.1 (2001), pp. 107–27.

2 See Ong, 'On Desdemona: In Response', *The Drama Review*, 45.3 (2001), p. 118; and Ong, 'Encounters', *The Drama Review*, 45.3 (2001), pp. 126–33.

3 Jean-Luc Nancy, *The Creation of the World, or Globalization*, trans. François Raffoul and David Pettigrew. Albany, NY: State University of New York Press, 2007, pp. 33–55.

4 For the Ibsen in China project, see http://ibseninternational.com/ibsen-in-china/ (accessed 20 August 2013).

5 See Ong Sor Fern, 'Too Many Things to Say, But No Idea What to Tell', *The Straits Times*, 10 June 2000, p. 8.

6 See Bharucha (2010).

7 Kathakali-trained dancer Maya Rao appeared as Othello's alter ego in *Desdemona*. Rao is known for her fusion of Kathakali with contemporary dance movements and is one of the few prominent female dancers in this traditionally male form.

8 See Banerji, 'Paratopias of Performance: The Choreographic Practices of Chandralekha', in André Lepecki and Jenn Joy (eds), *Planes of Composition: Dance, Theory and the Global*. Kolkata: Seagull Books, 2010, pp. 346–71.

9 Ong is referring to a renewed academic interest in the notion of 'affect' as elaborated by Deleuze and Guattari in *A Thousand Plateaus: Capitalism and Schizophrenia* [1980], trans. Brian Massumi. London: Continuum, 2004.

12

Hello Darkness My Old Friend: Alvis Hermanis in Conversation with Alan Read

Introduction

Stadsschouwbourg theatre, Amsterdam. Friday 8 March 2013, 20.00–21.30. Alvis Hermanis is in Amsterdam in 2013 as the unlikely subject of a festival titled: *Brandstichter*. Encompassing five of his works, drawn from a repertoire stretching back close to two decades, the epithet 'arsonist', or more theatrically in the legacy of Max Frisch 'fire-raiser' sits somewhat uneasily on the shoulders of the modest man now sitting in front of me, towards the quiet back of the Robozaal, in the upper reaches of the Stadsschouwbourg, where the evening's audience for his production of *The Sound of Silence* have just finished their drinks to enter the auditorium. When they return, for more drinks, this interview will be over. We are therefore talking in the time of a first act.

Hermanis has agreed to meet to discuss adaptation but with the qualification that we might not get to the question in hand (in preliminary communications adaptation and its various lives had elicited no direct response) and that he might be released at the interval to 'be with his actors'. Two conditions I am more than happy to concur with given that the actors have, in his work, always been the point, they have formed a continuous company of remarkable consistency since Hermanis took up the direction of the New Riga Theatre (Jaunais Rigas Teatris) in 1997, and recognizing that while 'adaptation' plays a central part in Hermanis's repertoire of novelistic interpretation and classic re-rendering, there might be something less obvious about 'adaptation to circumstance' at work in the current production of *The Sound of Silence* that provides at least a starting point for an act-length conversation.

Alvis Hermanis's work could be divided into three broad areas of interest without undue violence to the inherent, shared concerns across his oeuvre. Most prominently there has been a 'Latvian series' to which *The Sound of Silence* (2007) might be considered related, drawing upon something close to a documentary or even anthropological style described by some as 'hyperrealism'. Amongst these works involving long periods of research by actors and the inclusion of their experiences one might list: *Long Life* (2003), *Latvian Stories* (2004), *Latvian Love* (2006), *Grandfather* (2009), *Martha from the Blue Hill* (2009), *Black Milk* (2010), and *Graveyard Party* (2011). Second and more recently there has been a sequence of 'adaptations' of Russian classic novels including *Oblomov* (Ivan Goncharov) and *Eugene Onegin* (Alexander Pushkin) but also 'dramatic adaptations' of *Platanov* (Chekhov) and *Summerfolk* (Gorki). Breaking with this documentary, literary and dramatic repertoire, Alvis Hermanis's more recent work includes major operatic productions including, at the time of writing, *Gawain* by Harrison Birtwistle for the Salzburg Festival in 2013.

I had first encountered an Alvis Hermanis performance at the Avignon Festival in 2008 in a luminous production of *Sonya* (2006), an adaptation of the short novel by the Russian author Tatyana Tolstoya. The first line of the novel perhaps gives the best impression of what follows in Hermanis's production: 'A person lived – a person died. Only the name remains – Sonya.' In the apparent banality and eventless *bric à brac* of Kristine Jurjane's extraordinarily fecund setting, an action of sorts is brought into being with the arrival of what appear to be two balaclavaed burglars, though felons with a remarkable subtlety of theatrical presence and variety of character delineation. Reminding me of a theatre artist I had seen 30 years before in Amsterdam, Joop Admiraal, in his transformational work *You Are My Mother* (1983), one of the actors 'becomes' Sonya by assuming her clothes, her gestures and her memorabilia that threaten to engulf her in this restricted space.

Much of the vocal language of the work was beyond my comprehension but as in all the most engaging productions, the theatrical language that is brought to bear here is unmistakably the work of an auteur, a director whose understanding is resolute that the narrative might persist, be maintained, and suspended *in parallel* to the performance, and that the rend between the two, as in this production, might provide a melancholy gap within which the spectator's affective encounters with the work (of Hermanis and Tolstoya) are given room to play.[1]

Interview

Alan Read: Since *Sonya* I have been thinking about your work and wanted to take this opportunity to talk about *The Sound of Silence* and *Long Life* that follows it in the repertoire of the *Brandstichter* festival in two weeks' time. Perhaps we could begin with the work that chronologically preceded *Long Life*, but was in fact made after that work's broad European success, *The Sound of Silence,* if it is not too obvious to concentrate on one of your better-known works?

Alvis Hermanis: Well, *The Sound of Silence* is old and this is a 'funeral performance' that is taking place in Amsterdam tonight. I had not seen it for many years until last night, when you and I watched it, and when I saw it last night I realized how much time had gone by during its life. Women in this cast have been having families in the time of this production over the last 'how many' years, another form of evolutionary adaptation I suppose. Performances sometimes function like a computer but emotionally they are in a continuous state of drying up as they circulate. But *The Sound of Silence*, before this funeral, has had a great life. We have travelled through 25 countries from New Zealand to Canada and across Europe. And now the actors are getting older.

AR: How do you know it is a funeral for the piece? You talk about actors moving away from the work and having children. But is this theatre not a continuous process of adaptation to circumstance?

AH: In recent years I have been working in big German-speaking state theatres in Switzerland and Germany where a performance rarely survives more than two seasons. There is simply no room in their repertoire for such adaptation. They *stop* putting on performances when they are sold out. In Riga we have a repertory system that is state-subsidized, with permanent actors' companies, but we keep performances alive for up to ten years. Sometimes, I know it as an actor myself, there are performances when you as an actor can find out new things – you are continuously digging up something innovative as you proceed with the work. But there are other performances where actors are just part of a larger composition. In such a case it can become boring to continue and the performance becomes emotionally exhausted, you might say.

AR: I came to Riga in 2010 to give a talk about theatrical immunity and community.[2] And I realized immediately, on entering the bar and then the auditorium of the New Riga Theatre, the significance of the atmosphere of the space for your work. Could you talk about the significance of the space for you and how your work adapts to such spaces? The phenomenology of the space is of course resonant in Riga but your work travels widely across national boundaries. How does it adapt in such circumstances of theatrical transnationalism?

AH: In general the model of the British Theatre, like the Royal Court say, is not how continental European theatre makers treat the stage. Visual art in the theatre is a very important element for us and does not seem to be the same in Britain at the moment, in staged theatres at least. In my personal case, obvious in *The Sound of Silence* and *Long Life* where there are five apartments laid out on stage throughout the work, I have this obsession with *private* space, with living and private rooms. And I maintain this interest in a hyperrealist sense. I used this trick for years and only later realized that I had found a theoretical concept for it, perhaps because this obsession with private space is what we 'modern people' are all living. We are living *double lives*: one life is the life we maintain for entering the *sensorium* which is a 'directed theatre', where we know the rules and we behave nicely and obey those rules. And then, second, there is a secret life that we suspend in our little boxes that we call our 'homes'. When you meet a stranger you can spend several hours talking about your deepest and most intimate secrets but nevertheless the picture you could create of another person would be extraordinarily enriched if you had a chance to enter their private space. In a few moments you would have an obsessively detailed scanning of this person. These private spaces are the secret castles of our *demons*.

AR: Let me press you on the relationship between adaptation and *The Sound of Silence*? Here we are less talking about the re-rendering of one form to another (though the rendition of Simon and Garfunkel songs throughout the production does raise questions as to their adaptation to this specific setting) and more adaptation *to* one another? Socially I mean. Or, to take another word, there is an *adjustment* to one another, politically perhaps? Spatially, choreographically and architecturally the figures in this production resist and meld into each other. How people move around each other seems to be at issue here? How they adjust *for* each other in their accommodation, as a process *of* accommodation? Roland Barthes once titled it 'How to Live Together' for a course on 'idiorrhythmic communities' for the Collège de France in 1977.[3] The five apartments and their inhabitants play out a set of relations with each other spanning the stage. Is it a question of how to live together, as a utopian ideal? What I saw was a project within which we, the audience, were being given an opportunity to see this privacy being worked through and played out publicly. But for me it was also about the *shapes* of democracy we require to find a way to live. Does that make sense? Were we at the same production last night?

AH: No totally not. Even when I am showing my work abroad I have lost any sense of a *local audience* or how to enter the brains of audiences from different cultures. It is a 'blind date' and I am fine with this problem of the so-called transcultural potential of performance that does not seem to deliver on its promise. I have quite a substantial experience of working abroad, with 25 productions running in as many different countries, and you know with such an experience it is hopeless to understand what is going on inside the brains of those people in theatres that you visit. You can, of course, only guess. There are great misunderstandings, which is OK by me, and sometimes there are some very painful misunderstandings. For example, a performance which works in one city or country is a fiasco in another, in a different context, where it might solicit a wholly opposite reaction. A fresh and immediate experience was opening, just the other day, within the *Brandstichter* Festival in Amsterdam the production of Maxim Gorki's *Summerfolk* from the Schaubuhne in Berlin. In Berlin we had had the worst critical response in my experience, but here in Amsterdam, it was standing ovations and five star reviews all the way. Such a fresh example just a week ago emphasizes these cultural distinctions for me that theatre does little to 'adapt' to in the practicality and reality of its making.

AR: Indeed I was struck last night at the performance of *The Sound of Silence* by the warmth of the audience if one could call it that. But for those of us at a certain age, in my case mid-50s, and of course in Amsterdam perhaps more than anywhere, the piece plays to wonderful nostalgic possibilities, although none of us know the particular circumstances of the Latvian people in those apartments that we saw being adapted to life before us. I had been to Riga only once, for a few days, so knew nothing of this context but the soundtrack allows for this 'bridge over troubled water' into an imagined history. But then it plays a trick because once immersed in this soundscape politically and personally, it is very interesting where it leaves you as a performance. It leaves you beached in the disappointment of a failed utopia. It does not tell you anything about revolution but gives you the opportunity to live with these people for a few hours in their melancholy.

AH: I did not get a chance to participate in this party of 1968, this time is not documented in many ways for those of us in Riga and hence the tone of this work.

AR: Is it a dream, a hope for change, or a requiem, a funeral as you put it?

AH: When we started our work on *The Sound of Silence* our discussion centred on whether it was possible to make a piece of theatre *without conflict*, about happiness. In European theatre the drama is always about conflict, it is filled with artificial blows. There are angry people in the theatre with lots of issues, with Shakespeare central amongst them of course. How many corpses does he have on the stage at any one time? When someone has a problem the solution for Shakespeare is to *kill* somebody. Our question was, at the outset of *The Sound of Silence*: is it possible to invent dramatic forms without conflict? How to show happiness in the theatre would be, perhaps, the most boring thing for the theatre. And that was our conundrum. Another challenge would be for the professional actor to pass across the stage unnoticed. This would be the highest form, or quality, of acting we would say.

AR: What you have interrupted is *synthetic* conflict. What happens in *The Sound of Silence* is another kind of vital relation where conflict is present but differently so. For instance there is a certain softening through animism and the activation of the inorganic, where a book is opened by one of the apartment tenants and a leaf is inside which he gently holds, paper on paper. Or a feather held in the air by the breath of many becomes an opportunity for an immense choreography between the apartments, until then delineated and isolated. Conflict is operating here, but it is of a different, reticent, register I would suggest. To take a phrase from the Surrealists, it is 'infra thin'.

AH: That might be so, but people wrote to ask: 'Why did you not make *The Sound of Silence* shorter? Then it would have been a cute evening for the 1960s.' Advertising the *good* in theatre is just the first part of this show of course, in the second part the people lose their innocence, their virginity and there *is* conflict.

AR: The women are 'impregnated' with Simon and Garfunkel songs, literally in two cases with the antennae of a transistor operating as a prosthetic phallic extension, and that impregnation reflects the scene where a younger man 'drives' a red toy car between the legs of the older woman in the first seduction scene in the play? There is a violence in the work, that for all its whimsicality, and this is heightened by the romantic soundtrack, is not easy to watch. It has a veneer of happiness that is deeply turbulent and troubling. It is tender but aggressive. This charge is something that comes as much from the adaptation of scenes from the canonical films *The Graduate* and from *Blow Up* as much as anything intrinsic to the Rigan apartment scene.[4] There is an obvious and meticulously restaged underscore of adaptation from these iconic films of the 1960s. I saw these at the time as I suspect did many of the audience last night, with Vanessa Redgrave and Anne Bancroft, both of whom one could fall for as a teenager, and so there is of course a rupture, a kind of violence of adaptation from one milieu to another, one generational memory to another, one cultural site to another.

AH: It is perhaps simpler than that. Vanessa Redgrave visited Riga when I was a student. It was strange such a famous actress was visiting in the middle of the 1980s, when Latvia was still occupied by Soviets. She was sitting for hours in our theatre school in our class just watching our rehearsals: second year students, working on *Miss Julie* by August Strindberg, with Vanessa Redgrave just sitting there. After the rehearsal she presented me with a signed photo and she kissed me. I am wondering why she was there. It is hard to imagine.

AR: This brings me back to the technologies of memory that saturate the setting of this performance. Apparatuses of adaptation you could call them, of chrono-politics, the communication of the passing of times and events towards a mythic sense of a history of something that never quite happened. I wonder if you would say something about the equipment that is everywhere, here in *The Sound of Silence*, but also in other productions that I have seen of yours, such as the old gramophone in the production of *Sonya*? I was intrigued by the paraphernalia of trying to speak to somewhere else in another time. The wonderful scene for instance in *The Sound of Silence* where the red telephone upstage, towards the door, is dragged out of the room while being held by the woman, who is dragged into the doorway by a wire that seems to be being pulled from somewhere off, by some inexorable power beyond the woman but somehow connected to her conversant at the other end of the line. And the man, beautifully played by Andriss Keiss, with the amazing bonnet, the big hair, is drawn back into this seen world, through the physical proximity of the wire is brought into the room where he confronts his party line.

AH: I think this demonstrates the British observer in you, the British audience in you. I am not the best specialist on British theatre but once as an actor, in another production of *Miss Julie*, many years later than that first one Ms Redgrave saw, one British critic saw the production in Riga and our performance lasted four hours and I remember he said: 'In England this story takes a maximum of 1 hour 50 minutes.' 'There is a pause between every word, wasting so much time', he said. In my 'theatre religion' *sound* is more important than text. In British theatre it is the exact opposite, you have to *deserve the pause*. In mine you have to deserve the text; there must be something deeper beyond that text.

Tom Stoppard said laughing is like the first sign that communication is established in the theatre, if the audience are laughing then doors are open for more serious exchanges. In rehearsals recently I was in Berlin with German actors who were indulging in long, long pauses between the textual passages. Of course as an actor I understand this inclination well because an actor wants to prepare for the text in its density. Continental actors might learn from the British in some ways, even if your text is not prepared, you have to deliver it, because English audiences cannot wait if your 'inner kitchen' is too slow!

AR: Do you think then that cultural *differences* exist in a theatre, which has remarkably generic features across a landscape of European bourgeois sites and spaces? If so how might theatre adapt to such difference?

AH: Of course it has to do with mentality, local humour, how this communication in theatre is established between audiences and actors, this 'agreement', this silent agreement in each different country because, for instance in the case of a form such as Kabuki there is a very exotic agreement between audiences as to what is happening and what it is meaning. But while the same Kabuki might well be everywhere, Germans, French, Russians have their *own* Kabuki. Even critics are not able to understand this specific agreement between audience and performer. You can spend years working in these different contexts and this agreement between audiences and actors is *hermetic*.

AR: Do we then exoticize Latvia by suggesting it is peculiarly situated *between* cultures and unusually able to translate those cultures? There is a presumption that its geographical location between the cultures of Germany and Russia makes it an especially charged place for a theatre practitioner to work. Your work for instance has been described many times as being situated at a crossroads between these traditions, if such sites could be said to have a tradition?

AH: Historically that makes sense. Riga specifically and Latvia more broadly is located between two big superpowers and what is more two big *theatre* superpowers: Russia and Germany. Two conflicting theatre religions that it is impossible to mix. But today it does not make sense to judge whatever artist you might mention by such geographical qualities, because each artist who has a computer at home works in a *global* context.

Of course you watch a performance and you would not know whether the director was from here or there, how would you ask where he was from, from Barcelona, from Moscow? It is not so easy to say anymore, surely. This communication agreement between audience and actor, the way they give off their signals, is unique in each and every context. Let's say from a theatre arts side theatre is produced within a global context but consumed in a local context. Theatre is a conservative art, an old-fashioned art. Comparing it with music, with visual arts in the twentieth century, theatre is always 'climbing backwards'. Perhaps this anachronistic quality is to do with the story-telling that is about to happen, the audience is waiting to hear the *story*. That is the basis of theatre. It is simple. The difference with visual art and literature is that in the twentieth century these forms were more flexible and more irresponsible, whereas in theatre people enter a dark room and they want to hear the story, and they are not going away until they do.

AR: 'Hello darkness my old friend' is the first line of this show, because it is the first line of the Simon and Garfunkel song which starts the show. It is beautiful. It is the first line, and I am glad I am 'here' when I hear it. I am in the theatre, again.

AH: The same is true for the actor on the stage who wants to describe what he has formulated. Theatre is when a human being buys a ticket to see this dark space and to sit in a chair in this dark space to think about his miserable life. This marks the difference between theatre and the cinema where the spectator has to follow the story on the screen. In theatre you just follow the story in your own head. How else can you explain why, in recent years in Europe at least, the numbers for theatre audiences have grown and grown and grown? And at the same time theatre is not getting better, quite the opposite is the case of course. Theatre is getting worse, much worse, everywhere, but the audience is coming back for more, and more. Perhaps because they are living in the twenty-first century they have less and less reason to leave their house in the evenings because every form of art you can consume exists now in a digitized version. People in theatre are not going out for theatre at all, but to socialize, to 'smell the human flesh' as Platanov says in Chekhov's play.

AR: In the programme for your show someone had written that you felt there was a combination of laughter and tears when theatre was doing its best work. Did you write that?

AH: Yes those are my words. In moments when people experience their greatest joy they often experience something akin to their most intense grief. I am very old fashioned, and proud of it, and would say the highest form of acting is to achieve such a kind of moment where the audience is simultaneously able to have those two emotions, not one after another, but at the same time, as if those two masks were superimposed.

AR: Is that possible?

AH: Of course, beginning with Charlie Chaplin laughing and crying at the same time. Not surprisingly it has something to do with Jewish culture in which this simultaneity exists in everyday humour. That is why so many countries cannot imagine theatre communities without Jewish artists because this mentality is so close to how theatre works.

AR: Could I bring us 'back' to your performance *Long Life*?

AH: It was made before *The Sound of Silence*, and it just happened in the way that you will see it. People would recognize the same apartment, the five spaces as before and many of the actors. A silent, mute theatre, again I am afraid, with no text. These two performances that we have been discussing are the exceptions in my work, when people are *not* talking. Normally I have nothing against people talking to each other in the theatre.

AR: So, what next? How will adaptation influence your future work?

AH: Next year I will work only on operas, starting with Sir Harrison Birtwistle's *Gawain* in Salzburg. I have to visit him in England to plan this. In theatre I don't have the experience of working with live dramaturgs or playwrights as mostly I do classical plays and the writers are dead. So this meeting will be significant for how it affects what we do. I must add, I do realize that most of my performances are really long and boring; it is something like reading a thick book. You can make a very short version, an adaptation you could call it, of *Anna Karenina,* or a children's book version with nice pictures. I have directed performances of five hours and at the beginning it is unbearable, but after that the work seems to suck you in and it becomes like reading a thick book, the experience of duration creates an inner tempo that you deal with as time passes.

AR: The time of theatre is never the time of life. Is it not that it is quicker or slower, rather like the epileptic in their flickering state, time seems to 'escape' as though it never happened at all?

AH: This is the most crucial question for every theatre director in our day because in every rehearsal, through every moment, you have to make a choice between two different spectators. Those who are still reading books, and those who are not reading books, the ones who are consuming culture through TV. This is a two-speed audience not divided by generation, or by social class, but this division does have to do with the one categorization I have offered: they are either reading books or never reading books. And for every theatre audience in every rehearsal you have to make a choice. You cannot of course find a version that somehow theatrically pleases both groups.

AR: In *The Sound of Silence* it is books, amongst many inorganic things, that give off the music, like so many hand-held transmitters of hope and loss.

AH: Precisely, this was a homage to a generation that was always buying books. In Soviet times there was of course censorship, that makes the scene doubly poignant. Today I visited the flea market for books in Amsterdam. In places like this, most of those anywhere near the place are selling and looking for old books; they are all from that very generation. They fetishize the book, and for good reasons.

AR: Was the concert in Riga in 1968, by Simon and Garfunkel hinted at in *The Sound of Silence*, postponed, or cancelled? Are we seeing interrupted history here, or myth at work?

AH: It is a fake story! But of course in choosing Simon and Garfunkel and not the Beatles, this theatrical decision has to do with books, again. Simon and Garfunkel were an educated and intelligent Jewish duo who have a certain political quality. It is not like those musicians from Liverpool and their lyrics: 'Do you love me? Do you love me too?' It is about books, you can hear that from the texts on the stage.

AR: And then, in *The Sound of Silence*, after everything and the three hours traffic of the stage, having not yet heard our favourite of all Simon and Garfunkel songs, the man, finally, inhaling *Bridge Over Troubled Water* from the water in the bucket, dies at the end of the production, in the galvanized metal bath. What are we to make of this? Is this the image of a failed revolution?

AH: It's the interval. I had better go back to actors. Is that enough of an interview? What are you doing tomorrow?

AR: In the morning I'll go and see the sun rise on the grave of Rembrandt's wife, Saskia van Uylenburgh, at the Oude Kerk.

AH: [*Inaudible humming, as the audience enter the foyer.*]

Link

New Riga Theatre: http://www.jrt.lv/en/about-jrt (accessed 19 January 2014).

Selected bibliography

Kear, Adrian. (in press). 'Naming the Event: Alvis Hermanis and Jaunais Rīgas Teātris' *Sonja*', in *Theatre and Event*, pp. 92–118.

Marranca, Bonnie. (2010). 'The Poetry of Things Past: Alvis Hermanis in Conversation with Bonnie Marranca', *PAJ: A Journal of Performance and Art*, 32.1, PAJ 94, pp. 23–35.

Sacchi, Annalisa. (2010). 'False Recognition: Pseudo-History and Collective Memory in Alvis Hermanis' *The Sound of Silence*', in *Meno istorija ir kritika, Art History & Criticism*, 6, pp. 30–7.

Notes

1 See Kear, pp. 92–118.

2 See Read in Thea Brejzek (ed.), *Expanding Scenography, On The Authoring of Space*. Prague: The Arts and Theatre Institute, 2011, pp. 16–24.

3 See Roland Barthes, *How to Live Together: Novelistic Simulations of Some Everyday Spaces*, trans. Kate Briggs. New York: Columbia University Press, 2013.

4 See Sacchi (2010).

Part Four

Crafting Adaptations

13

The Novel as 'Obstacle': John Collins of Elevator Repair Service in Conversation with Aoife Monks

Introduction

John Collins founded Elevator Repair Service theatre company in 1991 with a collective of actors, designers, and co-directors and since then they have produced 16 shows. The company's performances are developed through mining popular culture artefacts: films, found-objects, dance forms, and theatre spaces, emerging as a mosaic of cultural and theatrical references. This approach underpinned their work on *Room Tone* in 2002, where they performed extracts from the early psychological studies by William James interspersed with Henry James' novella, *The Turn of the Screw*. This work paved the way for the trilogy on which this interview mostly concentrates; the staging of three 'Great American' modernist novels: F. Scott Fitzgerald's *The Great Gatsby*, William Faulkner's *The Sound and The Fury*, and Ernest Hemingway's *The Sun Also Rises.*[1]

ERS's production of Fitzgerald's novel, which they entitled *Gatz,* was set in a dingy low-tech office, with Scott Shepherd (playing Nick Carraway, the narrator), reading the entire novel aloud onstage alongside a cast of office workers who were slowly incorporated into the novel's narrative. The performance lasted almost eight hours including three intervals. The durational flair of this excessively 'faithful' approach failed to gain performance rights from the Fitzgerald estate, who had granted permission to a competing production, *Gatsby,* to be performed on Broadway, preventing the ERS show from performing in

New York until 2010, where it opened to great acclaim. The production, the company's eleventh show, was a huge international hit, and as Collins wryly suggests, made the company an 'overnight' success.

What made *Gatz* and the following two shows so interesting was their approach to non-theatrical material on the stage. ERS viewed the novel as posing a problem of form – how does one transpose the most literary of novels to the stage? This problem is nothing new. Currently, the London stage is populated by film adaptations like *The Bodyguard* or *Dirty Dancing*; and novels such as the National Theatre's *Warhorse* and the RSC's *Matilda*. In these productions, the commercial value of familiarity means that the source texts for these shows function like a libretto in opera, leaving the spectator free to take pleasure in the consumption of spectacle. The aim of these adaptations is to *overcome* the differences between the source material and theatrical form in order to promote absorption and participation through 'knowing the words'. The peculiarities of aesthetic forms then, and the work done to transform them, are sublimated to the spectacle.

This approach works in direct distinction to the theatrical context out of which ERS emerged. The company's 'ancestors', such as Richard Foreman, Robert Wilson, and the Wooster Group, are known for their attraction to non-theatrical materials and classic texts. But their approach to adaptation is radically different. Here, the gaps in the seams between forms often constitute the *work* of the performance, functioning as a useful 'obstacle', as Collins terms it, to the production of a fully realized illusion. Instead, these practitioners emphasize a rigorous emotional distance from the source material, requiring of their spectators a deep interrogation of the cultural freight that these texts bring with them to the stage. You might say that this attraction to non-theatrical source texts occupies a continuum with the employment of apparently non-mimetic bodies of children, animals and old people in the work of artists such as Pina Bausch and Romeo Castellucci. As Bert States suggests, these are moments in which the limits of theatricality are tested by incorporating things into the world of the stage, [illegible] novels and animals, that seem most resistant to theatrical mimesis:

'it is not the world that has invaded the illusion; the illusion has stolen something from the world in order to display its own power.'[2] Nick Ridout has argued, furthermore, that the resistant nature of these source materials and bodies demands an ethical response from the audience, which may require a reckoning with the peculiar responsibilities of being a spectator at the theatre.[3]

The work of ERS differs aesthetically from the formalist cool of their ancestors by producing a gentler, more awkward, and less deconstructive approach to the found objects of novels. There is nonetheless an on-going interrogation of Americanness that informs much of their work and underpins these shows. To perform 'Great American Novels' onstage, as ERS did in this trilogy, is to perpetuate the mythology and status of these books, while also exposing the limits to those myths. In this interview, Collins accounts for the ways in which performing these novels functioned to open out the gaps, flaws, and inconsistencies of the theatrical experience. By refusing to fully 'adapt' these novels, by enabling the peculiarity of their literary form to stand apart from the theatrical event, perhaps the gaps, flaws, and inconsistencies of the myths of America itself also came to light.

Interview

Aoife Monks: I'm aware that you may be slightly uncomfortable with just looking at the shows you've done that are focused on novels. Does it feel restricting?

John Collins: People will sometimes come up to me and say, 'Yes, I've seen all three of your shows'. We've made 16 … so there's a problem sometimes, when one kind of thing puts you on the map, but it comes later in your career. And in this case, the impulse that fuelled these later shows was in many ways the same as in our earlier work. From early on, we were looking to push ourselves to do something we hadn't dared do before. With adapting the novels, we wanted to do something that was difficult and unfamiliar, and like most everything else we've done, we wanted to get something on stage that didn't present an easy solution for being staged.

AM: Maybe you could begin by talking about your relationship to found objects and texts in your work prior to the 'novel' shows?

JC: We were always choosing material because of the kind of freedom it gave us, material that needed us to make some sense out of it. The most extreme example is *Total Fictional Lie* (1998), which was a show that we assembled in a sort of desperate state, because we got the opportunity to have a big international premier with rather short notice. We really didn't know what we wanted to make a show about, so we watched a documentary about vaudeville and we had a big wooden box, which we decided was going to be central, somehow.

AM: Where did you get the box from?

JC: We found it in a loft on 30th Street. We tended to rehearse in spaces where there was left-behind furniture. We used to start working on our shows by making little sketches so we tried a bunch of different things with the box. We had the box and we had a vaudeville documentary as well as some completely unrelated material that company members had brought in: a Nick Broomfield documentary about Aileen Wuornos the serial killer, a documentary about Paul Anka and a set of CDs of great speeches. So we were accumulating these things and trying to figure out what they had to do with each other and eventually we decided we just liked something about the way people behaved in documentaries. And that turned out to be the thing that held together a lot of far-flung choices. So, you put all these things together and you look for a logic. We don't try to invent a logic and then make things suit it.

AM: When you say 'we had these documentaries and we had CDs of speeches', what does that actually mean? Do people bring objects into rehearsal with them?

JC: Yes. Research, for us, just means, 'Oh, this thing reminds me of this other thing we're working on so I'm going to bring it in, let's just look at it and just mine it.'

AM: So as a director your work is responding to these materials, not finding the materials in the first place?

JC: Yeah, everybody in the company knows that anything they are curious about with regard to its form, if it has some kind of theatrical appeal, is fair game early on. Sometimes we just need a starting point. It's as if we were bringing these old machines in and taking them apart and trying to build a new one.

AM: As a source text, how might a documentary on vaudeville compare to the high status of something like *The Great Gatsby*? Are they equivalent as found objects to you, or do they have a different status?

JC: Well, I think they have a different scale. When we take a bit of found video, its utility is going to be very limited. We can extrapolate and expand from it, make movement, try out a certain gesture. But I think we treat everything as a found object, so that when we came to *The Great Gatsby*, it was an object too. It's a complicated object. The first lesson in working with that text, though, was that we weren't going to be able to pick it apart in the same way as a video. With a documentary, the material is not clinging to itself so strongly and so we can extract something from it, because it's a kind of fragment already. *The Great Gatsby*'s not a fragment. I think I stayed away from texts like novels for a long time because they have such a formal integrity, and I felt like there wasn't going be any room for me to move around. When Steve Bodow brought *The Great Gatsby* into rehearsal he said, 'Let's see what we can do with this.'[4] The way we made our work was to turn something inside out, pick it apart, tear it up, see how it fell back together, look for a new logic. And so we started to do that with *The Great Gatsby*. We had *another* idea about using junky found object puppets that we could clash together with the novel and hoped it would fall apart in a really interesting way. It wasn't even necessarily important to us at the time that we would say anything about *The Great Gatsby*. I think, though, that we began to realize, once we started, that we were dealing with a different kind of object that was going to determine a lot about the scale of what we did. I loved the book and I read it for the first time *for* that project in a day and a half. Of course I could have read it in a day, it turns out, out loud, and had time for dinner.

AM: So duration was an important aspect of the scale of this show?

JC: Yeah, duration was one thing but also the form, because it wasn't that it was just a really long play, with dialogue among three or four people and descriptions of settings that could be easily achieved. There was the sprawling scale of it, there was the literary form of a novel. I developed a frustration with editing it, because I didn't want to be making decisions on my own, I didn't want to just be picking what I *liked*, or trying to write an adaptation, I just didn't feel qualified and I didn't think anybody was. So we decided we would have the books around on stage, that the book would be this important object.

AM: Does that mean that the book is two kinds of object in *Gatz*? There's the found object as a stimulus, and the novel as a prop?

JC: It's an object among the many objects that form the show. Because we were going to have the book itself on stage, I thought we needed to ask permission from the Fitzgerald estate. I wanted the book to be governing the performance, I wanted the book doing that as an obstacle. I recognized that having to read from the book, having to use the exact words, was something we'd been resisting. I didn't think it was a good way to make theatre. But then when you resist something long enough, it becomes an interesting problem. So I was excited to have the book there as an obstacle to our show, not as a script for it, but as an obstacle that we had to work our way through. But also for that reason we felt we had to get permission. I was a little bit afraid of the money we might have to pay but I had no idea we would just get shut down.

AM: You seem to be the victim and beneficiary of the economic stakes around performing famous texts.

JC: It turns out the way that we were a victim also benefited us. Because, the first time, they stopped us from doing what would have been a much less substantial, much less ambitious and less serious project. When we came back to it a few years later, I let go of what had been the initial idea, which was this sort of dancing with puppets idea.

AM: When did you decide to set the novel in an office?

JC: When the estate told us we couldn't do it, we went on to other projects like *Room Tone*. After that was done we decided we were going to take a break. And so I came back to *The Great Gatsby* during that break and worked on it with the actors Scott Shepherd and James Urbaniak. We were renting out our rehearsal space to another company, so we met at the office in the Performing Garage where there's a small room and there's a big sliding door that opens into a bigger room, and we decided we would treat it as a found theatre.[5] And at that point, I had decided that we would try to do the whole book. So we started at the beginning and immediately we had to look for a rationale for why Scott would be reading the book, why he would be saying all the text. It came out of just making-do with what we had. We worked for a little while in the office, and I even considered performing it there.

AM: Why do you think your approach to doing the full novel specifically worked with that book – with *Gatsby*? Is it that Fitzgerald's novel suits itself to being told in full on stage, or rather that telling it in full on stage is the solution to the problem of Fitzgerald's novel for the theatre?

JC: Well it was a solution to the problem of the novel, and the way we came to it was not by evaluating the entire novel and then coming up with that solution. It was a proposition for how to get through it. As we worked our way through it I still thought that we were going to have to cut sections of it. But I had a sense that doing the novel in full was the right way to respond to his language, because I tried to edit his language and failed.

AM: So it's the dead-ends, it's the failures that helped you to find the solution?

JC: Yeah. There were some passages where I couldn't really see how we were going to stage them: I didn't know how they were going to work. And it's good that I didn't try to decide that in advance, because what we did with the more extemporaneous passages worked in the context of the larger project. I thought when we got to Chapter 4 we'd have to cut a lot of it, but then we got there and just kept working through it without having imagined already exactly how it was all going to work. That became the assignment: doing the whole novel was what we were making ourselves try to do. In retrospect I'd like to say that it was just part of our trajectory as a company because the three 'novel' shows were a way of rediscovering and re-energizing the impulse to make theatre out of non-theatre.

AM: You're suggesting that what was really energizing about *Gatz* was the impossibility of the project, the fact that you couldn't stage a novel in the theatre. So how do you tackle the next two novels when you know as a company that you *can* stage a novel now?

JC: We lived by the creed that you don't do the same thing twice, but for a couple of reasons we decided we *would* do the same thing twice. Because even though we had come up with a successful solution to the problem of *Gatsby* it would be absurd to think that was *the* solution to literature on stage.

AM: How did you come to Faulkner and Hemingway? Does repeating yourselves include working with modernist American writers?

JC: That wasn't the specific repetition we had in mind at first but I did have a positive feeling about modernist American writing, and realized that it did something that I loved, which was that it traversed period and felt contemporary. I was really happy and comfortable inside of that language. So we decided to find the Faulkner that seemed the most impossible to stage. We read *The Sound and The Fury* and read the notoriously difficult first chapter, and I actually understood it in a way that I had never understood it before. When we read it out loud I heard it rhythmically and musically in a way that had never worked when I was reading it silently and so I thought, 'OK there's something here'. During the process, I think I was still working out some ideas from *Gatz*. But *The Sound and The Fury* upset those ideas so much that eventually it forced me to let go of some of those tactics. We had big problems on our plate. The problem of the constantly changing voices and the temporal slipperiness of that book. And of course the problem of the narrator being mute. It was as if it was designed to thwart all of our solutions to *Gatz*. Nevertheless, when we came to Hemingway's *The Sun Also Rises*, I realized after *The Sound and The Fury* that I hadn't really successfully let go of the *Gatz* approach. So when we started reading some Hemingway, I knew I had to look for something else. What we found was Hemingway's dialogue. It just rang so true; it was just so much fun. But of course there was so much of that book where all our heads were dropping onto the table with boredom. I was beginning to think that we needed to try our hand at adapting. It really just meant, we were going to let ourselves edit.

AM: And how did that feel?

JC: It was the hardest thing to do. I mean it was the hardest assignment of all three. With Faulkner we could take on something like 21 different periods of time, but trying to make decisions about how to edit and deal with the Hemingway was *the* hardest thing we did and it took the longest. With *Gatz*, which was the longest show, the decisions came most quickly. We had set up this simple contrast with the office setting which was never going to change and we were never going to let ourselves cut the book.

AM: So your constraints helped you make the work? Did you have a constraint for *The Sun Also Rises*?

JC: The constraint there was the set. That was one important constraint, as it was for the other two as well.

AM: Scenography feels like a mechanism for both distancing and absorbing the audience in your work. There's something surprising about how naturalistic your sets are, to see real tables and chairs and teacups on your stage. The scenography feels like an interesting juxtaposition to the modernism of the novels, particularly the Faulkner.

JC: Yes we wanted to attach the weight of that set to the nimble way that Faulkner leaps around through different places, different times, and he only needs a word to free-associate himself from a fence, out in a field, to a living room, 20 years later. In the theatre it all takes place in that living room, it's trapped in this intimate, familiar world. The sets always emerge from real situations we are in. With Faulkner, it was just the way we found the rehearsal room that we were working in, which later became the set.

AM: The way that you recount the history and processes of the company is often through the spaces that you've occupied. It sounds like the biggest found object that you work with is the space you're in.

JC: That's often been the case.

AM: A lot of critics have said that going to *Gatz* or the Faulkner piece replicates the absorption of reading a novel. What did you hope for the emotional engagement of an audience with this kind of work?

JC: I think it's very different. It is a fundamentally different thing to hear something read aloud. When you're reading a novel alone, you know that you're looking at a page and your eye is aware of more text ahead of you. You can see that the next thought has already formed: it's already been considered, it's already been committed to writing. By contrast, the way we are accustomed to hearing people speak, is that it's like being there when the thought is first formed, and there's something unpredictable and messy about it. So, to re-cast written words in a spoken form gives you the sensation of them being imagined for the first time. It puts you in closer contact with the sensation of the words as thoughts and not as writing.

AM: But isn't there a difference between watching an actor speak the lines as if they were their thoughts, or watching an actor read the words from a book?

JC: In *Gatz* I wanted to dissect that process, to draw attention to the two things that were happening at the same time. I wanted to remind the audience constantly that this was already written down, so that the action would happen somehow in-between the speech and reading. It was a bit like a science experiment, in watching two ingredients interact, and so you are reminded always of the transformation. The first idea was that *everybody* was going to be reading the book, and then I let go of that and let it just be about one person's, Nick's, experience, and then eventually, by the end, he gets to be one of those people who is just saying these things too, he stops reading.

AM: He kind of gets absorbed back into the novel, doesn't he? You seem really attracted to distancing the audience, to drawing attention to the moments where the onstage action and the illusion disconnect.

JC: I think that what live performance can do best is show you the transformation of actor to character as it's happening. I don't think theatre's very good at asking you to take that for granted from the beginning. When those distancing things come in, it's like they're meant to kind of pry open the spaces between the things that we know are real, like actors and the set, and the things they are trying to become. Add to this the situation of the theatre – a room where these things happen in front of a live audience – which I find so compelling. I mean you can decide on your own as a spectator to disprove the reality of the illusion any time you feel like it. And I'm fascinated by the fact that a lot of theatre makers will try to talk you out of that, but there's no amount of money that you can throw at a piece of theatre that will prevent any audience member from saying, 'Oh, that's a light up there, that's a curtain, there's people sitting round me watching it too.' So that's the reality of theatre.

AM: And why is that reality so interesting to you?

JC: Because we believe the other stuff anyway. Because theatre can still be successful in those conventional ways. What's interesting to me about that success is the gulf that it has to cross, the gap that has to be bridged, and it's the bridging of it that's interesting. So I don't like to take for granted for too long that all those pretend things are true. It's the pretending that's interesting to watch. I try to keep pointing to whatever little reminders there are of the collision of reality and imagination.

AM: And this brings us to the thorny issue of adaptation. The term can suggest some kind of melding or blending, but your desire to keep things slightly apart seems almost to be an anti-adaptation stance.

JC: Well it depends if what you mean by an adaptation is that you create something that has redefined itself only in terms of its own medium. What's essential about theatre is all these uncontrollable imperfections, all these realities that are always going to interfere. So, you can do *The Great Gatsby* as a painting and you might really feel that you were just dealing with a painting. You know, it's controlled and contained and its medium of paint isn't really being much interfered with by anything going on in the world around it. But what's essential and fundamental about live performance is that it is always going to involve things that you can't control. So there *is* no adaptation that really works that way in theatre. Theatre's always going to be interfered with, theatre can't have itself to itself.

AM: Is the cultural status of these texts a factor in how you approach their adaptation?

JC: It seems like it must have been deliberate … We needed these works to have a kind of fierce integrity of their own. They had legendary status, and that guaranteed that they would put up a really good fight. I didn't want to work on a novel that anybody imagined needed improving on. I wanted something that was going to push back, so I wanted them to be *good* novels, I wanted to be impressed by them, I wanted to have reverence for them. I thought that was important because I knew I was going to be doing some kind of violence to them. Not out of contempt, but just because there was no other way to take something that was such a great achievement in its own medium and then try to bring it to another medium: inevitably, that was going to cause problems. I wanted something that we could throw ourselves up against and then bounce off and create an interesting gulf. Our project was not to knock it down and say, 'Look, we've got this great new thing here and never mind what it was before.' By contrast, the project we are working on right now *is* all about making something new, where we have text and a writer without an object that comes to us with the sort of integrity of a finished work. So I feel like we're in very new territory right now.[6]

Link

Elevator Repair Service: http://www.elevator.org (accessed 19 January 2014).

Selected bibliography

Bailes, Sarah Jane. (2010a). *Performance Theatre and The Poetics of Failure*. London and New York: Routledge, pp. 148–98.

—(2010b). 'Elevator Repair Service – *Cab Legs* (1997) to *Gatz* (2006) – Reversing the Ruins: The Power of Theatrical Miscomprehension' in

Jen Harvie and Andy Lavander (eds), *Making Contemporary Theatre: International Rehearsal Processes*. Manchester: Manchester University Press, pp. 81–100.

Coco, Fusco, Steve Bodow, John Collins and Rinne Groff. (1999). 'Elevator Repair Service', *BOMB*, 67, pp. 50–5.

Notes

1 *Gatz* was first performed in 2005. *The Sound and The Fury (April Seventh, 1928)* (2007) was a performance of the first section of Faulkner's novel, in which the role of Benjy was shared between the cast and the novel was passed from actor to actor. *The Select (The Sun Also Rises)* (2009), was an edited version of Hemingway's novel in which the object of the novel itself did not appear onstage.

2 States, *Great Reckonings In Little Rooms: On The Phenomenology of Theatre*. Berkeley, CA, Los Angeles and London: University of California Press, 1985, p. 34.

3 Ridout, *Stage Fright, Animals and Other Theatrical Problems*. Cambridge and New York: Cambridge University Press, 2006, pp. 96–128.

4 Bodow is a founding member and past co-director of ERS. He is also co-executive producer of *The Daily Show* with Jon Stewart.

5 The Performing Garage is the home of the Wooster Group, where Collins worked as a sound designer until 2003 and where Shepherd continues to work as a performer.

6 ERS are currently developing two new projects: *Fondly, Collette Richland*, the company's first collaboration with a playwright, Sibyl Kempson; and *Arguendo*, based on a transcript of 1991 court case, *Barnes v. Glen Theater*.

14

Doing the Impossible: Katie Mitchell in Conversation with Dan Rebellato

Introduction

Katie Mitchell is one of the most important directors to emerge in Britain – indeed in Europe – in the last 25 years. Her work is marked by a rich and profound realism; even in productions which are not in any conventional sense naturalistic, her work with actors and designers insists on a fidelity to the truth about human behaviour that grounds even the most experimental work. In her early career, Mitchell focused her attention on reviving plays from the European canon, with a particular emphasis on Northern and Eastern Europe. Increasingly over the last decade she has collaborated with actors to create devised adaptations of literary works and other sources. Often this source material might seem rather intractable to other directors – dealing as it does with inchoate and nebulous experiences like memory and consciousness – but Mitchell has developed a robust and rigorous methodology working with actors and increasingly with live video and Foley sound. In this interview, recorded at the Royal Court Theatre, London, in July 2013, and subsequently edited by Mitchell, we discuss the relationship between productions of plays and adaptations and the various techniques she has used to find theatrical form for experiences and perspectives not often shown on our stages.

Interview

Dan Rebellato: Can I talk about your production of *A Dream Play* in 2005? Let me confess something: I had a very complicated reaction to the production. I loved the evocation of dream imagery on stage, the precision, the atmosphere – but I was disappointed, because I was looking forward to finally getting to see Strindberg's *A Dream Play* and I felt I hadn't actually *seen* it.

Katie Mitchell: Even you!

DR: I know! And then, of course, it made me think in what sense do we ever 'see' the 'play'? We only see a *version* of the play and decisions have always been made that, in a sense, adapt the play to the purposes of the production. In other words, I felt your production of *A Dream Play* complicated, perhaps to the point of crisis, the borderline between production and adaptation.

KM: The thing that most fascinated me in the text was Strindberg's idea of bringing a dream to life on stage. In rehearsals we worked with one simple aim, that is, to make the audience believe they were watching a dream. To make this idea clearer we added the framing device of a dreamer going to sleep at the beginning and waking up at the end. All the scenes were angled around this central idea of the dreamer. He was based on one of the main characters in the play and we built his biography by combining facts about him in the play with details from Strindberg's own biography. In the early stages of rehearsals we analysed the composition of dreams. The actors tried to recall their dreams and re-enact them. We soon discovered that dreams are often a jumble of very concrete details from people's lives, mixed up with other surreal data.

When I was preparing the production I didn't know that we would depart from the original material as much as we did. In the end we only kept 40 per cent of the original text; 60 per cent was added material based on improvisations around the biography of the character from the play that we'd selected as the dreamer.

Caryl Churchill did the version of the Strindberg text for the production and she watched the process of cutting and pasting evolve through the rehearsal process. She was very torn between her loyalty to the original text and her interest in the new material we were generating. She is a very generous collaborator and she agreed to all the changes after careful and precise discussion. Looking back on it, I can see that in our enthusiasm to put a dream on stage we did depart from the original written material in a way that was understandably frustrating for those audience members who had come to see the original play. Really we should have called the production *After A Dream Play* rather than *A Dream Play*. After this we started to re-title shows that we were working on in this way so as not to confuse the audience, like the title *... some trace of her* [2008] for our adaptation of Dostoevsky's *The Idiot*.

DR: Did you come out of that experience any clearer about the difference between a production of a play and an adaptation of a play?

KM: Yes, absolutely, but with later productions it was harder to be so clear-cut about the difference. In many instances, like with *The Seagull* [2008] and *Women of Troy* [2007], I thought that I was directing the play but many folks viewed these productions as radical adaptations, and I got a lot more flak for these later shows compared to *A Dream Play*. With *A Dream Play* we did major surgery to the text and with *Women of Troy* and *The Seagull* there were only tiny textual changes made. There were clearly factors other than the text that were being responded to negatively.

DR: Maybe because the Chekhov is better known?

KM: Yes, and maybe because the production history of Chekhov is more deeply embedded in British culture. I did sometimes wonder if people were comparing the production I directed with productions in the past and not with the original text by Chekhov. You know the way that a rock at the seaside has all sorts of barnacles and seaweed on it; it's difficult to imagine the clean rock before it got any of those things grown into it and that is what can happen to old texts: the way the text is performed grows into the original text and creates a strange hybrid third piece of material and it is this third thing that people are actually coming to see. I think a lot of the time when people say, 'You're not doing the play', what they mean is, 'You're not doing the play like the productions I grew up with in the 1970s or early 1960s.'

I am working a lot in Europe now and it is clear that each country has interpreted these classics inside its own tradition, and each country's cultural approach to a classic like *The Seagull* has grown into how people understand the original text and what they expect to see from the productions they go to. If the German tradition of directing Chekhov were to butt up against the British tradition I could imagine a ripe old argument between the two sides each fighting for their cultural interpretation as the absolute truth of what the text is or what a production should be.

DR: Something else about *A Dream Play* that foreshadows later work is that it's absolutely about trying to capture a state of consciousness, a wholly subjective experience, and put it on stage in a public forum. And it seems to me that a lot of the later productions do something similar: *Waves* [2006], *Reise Durch Die Nacht* [*Night Train*, 2012] …

KM: Yes, you're right. All the multi-media shows in Germany – the ones you mention, plus *Wunschkonzert* [*Request Programme*, 2008], *Die Gelbe Tapete* [*The Yellow Wallpaper*, 2013] – are trying to represent consciousness and modes of perception on stage. The shows focus less on narrative and action, and more on behaviour and how a character looks out at the world. It's like the difference between being a documentary film-maker where you're an external eye putting together objective information about what human beings do and a film-maker who tries to get inside the head of the subject and show that person's uniquely subjective viewpoint.

DR: You are often drawn to material that some might superficially think is simply impossible to put on stage. *Waves*, for example, has these shifting internal voices, this play of memory, which is alien to a theatre of concrete, material representation, narrative three-act structure, and so on.

KM: Yes, I am very much drawn to texts like *Waves* which are more complex and layered. I am often struck by the way in which theatre practice has not completely embraced modernist texts from the twentieth century, and how mainstream theatre operates mainly inside nineteenth-century narrative structures. I often compare the way in which mainstream theatre has evolved in Britain with the way in which the visual arts or non-dramatic literature has developed over the twentieth and twenty-first centuries. *The Waves* was written in the 1930s and the idea that theatre attempted (and partly managed to 'do') *The Waves* 70 years later only shows how behind we are, formally. Questions like 'What is character?', 'What is narrative?' have been challenged and chewed over in other art forms for years now and yet linear narrative and traditional characters are the unchallenged staple diet of mainstream theatre practice. Germany re-imagined itself culturally after the Second World War and rejected many of these traditional components because they were connected to the way in which Nazism had unfolded itself. In theatre in the United Kingdom, we still insist on these old-fashioned rules that determine what theatre can or cannot be: it *must* have a story; it *must* be linear; there *must* be characters; there *must* be conflict; you *can't* do behaviour; you *can't* do states; you *can't* do anything deconstructed or broken down that gets closer to how you actually experience yourself in the world, not as a great hero in a linear narrative, with clarity and a fixed personality, but as an ordinary person living a much more fragmented, shifting sense of reality. Any attempt to represent that in theatre is frowned upon in Britain. Not so in literature; not so in the visual arts. And, interesting enough, not so in Europe: and for me that's a real problem.

DR: Do you think there's something here about gender? I wonder if some of the things that our culture seems to think are necessary on stage – linearity, clarity, action, conflict – are also what Western culture tends to think of as masculine virtues. I say that also because *The Waves* is both a modernist novel and a kind of feminist novel in its determination to use a different attitude to consciousness to structure its text. Do you think there's anything in that?

KM: Yes, there is something here about gender. It's very hard to talk along strictly gender lines because of course there are many women who do exceptionally beautiful work inside mainstream practice, with linear narratives, characters, and so on, and they would rightly dispute your point. But if, like me, you end up, after 30 years of work, coming to the conclusion that female perception and experience is maybe different from male perception and experience, then it follows that the theatrical forms you select as a woman may well need to be different to those chosen by men, and as the forms that dominate are male, then you may want to experiment with generating possible alternative forms for women's experience. And when some of those experiments are received in a rather … intense way,[1] one might end up believing what you just suggested. The narrative about my gender is interesting isn't it? Am I understood as a woman directing shows or just another person in the theatre? I've felt this question more and more intensely over the years; the more radical I've become, the more I've suspected that the forceful rejection of this radicalism, in Britain at least, is connected in part to patriarchal structures and systems, which lie invisible, somewhere deep in British society.

DR: Let me ask about *Waves*. Where do you start with adapting a novel like that?

KM: I had loved the novel from the moment I read the first page at University and over the years I had made several attempts to bring it to life, first during a period of research supported by a NESTA Fellowship and later in workshops at the National Theatre Studio. It was always tricky to find a performance mode that was true to its inchoate form. When we started rehearsals in London I didn't have a clue about how we were going to do the show. I had some starting points: a brilliant ensemble of actors, microphones, Foley sound effects, and live video. And I knew that the language could not be presented like a spoken Shakespearean monologue. The delivery of the text needed to have the speed and lightness of a thought as you experience it in your head. Before rehearsals I'd boiled the text down to a 40 page document to make the material more manageable. The main aim in rehearsals was to get our theatre production as close to the novel's stream of consciousness as we could. We soon realized that the only way to do this was to get close inside each character's head. This is where the video came in as it allowed us to get very close to each character's face, so close that the audience could see a thought flicker behind an eye or a tiny movement of one of the 200 muscles on the face. We used the cameras to get close to these tiny details and then we added the text as whispered quicksilver into the microphones to simulate thoughts.

DR: How did you boil *The Waves* down to that 40 page document?

KM: The book's about a group of seven people who go to the same school when they are very little and become friends for life. It charts the way that the friendships and lives of each character evolve until their deaths. Each chapter covers a different time in their lives so it is very easy to cut without dismantling the simple narrative drive. The 40 page document incorporated material from most of the chapters, favouring some like the early primary school experiences and middle age, more than others. This was because the workshops revealed the chapters which organically generated the most theatrical ideas. I also knew that the two dinners would be the main events of the production. Each section of the 40 page document had a simple title and an approximate date reflecting the book narrative. In each section I favoured more concrete text that was better for speaking than for reading. There are sections that are very slow, contemplative, with very long sentences, that would not really work theatrically and these were cut. The passages with shorter, punchier sentences, crammed with colour and metaphor, were selected.

DR: You've said that the use of video gives you the opportunity to offer extreme close-ups on the actors. Someone less sympathetic might ask, why not just make a movie?

KM: Film is a beautiful medium but it's totally *safe,* in that the images are pre-recorded and pre-edited. There is nothing live going on and although it can generate very strong emotions, like fear or sadness, it is not really happening. I love live performance and its edginess, how it teeters on the edge of possible collapse from moment to moment. I also love its collective nature with the strange contract between the actors and the audience. The work using video in *Waves* was done live, with live acting and live camera operating. The breathing of the live operator was present in all the shots of the actors, affecting the framing and the way the camera moved. The delicate dance between live operator and live actor is entirely theatrical and not filmic. In fact when a film-maker friend of mine, Grant Gee, first looked at one of the live video shows he said he felt physically sick. From his point of view the live operating put the film in jeopardy, frame to frame, and that was something he could not cope with being a consummate maker of pre-recorded film. The video also gives everyone in the audience access to the tiny details in the acting that normally are the privilege of the people watching in the first few front rows.

DR: When you first started using video, did you think this was a device with legs, that it would be very versatile?

KM: I hoped it would be versatile but I did not know. And it is a surprise to see how much work has evolved since *Waves* using the live video technique.

DR: It's going to be a bit of a leap from Woolf to Dr Seuss, but can I ask you about the children's shows? They're all adaptations in a sense.

KM: *The Cat in the Hat* [2009] was very much an adaptation but the focus of our work was on creating the cartoon-like pictures and not changing the text. The book was a classic picture book written for very young children who cannot read. Their experience of the book would be a visual one with parents reading as the sound track. We had to make the action on stage *look* exactly like the book, so that a child could turn the pages of the book whilst watching the show and the two would be an exact visual match. The main pressure was on the design: creating things like the outfit the cat wears or the tidying up machine at the end, and the choreography, or getting things like kites and flying objects to move through the air like they did across the white pages of the book. The children's shows that followed – *Beauty and the Beast* [2011] and *Hansel and Gretel* [2012] – were versions of existing well-known fairy tales and not adaptations of existing play texts. Here we did workshops with the actors and the playwright Lucy Kirkwood prior to the text being written. The workshops allowed us to test material in front of the age group selected for each show and to work out how to make the final production. We would work on things like how to make the beast really frightening or what sweets children thought should be on the gingerbread house. Afterwards, Lucy would write scenes to work on once rehearsals began and these would then be test-run in front of groups of children. The feedback from the children would determine how both text and production ideas evolved.

DR: *Hansel and Gretel* was also a piece of music theatre. How did the creation of original music figure in the adaptation process?

KM: In the workshop prior to the rehearsals we discovered how dark the material really is and how frightening it was for the children, not in a good way, so we were keen to present the frightening aspects of the story in brief moments and then use music to reassure the children that it was just a story told in a theatre. The text for the songs was written by Lucy before rehearsals began and Paul Clark then started composing. The songs, like the text, were tested out on children and modified and developed in response to their feedback.

DR: *The Rings of Saturn* [2012] was an adaptation of the book by W. G. Sebald. It's another example of choosing material about an individual consciousness. In a way someone might think of it as, if anything, *more* intractable than *The Waves*!

KM: When I first read *Rings of Saturn* it reminded me of Woolf's *The Waves* and I was delighted to discover later on that Sebald had been influenced by *The Waves*. The book combines a description of a man walking along the Suffolk coast with discursive passages about history, time and place. I decided before rehearsals that the material we would use would be the sections that described the man walking and the landscape through which he walked. Like *The Waves* this meant that I boiled the book down to a shorter document before we began rehearsing. The boiled-down document was divided up into sections with place names as their headings – Somerleyton to Norwich, the Victoria Hotel, Benacre Broad, and so on. I had done the walks he describes in the books so I had a clear picture of the places. The simple idea for the show was to transport the audience inside the head of the man walking and thinking. I wanted to use mainly sound to conjure up the actual sensation you get when you walk, like the way the sound of the landscape changes as the path changes from inland to coastal, or the way the blood pounds in the head if you suddenly see an unexpected sheer drop in front of you. The film-maker, Grant Gee, had also offered us his shots from his film *Patience – After Sebald* which we were planning to project alongside the sound world. The starting point for rehearsals was this filmed footage, the boiled-down script, a fantastic ensemble, a pianist, and one Foley artist, Ruth Sullivan, who was going to perform too. The show was going to be performed in German at the Cologne Schauspielhaus so I was also keen to look at the way in which the collaboration between German performers and British artists would reveal and shape the material. The first stage of the work started in Suffolk with the German and British team walking the walks described in the book. Of course the way in which a German experiences looking across the North Sea towards Germany is so utterly different from the way in which a British person does, and immediately the thoughts of our German colleagues revealed the book in an entirely different way. These experiences were to determine the emphasis of the adaptation that we later shaped when we started our rehearsals in Cologne.

DR: *The Yellow Wallpaper* is another fascinating, very 'subjective' novella. I'm usually struck that your taste in sets and designers seems to favour the solid and realistic; I felt like you could live in the designs for *A Woman Killed With Kindness* [2011] or *Three Sisters* [2003] or *The Seagull* [2008]. But in *The Yellow Wallpaper* we see the room around the protagonist through her eyes. We don't know what the objective truth of the room is. How did you get round that in your adaptation?

KM: In the novel the woman hallucinates and 'sees' a woman trapped behind the wallpaper. Finally she tries to 'free' the woman and strips off all the wallpaper. I wanted to understand more fully the hallucinatory aspect of the novel and how to present it, so the first thing I did was to ask a psychiatrist, Dr Neil Brener, to read the book and tell me whether the post-partum depression the book describes was literary fancy or psychologically accurate. He told me that these were textbook post-partum hallucinations and the novella must surely have been written by someone who had directly experienced them or been very close to someone who had. This made me realize that I had to create a world where we would represent the objective reality and also – more and more gradually – her subjective reading and interpretation of that reality. I should say at this point that this was a live camera show so we were already planning to use film special effects for conjuring the woman behind the wallpaper. The set consisted of two identical rooms, one with wallpaper and the other without wallpaper. The second room was used to shoot the action after the wallpaper had been removed and also as a location for the woman behind the wallpaper. We used gauzes, mirrors, and water containers to represent the woman's subjective view point and descent into madness. The script evolved alongside the set design process and the way in which the practical ideas for the special effects developed. The show was being made at the Schaubühne in Berlin and they had also requested that Lyndsey Turner (who was doing the adaptation) update the original Victorian setting to modern-day Berlin. This added a further layer of complexity to our adaptation.

DR: Your production of *Fräulein Julie* [2011] at the Schaubühne takes us full circle in this conversation: back to Strindberg, and another adaptation of a play. Is *Miss Julie* something you've always wanted to work on or confront?

KM: I've always wanted to direct this play 'normally' as a naturalistic proscenium show so it wasn't a natural choice for the live camera work but the Schaubühne wanted us to do it as a live camera show, so I thought I would give it a go. If we were going to do a big well-known title like that, I thought it could be a really interesting exercise in subjectivity. What does it mean to look at three characters in a play? Can we pick just one of them and look at the action through the lens of that character? How will our understanding of the play shift as a result of one subjective lens? Will the action still make sense or not? Will the audience fill in the gaps because it's a title that is so well-known or not? I chose the cook to be the person whose subjective point of view we presented because she is the character who has the least to do in the action of the play and is regularly absent. In the first draft of the adaptation I simply went through and cut all the scenes where the cook was absent. These cuts amounted to over 60 per cent of the play and it was with this cut text that we started rehearsing. It was enormously difficult to work out how to shoot all the action strictly from one character's subjective point of view and it was always difficult to resist the temptation to shoot the action of the scenes in a more objective fashion.

DR: All of that technical apparatus and the almost literally oblique angle on the play does something very specific to *Miss Julie*, which is one of the most openly misogynistic plays by one of the most openly misogynistic writers in theatrical history. In *Fräulein Julie*, you seem to me to have done something unthinkable, which is to create a feminist version of *Miss Julie* ...

KM: I was working in Denmark when I was preparing the adaptation and I had become very interested in Scandinavian feminism, particularly the poems of Inger Christensen. I thought it would be really interesting to crunch together her feminist text with Strindberg's nineteenth-century patriarchal viewpoint. So I used some of the poems from her book *Alphabet* to be the thoughts inside the head of the cook as she fried kidneys or sat waiting for Jean to return from the dance.

DR: And it worked very well. Many thanks, Katie.

Selected bibliography

Boenisch, Peter M. (2010). 'Towards a Theatre of Encounter and Experience: Reflexive Dramaturgies and Classic Texts', *Contemporary Theatre Review*, 20.2, pp. 162–72.

Mitchell, Katie. (2008). *The Director's Craft: A Handbook for the Theatre*. London and New York: Routledge.

Rebellato, Dan. (2010). 'Katie Mitchell: Learning from Europe' in Maria M. Delgado and Dan Rebellato (eds), *Contemporary European Theatre Directors*. London and New York: Routledge, pp. 317–38.

Shevtsova, Maria, and Christopher Innes. (2009). *Directors/Directing: Conversations on Theatre*. Cambridge: Cambridge University Press, pp. 177–205.

Note

1 Mitchell's work is popular with audiences and some critics, though she has received some ferociously hostile responses. In an interview at Queen Mary, University of London, in May 2012, she revealed that when her production of *The Seagull* was running at the National Theatre, she

received a copy of the programme in the post with the word 'RUBBISH' scrawled on every page. See also Martin Kettle, 'Hostages in the Hands of Overindulged Meddlers', *Guardian*, 1 July 2006, p. 33. I discuss some of her critical reactions in my essay in Delgado and Rebellato (2010).

15

There Are No Formulas: Emma Rice of Kneehigh in Conversation with Martin Welton[1]

Introduction

Kneehigh were founded in Cornwall in 1980 by Mike Shepherd. Finding themselves perhaps 'deliberately' distant from the capital, London, and even from other regional centres for theatre in the South West, such as Plymouth or Bristol, they built a reputation, and a methodology, out of being a Cornish company first. As both geographical and artistic outsiders, the company found a freedom to make works which were rooted in their Cornish locality and its historical and metaphoric landscape, as well as its continued location as one of the wild edges of an otherwise urbanizing nation. This wild, mythic outside informs the aesthetic of Kneehigh's productions, bringing a sense of passion and imagination to even their largest and more seemingly commercial productions.[2] However the same passionate force and free-ranging imagination also finds itself expressed in the visual eloquence of the onstage worlds audiences are invited into, and in the mercurial physical and vocal reach of the actors themselves.

Since their inception, the company have produced their work for and within their local community. Even as their national and international reputation has grown, this commitment to a shared sense of place outside the metropolitan mainstream, and of the vitality of a sense of 'being in common' between performers and audience has continued to inform their work. Paradoxically perhaps, given its passionately local roots, this work has grown to spread across the wider theatrical landscape in Britain, and increasingly, to represent it abroad. It encompasses works made for and with communities in Cornwall, nationally touring performances, and large-scale West-End productions.

Emma Rice joined the company in 1994, having worked as an actor with Theatre Alibi in Exeter, and with Gardzienice Theatre Association in Poland.[3] As she recounts below, she had no initial thoughts to direct, but when invited by the then company directors Mike Shepherd and Bill Mitchell to make good on her own 'bossiness' by doing so, she led the company in the development of *The Red Shoes* (2003), one of their most critically acclaimed productions to date. *The Red Shoes* announced Rice as a director able to draw a keen eye for design and *mise en scène* together with a similarly acute sense of musicality, humour, and narrative around physically adept performance. Like many of her subsequent works, *The Red Shoes* is an adaptation of an existing source – in this case a Hans Christian Andersen story – which has both mythic and popular resonances. Like *The Red Shoes*, in productions like *The Bacchae* (2004), *A Matter of Life and Death* (2007), *Don John* (2008), *Oedipussy* (a comic version of the Oedipus myth, with Spymonkey, 2012), and latterly *Steptoe and Son* (2012), Rice has sought to find her own particular, passionate relationship to her source material – what she characterizes as 'the itch' – and through collaboration with actors, designers and musicians, to translate this into a newly defined stage world.[4] These new theatrical environments are celebrations of the pleasures of theatricality itself, and in being so, act as an invitation to view the seemingly familiar from newly sharpened angles.

Interview

Martin Welton: Kneehigh have developed from being a company that was very much located in the South West to increasingly being one with both a national and an international profile, with shows on Broadway as well as in Cornwall.[5] Something that the company have become very well known and respected for is the range of works that they, and you, have adapted; from the poetic, in terms of *The Red Shoes,* through great classics like *The Bacchae* or *Don John,* right through to more contemporary classics with films like *A Matter of Life and Death* and *Brief Encounter,* and now your latest work *Steptoe and Son*. Given that diversity, is it fair to assume that you have a general set of principles that you're looking for when you approach a new source for a work?

Emma Rice: I think that there are lots of principles and voices that I listen to but there's never a formula. The minute you try to make a formula it falls down. The simple thing that binds all these projects together is that I wanted to tell 'that' story. I call it the itch. It's that moment when you wake up and think about Steptoe. You think, 'Why am I thinking about Steptoe all these years on?' Like a detective, you start to analyse what that itch is and what you're thinking about. And the next question is, 'Why at that moment do you want to tell that story?' and then the rest follows. The best pieces of work are the ones where at that moment of my life I wish to tell that story. If you can answer the question why, pretty much everything else falls into place in some shape or form, but there's no formula.

MW: Could you tell us a bit about the current production *Steptoe and Son* then? Because I think there's an extent to which those television programmes are lodged in the British national psyche. Even if that legacy wasn't immediately intimidating when you got 'the itch' presumably it was at least something that you were aware that you had to negotiate?

ER: Kneehigh have been together 32 years now. I haven't been there for the whole 32 years, but their history goes back that far, and there are times when we're a very happy family and there are times when we just want to get away. I suddenly thought this is *Steptoe*: you see actors needing to leave and actors coming back. I hope that it's a healthier situation than the Steptoe family, but

I suddenly thought, 'I completely understand', and felt that this was a story that I wanted to explore. The fact that there's a lot of cultural baggage I think is probably interesting because, although I know that story, I haven't seen it for decades. I think I always want to retell stories, and on some level that's what I consider myself to be, a storyteller. I see myself as just one in a long line of storytellers; so Galton and Simpson started that, I think Pinter copied, and then I'm picking up the baton. That's contentious, isn't it? But it is interesting that the first *Steptoes* were broadcast before Pinter wrote *The Caretaker* and you can't help but be interested in them.

The minute I decide I'm going to work on a story I keep it very, very simple. I'm very careful about what influences I let in. So the questions that I'm very rigorous about, are along the lines of 'What do I remember?', 'What do I feel?', 'What do I think my parents might feel?', then I begin to extend to the actors, what they might feel and what their experiences might be, so that those things are very, very tangible.

The one thing I knew when I got the itch to do *Steptoe*, was that, although it's a show about two men, I would need to have a woman in there, partly because I don't intend to ever do work without a female perspective or presence. My process became very much about how a woman might have changed that world or have been kept out of it. That became a really clear guiding point for me, and I cast a woman. At that point as a devisor I needed to give her things to do; you say I'm going to put a woman into this world, what happens at that point? We call it 'putting ourselves in the shit', and then when getting out of the shit you discover all sorts of things, and the ideas you discover surprise you.

MW: Was that decision to cast a woman into the world of *Steptoe and Son* something you decided before you began working with the actors, or something that arose out of working with them?

ER: Right at the beginning it was an original idea. I'm always really suspicious of any idea if I don't know how it starts and I don't know how it ends. I think that as a theatre maker you have to know what it is you want to do on some level and I was really clear that there was going to be this woman, and that she would be the lens on things.

MW: Once you've had the itch, and you've made those decisions about re-telling, how do you then begin to approach the work with actors, since presumably they come in with certain sorts of expectations themselves?

ER: We always do Research and Development, even before the show is programmed, and that's where I start to explore the ideas that I've had, and we decide, as a company, whether it's going to work, and it's from that point that my producer would then start booking a tour. From that R and D you really get a map as to how this project's going to work, what musical language you're going to work with, and what physical language you're going to work in. I make sure that the designer's there, and I get a team around me who might actually create this work. It allows the collective imagination to start, so that it's no longer just my idea, but also other people starting to fizz or react to it. I think that having actors involved at that stage really helps them as well. It's great practice to do an early R and D and then go into a show because they're very much in the DNA of it. Any actor who works with me doesn't come in with too much expectation. I always say don't read anything, don't research anything. I like to think of myself as being quite an enabling director who allows for creativity in the room but I'm very careful about how that creativity is born and what roots it comes from.

MW: You said that you'd also have other members of the team present, such as designers, and presumably they're not just sat there doing drawings on the side. Do you get them involved with the actors and vice versa?

ER: Well, I have no differentiation about people. If you're a part of making this piece of work then you're part of this work. Everybody who's involved in making work is welcome in rehearsals, always, and anybody who isn't involved is never welcome, so I keep the doors firmly shut on the process. I don't care where a good idea comes from, and my stage managers are part of that as well. It's the collective imagination that makes theatre really exciting. I do quite a lot of early work in which everybody is just exploring the world, of which everybody's the same, and having instinctive reactions to it. Then we start throwing things together, and then a lighting designer will pick up a torch and a musician will pick up a guitar but in many ways I wouldn't mind if it was the other way around. In that protective world there is a sense that anybody could do anything, so if an actor has a lighting idea they can get up a ladder and do it.

MW: Do you think that there's something quite special about Kneehigh's location in Cornwall in that respect, in terms of allowing that creative space? It reminds one much more of the European devising companies than most British ones. Has your background maybe fed into that process? You've worked with Gardzienice in the past; is something of that carried into your work with Kneehigh?

ER: Shall I start with the easy bit, Cornwall? It's extraordinary. You get on the train and you get off at St Austell and drive down ever-narrowing lanes, until you come to the top of the hill at Gorran Haven, and our collection of barns which we've had for probably 25 years. They're fantastic, beautiful. We've collected stuff over the years so on a really practical level we've got a props barn with lots of stuff to play with; we've got a costume barn with lots of clothes to dress up in; we've got a music barn with lots of cronky old instruments that anybody can pick up and play, and because there's nowhere to go we eat together, we all sleep nearby or in the barns. I think that it's absolutely key to what we do. When we're at the barns nobody's telling us off; there's no boundaries really. It's idyllic, but we've fought really hard for it. We've decided to make work away from London, away from where people see it, and certainly in the early days there was no external ambition in the company. We came together to just do this thing, to live together, eat together, and make work together, and that's been really hard to protect as the company became successful because people got other offers. There's a great romance about it but I actually think it's really practical. We kind of drop our lives for that creative period, whether it's a one-week workshop or five weeks' rehearsal, and simple magic happens. The simple magic really is simple, it's saying, 'I'm just going to do this with these people and enjoy it as well'.

In terms of the process, I think everything's always a cocktail. I'm absolutely inspired by my time with Gardzienice, who I trained and then performed with in the early 1990s. It's absolutely no coincidence, that they work in a tiny village outside Lublin. It's very isolated, and they absolutely used that in the same way that I use the barns. I stumbled down to these barns in Cornwall and thought, 'I'm home', and I haven't left.

MW: With *Steptoe* you're working with iconic source material, but in other work, like *The Red Shoes* there's also been a relationship to the archetypal, to something mythic and yet recognizable. Is developing that sense of tangibility for the audience something that attracts you to these sorts of source materials?

ER: There's a theory that there aren't that many stories out there and I think that's absolutely true. Those templates are there because we recognize them and because somehow they speak about a universal state of being a human being, and those are the stories I love. I think that I have quite a simple relationship to those stories. But the second thing that's interesting about them is that you need them at different times in your life and you understand them at different times of your life. Cinderella is one of those classic stories because it's about coming of age and feeling ugly and feeling unloved and feeling alienated from your family. I doubt there's a person in this room who hasn't felt those emotions at some point. It's a brilliant story that can be retold over and over again and it doesn't really matter whether it's my *Midnight's Pumpkin*, or a ballet or *Pretty Woman*, all of which are the same story, but that we kind of get it.

I never had any aspirations to be a director. I started work as an actor, devising with a storytelling company in Exeter called

Theatre Alibi. We did a lot of children's work which you will see running all the way through my shows because I loved it. Kids are fantastic audiences. They tell you when they're bored, and they tell you when they're excited, so you get very good feedback as a performer (and as therefore a director) about how to tell the story, when to bring on the next thing, when to expand and when to move on. When I ended up at Kneehigh they taught me to be funny; they taught me how to clown and how to enjoy performance in a way that my Polish background hadn't allowed me to, and they said, 'Just direct a show'. I said, 'I can't direct', and Bill [Mitchell] said, 'Well if you were to direct a show what would you direct'? And I said, '*The Red Shoes*'. Now I promise you that I had never seen the film, and I couldn't have told you what the story was. My mouth opened and the words came out. They said, 'Brilliant, you're doing it next year!' I think I had heard the David Bowie song so that was probably my best reference, but the first thing I did was watch the Powell and Pressburger film [1948]. I thought, 'What have I done? This is the most complicated, massive, operatic show!' I was just an actor at that point, and I thought, 'Bloody hell, I'm really in the shit now!' I went to the library and got the Hans Christian Andersen out and I wept at the amazing relevance to me at that time. My marriage was breaking up, I was bursting with a volcanic energy as a person, and it became a directorial energy. I was bursting out of my skin and here's this story which is about female passion and the expression of it, and also about what rules have to be broken to feed this passion and what the price of it is.

It was important for Kneehigh. It won lots of awards, and it was an extraordinary explosion of passion, but it's really my guiding light because of that instinctive edge which I hadn't even put a context around, which I hadn't even named, but that came out of my mouth, and I caught it. It's a really good map to remember how raw that piece of work was. When I knew I was going to do it, man, I knew I was going to do it, it was a very clear vision. There's something about that instinct that I feel very, very protective of, but it's harder and harder to explain.

MW: You've touched on the sense of a sort of willpower in the piece, and there's a darkness to it as well, but what's also striking to me about it is that there's a very strong sense of humour in it. Do you think that a sense of humour is something that's important when dealing with that sort of material or is it just present because it's there in amongst the company?

ER: I don't know that there's a simple answer to that. I find life quite funny and I really like to be entertained in the theatre, so if I'm directing a piece and I'm watching and I'm thinking, 'Gosh this is getting a bit dull', I think it's time for a song and dance or a joke. I really stand by that. It's entertainment ultimately. People are paying money, and I want them to feel the patina of what it is to be human, and there are lots of funny and eccentric things about it too. Funny things happen and I like to catch them.

MW: I was thinking, in a not dissimilar way, that there's also lots of music in your work. Again is that something that's an active choice, or is it something that just keeps coming back in the shows that you do?

ER: No it's a completely active choice, although it's developed through the years. As a theatre maker I think I'm always telling a story, and I would always say only use words when all other avenues have failed. Music can tell a story; design can tell a story; film can tell a story. There are moments when you do need to speak, but I don't buy into the wall of words that is our heritage.

MW: You described yourself as a re-teller of stories earlier on. You're not just re-presenting the story though: the music, the projection or whatever is always a means of re-telling. In your production of *Brief Encounter* there's a very large-scaled back projection of the train which is from the David Lean film [1945], although that, in turn, was adapted from Noël Coward's play, *Still Life* [1936]. This kind of multiple re-telling runs across the whole aesthetic of the piece. Did you feel that you not only had to retell the story but also somehow the film too?

ER: You can't just re-create; you have to reference the roots. In *Brief Encounter* I used the [soundtrack by] Rachmaninov throughout, although nothing else really from the film. The character Laura says that she was a pianist but that her husband didn't enjoy music very much, so that's what I brought to it: she plays the Rachmaninov at the end, so that we actually get a sense of her explosion, of what she could have been [had she not been trapped] in this marriage.

MW: Looking back over the history of the company and your work with them, I'm really struck by the extent to which it seems to encompass pretty much the whole ecology of the British theatre – from site-specific work, to fringe venues, to regional producing houses, right through to really large-scale commercial theatres. Is there a sense in which you're having to adapt the work for those different sorts of venues and stages? Is it important that it gets to be explored in Cornwall first?

ER: Certainly the healthiest way to make our work is to make it in Cornwall and have that protection, because nobody comes apart from our community and our peers. We do huge amounts of work in those early stages before the critics and the industry come in and judge us to be successful or not. I never think about an audience really, I only ever think about the work. I treat every audience as if they're me because I can't look at life through any other eyes. So if I believe it, if I'm entertained, if it's absolutely revealed to me, if I'm moved, then we do it.

MW: I was wondering about some of your larger-scale works, say, *Umbrellas of Cherbourg*, and if there's perhaps a difference between the way in which you get to work on adapting a film like that, where you've got already this very large-scale set of production guidelines (and presumably a much bigger crew), and your approach to a piece with a smaller company such as *Midnight's Pumpkin*.

ER: Well, I'm sounding like a broken record, but I work very hard for there to be no difference. The creative team is just as welcome in a big show as they would be in a small show, and we try and work in Cornwall and break those barriers down. We stand up, expose ourselves, and people decide whether it works or not, it's a genuinely terrifying thing to do. In all my processes I work very, *very* hard to relieve and remove the fear. Even in a big West-End production I force everybody to play games. I make everybody join in, to remove those triggers of fear. And you can do it; they're very easily diffused.

MW: Could you tell us something about your new mobile venue, the Asylum. Presumably this has come about because of the increasing success of the company, but does having this sort of portable facility also help you to think about the way you want to continue to make work?

ER: Well for those of you who don't know what the Asylum is, three years ago we raised money for a big tent. Kneehigh's been going for long and there was certainly a moment five or six years ago, when the work was really taking off and the opportunities for the work were threatening to shatter the company. So that was when we decided to build a tent so that it was nomadic, but also because tents are magic, aren't they? When you see a circus tent as a child you are excited by going in, and you feel that you can go in. Whereas I think theatres are quite daunting. Tents have none of that. You can feel the earth, you can open the flaps and let the rain in if you want. It's a gift to ourselves and it's a gift to Cornwall, because we can move it and put up a bit of Cornwall and Kneehigh in New Zealand if we want to.

MW: Are there any questions for Emma?

Audience member 1: I was wondering about the process that you use to develop your dramaturgical approach to the source. For example you've done *The Bacchae*. Did you have a script beforehand or did you go into rehearsals to devise it?

ER: On devising a project like *Don John, The Bacchae, Red Shoes,* or *Wooden Frock* [2004], having done the 'whys', I'd then work with the creative team, such as the musicians, on themes. So I might say, 'Can we do the theme of the devil, the theme of dance, or the theme of the girl who's lost her father, her mother', to develop a palette of musicality without prescribing where it goes. Similarly with the writer, I nearly always say, 'Write poems, not text', because it frees them too. So in *The Red Shoes* I might say, 'Write me the poem of the butcher' to try to take it away from being too literal. It's the same with the designer, so that by the time you go into rehearsals you've got a palette of stuff which is quite finely tuned.

Audience member 2: Can you elaborate a little bit more on the role of the text and the role of the writer?

ER: I work with two writers in particular – Carl Grose and Anna Maria Murphy – both of whom are Cornish writers and performers, and both have come through the company. They've developed the process with me. I choose what we're doing, and they work very much like an actor would improvise, so I say, 'Write me this', or, 'Write me that', and they respond. Sometimes it's a tricky relationship in that I think I'm the author of my work and those two writers completely accept and understand that, but it is much easier to work with dead writers, such as Shakespeare, because you don't have to deal with them.

Link

Kneehigh Theatre: http://www.kneehigh.co.uk (accessed 19 January 2014).

Selected bibliography

Georgi, Claudia. (2013). 'Kneehigh Theatre's *Brief Encounter*: "Live on Stage: Not the Film"' in Lawrence Law and Defne Ersin Tutan (eds), *The Adaptation of History: Ways of Telling the Past*. Jefferson, NC: McFarland, pp. 66–78.

Lane, David. (2010). 'Adaptation and Transposition: Reinterpreting the Past' in *Contemporary British Drama*. Edinburgh: Edinburgh University Press, pp. 157–87.

Radosavljević, Duška. (2010). 'Emma Rice in Interview with Duška Radosavljević', *Journal of Adaptation in Film & Performance*, 3.1, pp. 89–98.

Notes

1 This interview was part of the Leverhulme Olympic Talks on Theatre and Adaptation. It took place at Queen Mary, University of London, on 9 October 2012.

2 *The Umbrellas of Cherbourg*, for example, was produced in association with Daniel Sparrow and Mike Walsh Productions, City Lights, and Curve Leicester. It opened at the Gielgud Theatre in London's West End in March 2011.

3 Founded by Wlodzimierz Staniewski, a former collaborator of Jerzy Grotowksi, in 1977, Gardzienice makes work that is characterized by rigorous physical and vocal training. They use the songs, myths, and rituals of the communities with whom they work.

4 Written by Ray Galton and Alan Simpson, *Steptoe and Son* was a popular British television sitcom in the 1960s and 1970s, depicting the bickering but loving relationship between father and son rag-and-bone merchants, Albert and Harold Steptoe.

5 Having toured in Great Britain, before opening at the Haymarket in London in 2008, in 2009 *Brief Encounter* transferred to St Ann's Warehouse in Brooklyn. In September 2010 it opened on Broadway at Studio 54.

16

'Expert' Dramaturgies: Helgard Haug of Rimini Protokoll in Conversation with Margherita Laera[1]

Introduction

Rimini Protokoll are a German/Swiss theatre director collective founded in 2000 by Helgard Haug, Daniel Wetzel, and Stefan Kaegi. Now based in Berlin, they met in Giessen where they studied and started doing experimental performance work. The disillusionment with classical forms of theatre and traditional dramaturgies developed their taste for the blurred geographies of everyday theatricality, where fiction and reality meet. By working near-exclusively with non-professional performers, whom they call 'experts', Haug, Wetzel, and Kaegi have created new methodologies for collaborative devising and dramatized private and working lives of ordinary people. So far, amongst others, they have investigated the professional worlds of trade (*Market of Markets*, 2003), diplomacy (*Schwarzenbergplatz*, 2004), call centres (*Call Cutta in a Box*, 2008), journalism (*Breaking News*, 2008), videogames (*Best Before*, 2010) and most recently the politics of war (*Situation Rooms*, 2013). Another consistent strand in Rimini Protokoll's work is the 100 Percent city series, where the company's passion for statistics and numbers emerges in an almost obsessive manner. It began with *100 Percent Berlin* in 2008, where Haug, Kaegi, and Wetzel directed a heterogeneous chorus of 100 Berliners statistically selected (not directly by the authors) to represent the city in its complexity, then indulged in the visualization of data about the German capital, its composition, and the opinions and desires of its inhabitants. This model was subsequently applied to 11 cities, from Vienna (2010) to Melbourne (2012) and San Diego (2013). In this interview, Haug discusses another strand of Rimini Protokoll productions, which can be thought of as adaptations: *Wallenstein: A Documentary Play* (2005), based on the Schiller drama; *Karl Marx: Das Kapital Volume 1* (2006), inspired by one of the most influential books in recent history; *Prometheus in Athens* (2010), adapted from Aeschylus' tragedy; *Herrmann's Battle* (2011), a rewriting of Kleist's play of the same name; and *An Enemy of the People in Oslo* (2012), based on Ibsen's text. Juxtaposing the experts' biographies to existing pieces of dramatic or scholarly literature, these performances playfully displace and confuse the opposite poles of authenticity and make-believe. Starting from an engagement with the themes raised by the chosen source, Rimini Protokoll go to great lengths to find the right cast members for their productions. The experts' biographies, which are evoked and performed on stage, constitute the pivotal points around which revolves the adaptation process. Parallelisms and analogies are sought between the fictional plot or themes and the performers' life stories, which enrich the world of illusions with a puzzling sense of truthfulness. The source text's dramaturgy is used as a structure and springboard to organize the personal stories on stage, highlighting the resonance of 'classical' narratives with individual ones.

Wallenstein, the first adaptation project ever completed by Haug and Wetzel, was commissioned by the 13th Schillertage Festival in Mannheim and starred an ex-aspiring local politician, Dr Sven Joachim Otto, who, like his counterpart Wallenstein, had been betrayed by his own allies. Thomas Kuczynski, a Marxist scholar and author of a new edition of *Capital*, was among the protagonists of the second adaptation, alongside a political protester, an interpreter from East Germany, and a blind DJ, unaffected by visual branding and advertisements. In *Prometheus in Athens*, performed for one day only at the peak of the European financial crisis, 103 Athenian citizens were chosen to 'represent' the Greek capital with some statistical accuracy (three were illegal immigrants, unaccounted for in official statistics).

Prometheus was played by several 'experts', including Konstantina Kouneva, a migrant cleaning labourer who had been attacked with acid for exposing a case of corruption in her trade-union work. A year later, *Herrmann's Battle* featured witnesses of war, including a young Egyptian/German woman who had taken part in the Tahrir Square protests. By casting 100 citizens of Oslo to debate public issues, *An Enemy of the People in Oslo* focused on the question of how public opinion can be manipulated taking inspiration from the Ibsenian plot. What makes Rimini Protokoll adaptations distinctive are, above all, the personal stories interweaved with the well-known narrative structures. As Haug explains in this interview, the process of their 'theatricalization' is complex and laborious, but always surprising and unexpected.

Interview

Margherita Laera: Why do you work with non-professionals?

Helgard Haug: I think it has to do with the process with which we work. At the beginning of a project, we go through a period of research and meet a lot of people. For *Kapital*, for example, we knew we wanted to work with people who had different perspectives onto a text that most haven't read, but pretend they know or have on their bookshelf. Those we talked to were either recommended to us or we found them through our research, or had particular experiences that we'd heard of. This process lasts about a year, after which we start rehearsing with the chosen individuals and writing the script based on our meetings. While doing research, we ask ourselves which of the people we met would be good on stage. So it's not only about how well they perform themselves on stage, it's about their experience, their story, their content. When we started working like this, I was really fed up with traditional acting in Germany. I just didn't think it was productive for me as a director to work with people that are so well trained and skilled but not really linked to the content of a production. That was the main problem: in traditional theatre, a person performs something beautifully but the whole link between them and the content is fabricated. When we met, my colleagues and I all had the same problem: we wanted people on stage that we could have a conversation with. The experts step out of their professional life to go on stage and talk about their expertise, for instance, but also about private episodes – they take a risk. We wanted the 'I' on stage to be identical to the 'I' who talks about her or himself, but of course there is fiction in the mix, too. This way it can be a really powerful combination of reality and make-believe. But above all I like what people talk about, their biographies, their experiences; I just like those moments. It's about the pleasure of researching the text in question, but it's also their whole body language, voice, the experience of somebody addressing the audience directly. It's not like with professional training which is all about skills and creates distance from the audience.

ML: How do you approach rehearsals? Non-professional actors don't have experience of that, I suppose.

HH: After the period of research through interviews, where we also choose the performers, we start to write the script and rehearse. It's a work that takes place around a table, while we chat, ask questions, and make notes, writing what we call our 'protocols'. Essentially we're trying to capture the experts' sentences – their way of thinking. Then we transform the words and write a text. We play that text back to the person, and ask that person to perform that text, and only then it's really clear to the experts that they're entering the next level and now it's about rehearsing those words they have already said beautifully and spontaneously. They learn their lines by heart. They rehearse them intensively but they're still very flexible to improvise as well, which is really nice. I would really describe it as a process that we share with the protagonists. Often the two phases overlap; sometimes the cast is completed only two weeks before we actually have the opening.

So it's a growing process: we start talking to people and only then do we realize who's 'missing'. It's a very open way of working actually.

ML: Do you ever comment on their acting style and the way they talk? Because it seems to me that as soon as you step on stage, you start performing someone other than your 'everyday self'.

HH: We mainly tell them what they shouldn't do, for example don't try to be an actor when you are on stage. It's awkward to stand on stage, and they are not used to microphones, so we advise them or we try to find the right way for them to do it. It is a problem when we take a piece on tour for a long time, as even if at the start they tried to play themselves naturally. If you have to say the same text 30 times, you start to build a character. And that's where we try to interfere again – in order to make it a unique evening and not a reproduction of something …

ML: You have different methodologies to select your experts, so how do you go about picking them?

HH: For projects like *Prometheus in Athens* and *An Enemy of the People in Oslo* which combine adaptation with the 100 Percent series concept, it is on the one hand about trying to get a cross-section of the population of a specific city, like Athens or Oslo, and on the other hand we try to find people that point out specific questions and that can represent themselves on stage. So, we look at statistical data, the age structure for example, and we see what the gender ratio is. And then we look at where people live in the different districts; we look at nationality or ethnic background, marital status, etc. Then we have all those numbers, for example here in London you need 2 per cent of people with Irish background, so you need to have two people from Ireland on stage. So that's a very abstract way of finding people, but in Athens and Oslo it was a combination of numbers and content. In the 100 Percent series it's only numbers so we only cast the very first person, and often that's a person who works with statistics. And then we tell that person, 'You have 24 hours to find the next one.' The other way is, for example, the one we used in *Wallenstein*. We followed many leads replacing the characters of the play with today's people. For example we asked the director of the Nationaltheater Mannheim, who had invited us to do this project, if he knew any powerful people in that city. So he looked through his contacts, for instance those who had donated money to the venue. There were of course people who had big companies or were politicians, so he just put us in touch with them. We also had other advisors, and then obviously there's the internet, so we try to find people ourselves. And often by meeting someone, we ask them for recommendations. When we have a topic, we try to speak to people who have different roles and positions in relation to this topic.

ML: Most of your performances are based on your 'texts' or, as you call them, your 'protocols', that is, patterns that guide everyday life and behaviour. However, some of your projects are specifically inspired by 'classics' of the Western canon. How do these adaptation projects differ from other works that you do?

HH: The first adaptation was actually *Wallenstein*. Before then, a lot of theatres kept asking us to take a drama or tragedy and confront our experts with it, but we didn't like the idea. We were more interested in finding new dramaturgies and structures. There is for example the funeral protocol: you could take that as a dramatic text or structure. You could talk about the experts' professional life, for example. But then they invited us to the Schiller festival and it was quite a nice challenge: there are Schiller productions from all over the world, from India, Nigeria, and so on, and I think it's really interesting to see how these international theatre groups deal with old and dusty texts by Schiller. So we finally agreed to do it and we immediately asked ourselves what would be our approach. We thought we should use one of the Schiller texts that was hardly ever staged. At the beginning of the Nazi era there were 100s of performances of *Wallenstein* because they are about a hero and national identity. You could strongly misuse that text, which was interesting. But it's very long, so if you read every word, it would take eight hours. It was clear that we couldn't deal with the whole text. We looked at the characters and their positions and professional profiles. We saw there was an astrologist in there, for example, so we met local astrologists to see if they were interested. Then there's a character who arranges, or tries to arrange, a love affair between two other characters, and so we met someone who does that for a living. One of the main characters is back-stabbed by his own people after trying to force his ideas on them, so we tried to find someone powerful who had been betrayed by his own allies. So it was really about profiles and meeting people. And then we talked about their biographies and always linked them to the text. We showed them quotations, and read texts together. There were hardly any Schiller lines performed in that piece but the play was a guideline through the whole evening for us. And people who knew the play could easily link it to the original. The combination of experts on stage shows where you are in the text, and you could actually follow the play through the problems or questions that are discussed by the experts.

ML: Tell us about the process of creating *Wallenstein*.

HH: We had a Schiller fan, Friedemann Gassner, in the production, and he was one of the rare examples of people who applied to be part of it and was later cast by us. He's actually a mechanic who didn't go to university, but he says Schiller saved his life. And at every occasion he would quote some Schiller. We liked his enthusiasm about the text; he's so emotional about it, so he opened the show. And then we met Sven Joachim Otto. The artistic director of the theatre said, 'You should meet him but please don't work with him.' He was a very unpopular but well-known figure. In his mayoral election campaign, the city was covered with his face on posters. Mannheim, where we opened the show, is a traditional working-class left-wing city, a Social Democrat stronghold. Otto was a Christian Democrat and tried to exploit the Social Democrats' weaknesses to gain votes. He didn't win, but the percentage was extremely high. But then his own party got fed up with him and decided not to support his candidacy for a prestigious position on the city council. His own party betrayed him at a moment when he was very powerful. When we met him, nobody talked to him anymore. His political career had ended and he was desperate. He said, 'I made mistakes but I never thought my own people would do this to me.' We thought we would risk it. We openly told him that our fear was that he would use the stage for his personal reasons and not so much because he wanted to be in a team. In a project with ten people on stage there can't be a superstar. But he convinced us because he was able to question himself. I've never met any politician who would take off his mask and reveal all the lies he had told everyone to get votes. We showed the play at an experimental venue, the Mannheim Nationaltheater. Just a few months earlier he had declared he wanted to close that venue, because it staged too many avant-garde projects: 'We don't need that crap – he said – we need opera.' So for the whole creative sector, he was just the devil. Only half a year later he stood on that stage, in the theatre he wanted to close, doing an experimental theatre piece, and telling us about a really personal experience. I think that throughout the play people changed their opinion about him, and they realized that you could actually empathize with him.

ML: Do you think that there are some source texts that are more adaptable than others? Did you find *Capital* particularly difficult to mobilize on stage?

HH: Yes it was difficult, but of course that was the point. It was clear that we wouldn't be able to stage the whole of *Capital, Volume I* – you just can't do it. It's a long, complex, partly very boring text, so we really needed the perspective of people who would command it, pull it out of the bookshelf and use it very freely. We have eight protagonists for that play: one, Thomas Kuczynski, is a book editor, and at the time he was compiling a new edition of *Capital*. There are lots of stories about the different editions and what Marx actually meant, which was often misunderstood, but Kuczynski was very interesting for us on stage. You could ask him everything, for instance, 'Where was that passage about … whatever', and he would say, 'Oh yeah, it's here on page 280, you need to read this other chapter to understand that.' And then we had other people, like Jochen Noth, whose experience of *Capital* was as a political protester in the 1960s, when he was reading and using *Capital* to fight for a different society. And then to avoid being jailed in Germany, he went to Beijing and lived there for about eight years and came back to Berlin in order to become a manager. Then there is a blind man that we chose because he's not influenced by brand culture. He's a DJ and he talks a lot about not being part of the visual world. There was also a young woman, Franziska Zwerg, whom we got in touch with because we needed an interpreter for Talivaldis Margevics, a historian and filmmaker from Riga who talks Russian on stage. He was forced to study *Capital* several times, and when we asked her to translate we realized she came from East Germany and she had always hated reading *Capital*. So you have different generations, backgrounds and involvements in the text.

ML: What drew you to *Capital*? No one to my knowledge had ever tried that on stage before.

HH: It was a provocation. We were asked by a theatre to undertake a new project, and we had this idea one evening. You look at the season programme and there are all those proper plays and then in the same brochure you find *Karl Marx's Das Kapital – Volume I*. What would people expect? And then we started to do some research; we liked the fact that we didn't know the text at all. Because in Germany our parents' generation read it, but we didn't come across it. By then it was out of the whole system. And to carry out a theatre project to read such an influential book, that was a nice idea, we thought.

ML: Even if you take a lot of liberty in adapting your texts, you follow quite closely the dramaturgy of the 'original'. In *Prometheus in Athens*, for instance, your opening scene runs in parallel with

Aeschylus' prologue: there are Cratus and Bia, and Hephaestus chaining Prometheus to a rock following Zeus's order. In your piece there are two experts who represent those characters: a prison guard, Yannis Milonas who identifies with Cratus, and Fanie Mamalaki, an HR manager who identifies with Hephaestus because she followed her bosses' order to fire people during the crisis. So there's a polarity in your work between taking the liberty to adapt the work quite radically, and then recreating the structure quite carefully. It seems that the notion of authenticity in this particular work is important. You cast three people in the role of Prometheus, and one in particular, Konstantina Kuneva who wasn't actually on stage. She was there by proxy through a friend of hers who was wearing a mask representing her, and was in constant connection with her by telephone to respond to the prompts on stage. Konstantina was in hospital because she had been attacked on the street with acid.

HH: Yes, she is a trade unionist. She discovered a case of corruption and she revealed it. She was attacked so she was in intensive care in hospital but she wanted to participate in the project. She was a popular figure at the time. She was in the news a lot, and of course she almost died and she lost half of her face. We built this mask for her friend to wear, which is inspired by an ancient Greek mask, but one half is disfigured.

ML: There's a sense in which the biographies of these experts and specifically this one is emblematic. These life stories authenticate these fictional narratives that you tell, so I wondered, what is the relationship between your work and the notion of authenticity? Is that something that you talk about?

HH: We try not to. Of course it's there; it's the big word. Like I said, as soon as somebody is on stage, you're turning them into somebody else, but is that more or less authentic? It's a version of yourself, but it's made to communicate outside. Maybe Konstantina's testimony was authentic because we used that tape when she was in her living room and she just talked to us. Again it was re-worked, but we couldn't use it exactly as we recorded it. Generally I don't like to use the word authenticity.

ML: In your project based on *Herrmann's Battle*, which was performed at a Kleist festival, you cast someone who had taken part in the Tahrir Square protests in Egypt, a woman who had experienced violence in the Bosnian war, and two computer hackers. What did they have in common?

HH: They did not have so much in common but we were looking at different forms of war and different roles in a war. There's a retired Colonel as well in the cast, Karl-Christoph von Stünzner-Karbe, who was part of a UN Peace Mission, an experienced strategist, but who thought that UN Peace Missions didn't work. Nathan, the young hacker, talks about forms of internet-based war, such as when secret agencies switch off power plants in other countries. He discusses the possibility of recruiting soldiers and machines on the internet. The protagonists didn't know each other of course; they only met at rehearsals. Barbara Bishay, the half-German half-Egyptian woman, talks about when the revolution first erupted in Cairo. She was following it from Germany. As a script we used her Facebook posts about Cairo. She was constantly writing comments from Germany, and then finally just two days before the big riots, she flew to Cairo and was really shocked by what she saw and how people had changed. She couldn't believe the risks people would take for their families and lives. So she thought, 'I don't know if what is happening is good.' It was the foreigners that kept telling her, 'Yeah, go for it, you just have to be in Tahrir Square.' But she had the feeling that the future alternative to what she used to know in Egypt was not very promising either. When she posted her thoughts, she was blamed and a kind of Facebook riot erupted. So the show was really about different forms of mobilization. Again, we were overwriting the Kleist-text, which is about a person who wants people to fight for an idea, more than for anything they know or possess.

ML: Can you tell us about the process of making *An Enemy of the People in Oslo*? How did you work with the experts there?

HH: The fourth act of Ibsen's *An Enemy of the People* stages a meeting of the inhabitants of a town gathered to vote on Dr Stockman's plan. Earlier he had discovered that the town's public water was contaminated. He wanted to find a solution because that same water was also commercialized as having healing powers. At first he had many allies but later almost all turned away from him, persuaded that solving the water problem would mean changing their life-style. Nobody wants to lose their standard of living. In the assembly the citizens decide whether to vote for Stockman and the truth, or for his brother who promises to keep things as they are, and of course the brother wins. We took this moment of a city that is having an election and stretched it for an evening that questioned 100 people who represent the city of Oslo. We replaced the water theme with questions focusing on oil production, for example, or on the question of how the fastest-growing city within Europe tries to maintain standards of living. During the play, people vote for certain resolutions and the audience could always see the results. At one point members of the audience could also vote themselves.

Audience member 1: To what extent are the experts influencing the devising process? Do you find that you end up with something that you hadn't quite planned when you began?

HH: Yes, the result is always something we couldn't have thought of without the participants. We start with a conceptual idea and then develop the play with the protagonists. It's really a process. The best projects are those where we build the show within the same room it is going to be performed in. I really hate it where you have to rehearse somewhere else and then you need to move a couple of days before the opening, I think that really kills every kind of development that you might have made. In the case of *Kapital* and *Wallenstein*, we had six weeks in the venue, with the people coming and going, but we could always be in the space, develop the right sound and lighting, and give that as much time as everything else.

Audience member 2: In rehearsals do you ever get to the point where the experts feel exposed and don't actually want to go on?

HH: Yes, that happens. When they say, 'No, I don't want to say that in public', if we think it's really important, then we just try to find the right way to say it so the protagonist feels comfortable with it. But often it happens the other way around as well, where experts want to expose themselves and we feel we don't want to cross that line. So it happens on both sides. We once did a project with diplomats in Vienna, and it was really striking because they told us really interesting stories in the cafeteria, and then when we began rehearsals and asked them to say those lines, they told us, 'We're not saying that on stage'. So at the end it became a strange play about things that they could not say in public.

Audience member 3: Do people get paid?

HH: Yes, that's something we think is really important because it turns the experts into professionals and it allows them to cut down hours on their job for example, or to use that as a job. Development, rehearsals, and tours are paid as well.

Audience member 3: So if the experts get paid then they are in a sense professional actors.

HH: Well, yes they are professional stage figures. They are giving their time and energy and I think it's fair enough to pay them like everybody else.

Link

Rimini Protokoll: http://www.rimini-protokoll.de (accessed 19 January 2014).

Selected bibliography

Boenisch, Peter M. (2008). 'Other People Live: Rimini Protokoll and Their

"Theatre of Experts"', *Contemporary Theatre Review*, 18.1 (February), pp. 107–13.

Dreysse, Miriam and Florian Malzacher (eds). (2008). *Experts of The Everyday: The Theatre of Rimini Protokoll*. Berlin: Alexander Verlag.

Laera, Margherita. (2011). 'Reaching Athens: Performing Community in Rimini Protokoll's *Prometheus in Athens*', *Performance Research*, 16.4, pp. 46–51.

Note

1 This interview was part of the Leverhulme Olympic Talks on Theatre and Adaptation. It took place on 19 June 2012 at Queen Mary, University of London.

17

Theatre as an Intellectual Concertina: Simon Stephens in Conversation with Duška Radosavljević

Introduction

Since 2001, Simon Stephens has had at least one highly acclaimed UK premiere of a new play each year. Following his residence at the Royal Court in 2000, he also served as the Writers' Tutor on the Royal Court Young Writers Programme between 2001 and 2005. In 2006 he won his first Olivier Best New Play Award for *On the Shore of the Wide World*. In addition, Stephens has eclipsed any other contemporary British playwrights in his popularity in mainland Europe, specifically in Germany where he maintains an on-going working relationship with director Sebastian Nübling since their first collaboration in 2003. In 2010 he wrote *The Trial of Ubu* which was directed by Nübling and premiered at the Toneelgroep Amsterdam. Although this was a new play inspired by a classic, it appears to have set a new trend for Stephens which led to a translation of Jon Fosse's *I am the Wind* in 2011, directed by Patrice Chéreau at the Young Vic in London, and to a translation of *A Doll's House* directed by Carrie Cracknell at the same venue in 2012. In 2012 Stephens had no less than five major productions in London,[1] a feat crowned with another Olivier Best New Play Award, this time for his adaptation of *The Curious Incident of the Dog in the Night-Time*, directed by his long-term British collaborator Marianne Elliott for the National Theatre.

Despite – or because of – this, Stephens defies the British notion of 'new writing' as defined by critics such as Aleks Sierz.[2] In his 2011 lecture 'Skydiving Blindfolded', he championed the virtues of the continental ways of theatre-making, namely the emphasis on physicality, collaboration, theatre as art, and the musicality of language, while also criticizing the arrogance of the English and the Royal Court's 'imperialism'.[3] Similarly, in 2013 he provoked some controversy by downplaying the significance of winning the South Bank Sky Arts award for his adaptation of Mark Heddon's novel,[4] in order to emphasize the importance of collaboration and the fact that 'the creation of the work was of far greater significance than any physical accolade'.[5] That this was not a matter of empty posturing or false modesty is confirmed by his frequent relinquishing of authority.[6] In the interview that follows Stephens likens himself to a language designer and his relationship to the director as being analogous to that of an actor who 'want[s] to do what the director wants you to do as well as bringing yourself to it'. Admittedly this refers to his translation work rather than original creations. Nevertheless, Stephens once again highlights a different slant on the quintessentially British practice of versions commissioned from renowned playwrights rather than translators. At the core of it – whether he is discussing his translation and adaptation work or his own work in translation – is always an inherently dramaturgical rather than a solely literary concern with playwrighting and theatre-making. This interview took place in November 2012 in London.

Interview

Duška Radosavljević: You adapted *The Curious Incident of the Dog in the Night-Time* for the stage at the invitation from the novel's author Mark Haddon. What was your approach to the task?

Simon Stephens: The conditions of doing the work allowed me to feel rather free. I read the book before I met Mark. It was interesting that it was a book that had played a very big part in my own writing in that it really did help me crystallize the character of Lee in *Motortown* [2006], so even before I met him, that novel in some way had an osmotic relationship with my work. Mark and I worked at the National Theatre at the same time, both of us on attachments. He'd been to see a few of my plays and was always very generous about them. He rang me to ask me to do the adaptation and I was immensely flattered because, until *Fifty Shades of Grey* was published, it was the best-selling adult book in the UK by a living author (so not including J. K. Rowling and children's books). I told him I'd do it on the understanding that I didn't take a commission and that I just did it as an experiment in process. I thought: I'm not going to be able to do this if I have the pressure of a commissioning theatre on my neck. He was very happy with that and that's what I did.

One of the challenges of the book is that Christopher's interior voice is so remarkable and compelling and original you can be seduced away from the action of the narrative into looking at his worldview, and the worldview lends itself beautifully to the novel, but it's fundamentally not dramatic. What felt important was to separate his perspective from the stuff that happens – the work of the playwright, I think, is the consideration of the stuff that happens and the things that people do. I made two lists, one was the events that happen in the present tense of the book, and one was the events that happened before the book started, and I made one chronology and put them together. So I had a sense of the book as being a sequence of actions rather than just a worldview from this remarkable mind.

The second thing I did, which was very pragmatic and didn't take long at all but became absolutely fundamental, was to transcribe the direct speech – and unlike a lot of novelists, Mark's direct speech is actually innately dramatic. A lot of novelists' direct speech is often exploratory or tonal or expositional or intellectually searching, but Mark crystallizes his intellectual search and the tone and the exposition and the backstory in action like a dramatist. He's written for screen before and he's written for stage, so he's a dramatist. I had this document which was just a series of conversations and I took that to the National

Theatre Studio and just spent a morning with some actors who were working in the repertory reading the conversations.

The dialogue in itself had dramatic charge but it needed to be shaped and given a dramatic structure. In the end I decided that I wasn't going to change the chronology that Mark presented but was going to have this fractured chronology – so when the audience watch the play it does leap backwards and forwards in time. The biggest problem was the question of what to do with the letters, which was a really key moment in the novel – the moment when Christopher realizes that his dad has been lying to him and that his mum is alive. Finding a dramatic language for the letters was really important. Another fundamental challenge was that while the dialogue worked well, you palpably missed Christopher's voice – so do you dramatize Christopher's interior voice, which is the one thing that readers of the book remember?

In my memory a real epiphany was to realize the book is a book about writing a book, and the way Mark presents the book is from Christopher's point of view absolutely, as though it is a book that Christopher's written for his teacher.

Then I thought: there are three people who read the book. Christopher's relationship to his writing and to reading his own writing isn't dramatic because he doesn't really understand the gap between what he's presenting and the truth of the world. The other two people were much more interesting: one was Ed, his dad, whose relationship with the book is immensely dramatic because when he reads it, he realizes that his son has rumbled him; and the other is Siobhan, the teacher. I experimented with Ed doing some narration and with Christopher doing some narration, but I think the biggest breakthrough was to give the narration to Siobhan, because she's the one who is most like us. I think most people reading the book kind of fall in love with Christopher but, unlike Ed or Judy, don't have to live with him. Siobhan can love him without having to live with him. But also she understands stuff about Judy and about Ed that Christopher doesn't understand. She was very useful when it came to the letters because in his book Christopher transcribes the letters from his mum.

Two other decisions worth talking about: one was I really loved reading the book and then you get to the end and there's the Appendix where he describes how he did the maths A-Level. You read it and you just can't follow it, and I thought I'm definitely going to keep that because that's really joyful – to go through this whole story and then be presented with a little bit of his genius. One of the things that Mark said to me when we first met was that he was really interested in Simon McBurney's *A Disappearing Number*; the video and projection work in it he thought was amazing, and that maybe we could think about that. And my line to him was actually: you know what, we should write this play so that people can do it in their school hall – so you don't need to be fucking Complicite to do a version of this play! I just wanted a dead simple script and that's what we wrote – although Finn Ross, the projection artist who worked on *A Disappearing Number*, did end up working on *The Curious Incident of the Dog in the Night-Time*. But the one thought I had was: the one time when we pull all the stops out and we use all the bells and whistles should be for the Appendix.

The final element in this story was the idea of staging it as a play – the play within a play, which came quite late on. Sean Holmes read a draft of it and he said, 'That was really good, you should make that much bigger.'[7]

DR: Yes, because if the novel was a meta-novel you made the play a meta-play.

SS: Exactly! What I liked about it was: although it's a real invention and an addition to the novel, it feels completely in the spirit of the novel.

DR: What happened in the rehearsal process? Were you involved at all?

SS: I was in the rehearsal for *A Doll's House* and for *Morning* [2012] at the same time, so I wasn't there as much as I'd have liked to be. I was there at the beginning, with Mark, for the first read-through, which was just joyful, and he was just really gorgeous, so happy with it. And then I kind of dipped in and out very briefly. So much of the rehearsal was technical, and a lot of it was physical, dominated by Steven [Hoggett] and Scott [Graham] getting the actors into a physical position where they could do all the work, especially Luke [Treadaway], whose physical work is astonishing. I've talked about the way Marianne arranges the rehearsal room. At one end of the rehearsal room there will be the various designers. She'd have the set designer and the lighting designer and the sound designer and the composer and the video designer, and I'd sit with them. We'd all get our little laptops out and we'd be sitting there watching and making notes, and I kind of thought: 'Yeah, I'm just the language designer here! That's what I am', which I quite liked; it was quite enjoyable.

DR: That's really interesting. Would you say that applies only to your adaptation work, or do you feel like a language designer even when you write plays?

SS: Well, it's a really interesting question. The difference would be: when you write a play, normally you have to invent characters and actions and situations and story, so it's actually harder to be a language designer because it's so inextricably connected with the invention of character and action and situation, and when it's an adaptation, that burden has been taken from you so you can just look at the dramatic structure and the dramaturgy.

In a sense the two different adaptations were fascinating, rehearsing in the same day – *A Doll's House* was in the Jerwood Space and *The Curious Incident* was in the National. I'd just cycle up the length of The Cut, and I'd be in one rehearsal room in the morning and the other rehearsal room in the afternoon. They're completely different rehearsal processes and completely different processes of adaptation. Both with *A Doll's House* and *The Curious Incident*, what was important to me was the certain fidelity and loyalty to the original writer's vision – I didn't do anything bombastic with Ibsen or with Mark Haddon. But with *A Doll's House* the dramatic structure, the characters, the action, the situation, the number of scenes and the order of events in the scenes are all there. So my work on *A Doll's House* was entirely linguistic, all I was thinking about was the language which is a real luxurious exercise for a playwright whose work normally incorporates the invention of characters, situation, action, narrative, structure and language. It was great to take five of those six things away and just look at the language. *The Curious Incident*, on the other hand, most of the language in it is Mark's. I don't know statistically but I would speculate that something like 80 to 85 per cent of the actual language used in the play is Mark's. So my work on that was entirely to do with structure and with the design of the language rather than the invention of the language.

DR: How did you work on the translations?

SS: I worked from literal translations – Øystein Ulsberg Brager's for *I Am the Wind* and Charlotte Barslund's for *A Doll's House*. I subsequently went to meet Øystein. I met Jon [Fosse] as well – that was the really big difference, I never met Henrik!

I went over to Bergen with Patrice Chéreau, and had a great time with the two towers of European theatre! I really, really like Jon. We got on very well together. We stayed up quite late drinking and talking about depression, and there was an invaluable breakthrough with him just to get to the heart of his linguistic concerns.

The main thing that was useful about that night was understanding what Jon Fosse meant by the word 'yes'. His plays are mainly translated by May-Brit Akerholt, a Norwegian woman who lives in Australia. And what strikes me about her versions is she always translates the word 'yes' as 'yes' – 'y-e-s'. Now, in English, if you say the word 'yes' there's something very definite, something finite and something certain and completed about it. It's actually very rare in conversational English to complete the word 'yes' with an 's' at the end. Normally you would say, 'Yep', sometimes you'd say, 'Right', or 'OK', and sometimes you'd say, 'No' actually! Which is true if you're agreeing with somebody in the negative: if somebody is saying, 'I don't want to go to the doctor's', you would say, 'No', as in, 'No, of course not!' But in Norwegian it would be translated as 'yes', and it's used all the time in his plays. So you get this very strange energy where the characters are saying, 'Yes, yes, yes, yes'. 'I don't want to go to the doctor's – yes'. What does that mean!? And Jon said, 'What's important is that you get the rhythm and a lightness to it, a sense of poetry, and English is a much more fluid language than Norwegian, if you've got other words, you have to use those.' With that play the subject is so dark that I thought the language needed a tone that juxtaposed with the content, rather than underlined the content. What needed to happen was to create a language that was lighter and more human and did have the poetic quality that Jon's talking about.

DR: Were rehearsals part of your process on *I Am the Wind*?

SS: I was rehearsing two plays at the same time then as well. In that one, both *Wastwater* [2011] and *I Am the Wind* were rehearsing in the same building, the Jerwood rehearsal rooms, so I didn't need to get on my bike, I just went up and down stairs. I was working with Katie Mitchell in the morning and Patrice Chéreau in the afternoon. Chéreau was very interesting because, I think, especially with male collaborators, he's quite avuncular, and especially with those two boys [the actors], he was very protective – a little bit like a kind uncle. He brought me into this circle of people and created this atmosphere that was very tender. He'd be doing line readings with Tom [Brooke] and Jack [Laskey], and in the rehearsal he had the German, the French, the Norwegian, my version, and the literal – five versions.

DR: So the text was really important to him?

SS: Yeah really, really important. And on the whole he was very complimentary. But then when he hit a corner, he'd go from being very avuncular to just being like, 'That's not right, we've got to get it right!' There were only three or four lines that I needed to rework and rework and rework – and I'd be emailing Jon from the rehearsal room, 'What do you think about this bit?' – because, for Chéreau, what was key was the psychological precision of the language. Every phrase and every syllable had to have a psychological truth to it that he understood and that made sense to the characters. When I'm doing a version, quite often it's initiated by a director wanting to do a play. So just like an actor in a rehearsal room – if you're a good actor – you're working with the director, and you want to do what the director wants you to do as well as bringing yourself to it. I think, certainly in my translation work, it's been the same.

DR: How did *A Doll's House* come about?

SS: I think it actually came about from a conversation between Jon Fosse and David Lan, Artistic Director of the Young Vic, about *A Doll's House*. Jon made the observation to David that there's a dramatic history in the United Kingdom of receiving that play as being an iconic celebration of the liberation of women. That tradition was initiated around the time when George Bernard Shaw started bringing Ibsen over to the United Kingdom. This filtered Ibsen through Shaw's concerns, which are more overtly about female emancipation, but in Norway the play's not received as being about female emancipation, and actually Ibsen never wrote it as such. If you read his journals, his diaries and his letters about the play he never talks about wanting to celebrate female emancipation. He writes again and again about the autonomy of individuals, and it's about individuality rather than gender liberation. You get the sense that Nora was a representation of him as much as anything.

I thought it was a really fascinating time to be considering a play which the writer perceived to be about celebration of the autonomy and a call for the emancipation of individuals and individual free will because, it strikes me, so many of the political and socio-economic catastrophes facing us as a species now are, if anything, born out of an over-indulgence in individual emancipation and autonomy and a refusal to take a collective responsibility. We have all in the last 100 years been defined by our pursuit of what we want that the two big burdens facing my children's generation now are economic and ecological catastrophe, both of which, you could argue, are a direct consequence of the post-Milton Friedman neo-liberalism of economics introduced by Reagan and Thatcher in the 1980s and then taken up by their descendants. It struck me that there's a remarkable and chilling line that runs from Nora to Thatcher! And it all crystallized around this moment that Nora has this speech where she says, 'There's no such thing as society, I don't believe in society anymore.' And I remember a woman saying, 'There's no such thing as society'…

The work with Carrie, rather than the kind of linguistic precision of Patrice Chéreau, was in cleanness and direction of action, and getting the language as simple and uncomplicated and as uncluttered by specific references to period as possible. Taking out references to currency, just keeping it as clean as possible, so it's all built around very clean moments of psychological action.

DR: To what extent is language or any aspect of it important to Sebastian Nübling, who has directed your plays in German translation?

SS: It's a very interesting question because I think on one hand language is completely fundamental to his thinking about the world. Although he's German, he lives on the border of Switzerland. The city he built his career in is Basel. I always think there's something kind of Swiss about him in that he speaks five languages fairly fluently. His English is good enough to direct in; he speaks conversational Italian, fluent French, fluent German, Swiss Deutsch. He has a real fascination with language. If he was talking to you he would be really interested in where you were from and what language you speak too. If an actor brought a linguistic faculty into the rehearsal room, if they were half-Serbian or half-Italian or half-Turkish, they would definitely have a bit of their performance in their original language. He did a co-production of *Herons* [2001] with the Junges Theater in Basel and with the Stuttgart Schauspielhaus. The children in it spoke in Swiss Deutsch and the adults spoke in German, and when we played it in Stuttgart there were subtitles for the children. *The*

Trial of Ubu – there must have been eight different languages spoken during that evening. In *Pornography*, there were at least three. And in *Three Kingdoms*, five or six languages …

But unlike, say, Chéreau, what he doesn't do is concern himself with the minutiae of psychological action brought about by linguistic nuance. So working with Chéreau, or with Katie Mitchell, or with a lot of the directors in the post-Royal Court Lindsey Anderson/George Devine/Bill Gaskill school of direction, there will be a lot of time spent looking at play scripts going, 'Oh why has the writer chosen this word as opposed to this word; why is the character saying yeah and not yes?' That would be the kernel of the director's work. Nübling doesn't do that. He's not interested in that. He's got much more interest in the sound of a sentence and the sound of a phrase, and that is really central to my writing.

DR: The musicality that we talked about before.[8]

SS: The musicality exactly, it's really key to me. So sometimes working with him can be really frustrating because he will get actors to improvise text in the scene. And normally I'd let them do it, but then in performance it's still jarring. With *Three Kingdoms*, when it came to the previews in the United Kingdom, I think there were three lines where I said to him, 'I've just got to change these lines, because I just hate the way it sounds, do you mind if I do that?' and he looked at me as though it were just the stupidest question ever!

DR: So what does he take from the text?

SS: The idea. The idea and the possibility for manifesting that idea, image, and action. He is using the language and the text as a starting point for image and action.

DR: What's been your relationship with your German translators?

SS: I've only got one German translator, which is really essential and really key. It's a woman called Barbara Christ who has now done 17 plays of mine. She has a doctorate in dramaturgy or translation. We're very different people in a lot of ways but I think we're quite close. She's very cerebral; she's very sober – which are very good qualities – and our working relationship tends to be based on the fact that she's done so many of my plays now. She really knows the metabolism of my thinking and how my thinking is manifested in my word choice. She knows that instinctively now. So she will write me emails at the end of the first draft with all of her questions. And I really love her questions actually; they're fascinating. A lot of them will be about what I mean grammatically by certain decisions that I have made intuitively and that's always a healthy process to go through …

In *Three Kingdoms* there was a real problem with translation for detective Steffen Dresner because the way Dresner speaks to Charlie and Ignatius is very unorthodox. Some of the original speeches are just untranslatable because he swears so much and he's so aggressive and dirty to them, but he's a cop. Barbara said, 'There's no way German police would ever talk like this, you can't translate that so I don't know what to do.'

DR: That's a very interesting problem. What did you do?

SS: She did quite a clean translation and then Sebastian and Steven Scharf, the actor playing Dresner, really reworked it and brought it together and invented words.

What's really, really central is that all theatre is adaptation. Every time one makes a process of theatre – you're adapting something, and every time you write a play – you're translating something. My 14-year-old son had a brilliant image: he said that theatre for him was kind of like an intellectual concertina so a writer takes a thought and compresses it into an image that's then compressed further by the director and then further by the actors and designer, and then that expands out into the audience again. Which I thought was an amazing thing for a 14-year-old to come up with, but it's kind of true – it's no different from me adapting *The Curious Incident*, or *A Doll's House*, or *I Am the Wind* than writing *Wastwater* or *Three Kingdoms*. It's not true that when you write a play as a playwright there's a purity of experience, because

> I adapt my own thoughts into scenes and image and action. And then the director will adapt the script through the bodies of the actors and the image of the designer, and the audience will interpret that adaptation through their own experience. This is why writing for theatre is different from writing a novel because it's dependent on translation and adaptation and interpretation. There's no purity of text which is received by a reader.

Link

Simon Stephens on Twitter: www.twitter.com/StephensSimon (accessed 19 January 2014).

Selected bibliography

Bolton, Jacqueline. (2013). 'Simon Stephens' in Dan Rebellato (ed.), *Modern British Playwriting: Voices, Documents, New Interpretations: The 2000s*. London: Methuen, pp. 101–24.

Fosse, Jon. (2010). *I Am the Wind*, trans. Simon Stephens. London: Oberon.

Ibsen, Henrik. (2013). *A Doll's House*, trans. Simon Stephens. London: Methuen.

Innes, Christopher. (2011). 'Simon Stephens' in Martin Middeke, Peter Paul Schnierer and Aleks Sierz (eds), *The Methuen Drama Guide to Contemporary British Playwrights*. London: Methuen, pp. 445–65.

Radosavljević, Duška. (2013). 'Appendix 1: Simon Stephens – Interview' in *Theatre-Making*, pp. 197–210.

Stephens, Simon. (2010). *The Curious Incident of the Dog in the Night-Time*. London: Methuen.

—(2010). *The Trial of Ubu*. London: Methuen, 2012.

Notes

1 Theo Bosanquet, 'Brief Encounter with … Playwright Simon Stephens', *What's On Stage*, 30 January 2013, http://www.whatsonstage.com/west-end-theatre/news/01–2013/brief-encounter-with-playwright-simon-stephens_1382.html (accessed 5 August 2013).

2 According to Sierz, 'new writing' as a quintessentially British practice is 'pragmatic, not ideological', 'tolerant, not autocratic', 'fair-minded, not political', 'metropolitan, not regional', 'literary, not performance-based', and developed in theatres 'created by eccentrics'. See Sierz, *Rewriting the Nation: British Theatre Today*. London: Methuen, 2011, pp. 43–4.

3 Stephens, 'Skydiving Blindfolded: Or Five Things I Learned From Sebastian Nübling', *Theatertreffenblog*, 9 May 2011, http://www.theatertreffen-blog.de/tt11/artikel-zu/stueckemarkt/skydiving-blindfolded/ (accessed 5 August 2013).

4 Tabard, 'Curious Incident of the Writer who Scorns his Flatterers', *The Stage Chit Chat*, 18 March 2013, http://www.thestage.co.uk/columns/chitchat/2013/03/curious-incident-of-the-writer-who-scorns-his-flatterers/ (accessed 5 August 2013).

5 Ibid.

6 For example he has said of his play *Three Kingdoms*: 'I wasn't the author of the piece; my role was never authorial' and 'I think we produced something that none of us could have produced in isolation'. Stephens, 'Preface', *Three Kingdoms*. London: Methuen, 2012, pp. vi–viii.

7 Sean Holmes is the director of the Lyric Hammersmith Theatre in London.

8 See Radosavljević (2013), pp. 197–210.

Notes on Contributors

Paul Allain is Professor of Theatre and Performance at the University of Kent, Canterbury. As well as writing about Tadashi Suzuki, he has published extensively on Eastern European and Russian theatre including Grotowski, Gardzienice, and Andrei Droznin. He has recently led AHRC- and Leverhulme-funded research projects in collaboration with the Moscow Art Theatre School and the Grotowski Institute, Poland. In 2009 he received an award for services to Polish culture.

Peter M. Boenisch is Professor of European Theatre at the University of Kent, Canterbury. His primary interest is in the aesthetics and politics of theatre, dramaturgy, and dance-theatre. He is the author of *Regie: Directing Scenes and Senses in European Theatre* (2014) and co-editor of a special issue of *Contemporary Theatre Review* entitled 'Border Collisions: Contemporary Flemish Theatre' (2010). Peter is currently working on a monograph on the German director Thomas Ostermeier.

Nadia Davids is a South African theatre maker and scholar. She lectures at Queen Mary, University of London, where she researches and teaches around the intersections between performance, cultural practice, and political intervention. Her articles have appeared in *The South African Theatre Journal*, *Safundi*, *The Social Dynamics Journal*, and *The Drama Review*. Her plays have been staged at The Market Theatre (Johannesburg), the Southbank Centre (London), and the Frascati Theatre (Amsterdam).

Miguel Escobar is a PhD candidate at the National University of Singapore. His research investigates the intersections between digital media, cross-cultural communication and art. He has explored these intersections as a performer, teacher, translator, video producer, and web developer while living in Mexico, the Netherlands, Singapore, and Indonesia.

Jean Graham-Jones is Professor of Theatre at the CUNY Graduate Center, where she currently serves as Executive Officer of the PhD Program in Theatre. A scholar and translator of Argentine and Latin American theatre, she has published *Exorcizing History: Argentine Theater Under Dictatorship* (2000); *Reason Obscured: Nine Plays by Ricardo Monti* (ed. and trans., 2004), *BAiT: Buenos Aires in Translation* (ed. and trans. 2008), and *Timbre 4: 2 Plays by Claudio Tolcachir* (ed. and trans., 2010).

Jen Harvie is Professor of Contemporary Theatre and Performance at Queen Mary, University of London. She is author of *Fair Play – Art, Performance and Neoliberalism* (2013), *Staging the UK* (2005), *Theatre & the City* (2009) and *The Routledge Companion to Theatre and Performance* (co-author, 2006). She co-edits Palgrave Macmillan's *Theatre &* series and co-edited *Making Contemporary Theatre: International Rehearsal Processes* (2010). She is collaborating with Lois Weaver on a book on Lois's practice.

Dominic Johnson is a Senior Lecturer in Drama at Queen Mary, University of London. He is the author of *Glorious Catastrophe: Jack Smith, Performance and Visual Culture* (2012) and *Theatre & the Visual* (2012). He is the editor of four books, including most recently *Pleading in the Blood: The Art and Performances of Ron Athey* (2013) and *Critical Live Art: Contemporary Histories of Performance* (2013).

Margherita Laera is a Lecturer in Drama and Theatre at the University of Kent, Canterbury, UK, where she is a member of the European Theatre Research Network based in the School of Arts. She is the author of *Reaching Athens: Community, Democracy and Other Mythologies in Adaptations of Greek Tragedy* (2013). Her current research explores the politics of affect in transnational performance processes. She has published articles in *Theatre Forum*, *Contemporary Theatre Review* and *Performance Research*. Her stage translations from English and French to Italian have been published and performed across Italy. She is the London Theatre Correspondent for the Italian theatre review *Hystrio*, and is a regular contributor on arts and culture for the weekend magazines of the *Corriere della Sera* and *Repubblica*.

Aoife Monks is Senior Lecturer in Theatre Studies at Birkbeck, University of London. She is the author of *The Actor in Costume* (2010), co-editor of the journal *Contemporary Theatre Review*, and director of the Birkbeck Centre for Contemporary Theatre. She has published in journals such as *Modern Drama*, *Theatre Journal*, and *TDR*. She is currently working on a new monograph on virtuosity in performance.

Diego Pellecchia holds a PhD from Royal Holloway, University of London. He practices Noh theatre with Master-Actor Udaka Michishige and has performed in Japan and abroad. His research focuses on aesthetics and ethics in Noh. He has been a Visiting Lecturer at Royal Holloway and East 15, University of Essex.

William Peterson is Senior Lecturer at Monash University. Author of *Theatre and the Politics of Culture in Contemporary Singapore* (2001). His articles on the Philippines focus on community-based performance, identity, and happiness. He has published widely on intercultural and transnational performance, theatre in Singapore and Aotearoa/New Zealand, and international arts festivals.

Duška Radosavljević is Lecturer in Drama and Theatre at the University of Kent, Canterbury. She has previously worked at Northern Stage and the Royal Shakespeare Company and has written extensively for the Stage Newspaper since 1998. She is the editor of *The Contemporary Ensemble* (Routledge, 2013) and the author of *Theatre-Making* (Palgrave, 2013). Her publications also include articles on translation and adaptation.

Alan Read is Professor of Theatre at King's College, London. He was Director of Talks at the Institute of Contemporary Arts and the first Professor of Theatre at Roehampton University in the 1990s. He is the author of *Theatre and Everyday Life: An Ethics of Performance* (1993), *Theatre, Intimacy and Engagement: The Last Human Venue* (2008) and *Theatre in the Expanded Field: Seven Approaches to Performance* (2013).

Dan Rebellato is Professor of Contemporary Theatre at Royal Holloway, University of London. His research focuses on post-war British theatre, playwriting, and politics. He is the author of *1956* *and All That* (1999) and *Theatre & Globalization* (2009) and editor of *Contemporary European Theatre Directors* (2010), *The Suspect Culture Book* (2013), *Modern British Playwriting: The 2000s* (2013) and the *Theatre &* series for Palgrave Macmillan. He is also a widely performed and award-winning playwright.

Nicholas Ridout is Reader in Theatre and Performance at Queen Mary, University of London. His research is concerned with a political understanding of the theatrical event as an instance of cultural production, an affective experience and a mode of social organization. He is co-author of *The Theatre of Socìetas Raffaello Sanzio* (2007), and author of *Stage Fright, Animals and Other Theatrical Problems* (2006) and *Passionate Amateurs: Theatre, Communism and Love* (2013).

Martin Welton is Senior Lecturer in Theatre and Performance at Queen Mary, University of London, and the author of *Feeling Theatre* (2012). Martin's research centres on the senses in performance, considering sensory engagements and encounters on the part of audiences and actors alike. Martin has worked as a performer and devisor with Sound and Fury Theatre Company (UK) and Theater ASOU (Austria).

Penelope Woods is a Research Associate at the ARC Centre of Excellence for the History of Emotions 1100–1800, University of Western Australia in Perth. She has contributed to *Shakespeare and Audience in Practice* by Stephen Purcell (2013) and *Moving Shakespeare Indoors* (2013) edited by Andrew Gurr and Farah Karim-Cooper. She sits on the Architectural Research Group at Shakespeare's Globe in London.

Index

This index categorizes the principal subject matter of adaptation in the theatre as a general topic, and in more detail by different terms.